Economic Rights of Women *in Ancient G.*

. . . .

for my parents

HARRY M. SCHAPS

and

ZELDA L. SCHAPS

Economic
Rights of Women
in Ancient Greece

∴

DAVID M. SCHAPS

. . . .

at the University *Press*
Edinburgh

© David Schaps 1979
Edinburgh University Press
22 George Square, Edinburgh

First published 1979
Paperback edition 1981

ISBN I 597406899

Printed in Great Britain by
The Scolar Press Ltd
Ilkley, Yorks

Preface

· ·

The question of women's property rights was most recently raised by Mr G. E. M. de Ste Croix a few years ago, 'in the hope of stimulating a thorough inquiry into the whole subject'.[1] I have enlarged the field of inquiry — he was discussing only classical Athens — but his article has remained the basis of my investigation. Other scholars have discussed various aspects of the problem, but there has been no comprehensive treatment since the unpublished thesis of Maud Thompson in 1906,[2] and many areas have been almost entirely neglected. For the questions of Attic law I have availed myself of the standard works by Beauchet[3] and Lipsius, and of the more recent work by Harrison, unfortunately left incomplete at his death. Of particular value has been the edition of Isaeus by Wyse, whose copious notes serve as a constant reminder that we are dealing with the speeches of a paid advocate whose job is to persuade the judges and win cases, not — unless that will help him — to enunciate law and speak the truth.

Of the three most characteristic — to us — features of Greek property law relating to women, one, the dowry, has received its definitive treatment (at least for the present) from Wolff, RE; the epiclerate[4] has been discussed by many scholars, none, in my opinion, offering a satisfactory explanation;[5] and the last, the economic power of the *kyrios*, has never received the serious attention it deserves.[6] Lacey's study of the Greek family has been useful, mostly in an indirect fashion; the direct effects of the family on women's property ownership are there discussed (as is reasonable in so broad a study) only sketchily. As for the direct uses of property by women, its acquisition, management, and disposal, the only discussion of any particular value is that by Herfst, whose thesis has deservedly been the source of all later treatments of his topic, including my own.

This book as originally planned was to deal with women's property in what seemed like a sensible order, beginning with its acquisition, continuing through exchange and ending with disposition. The nature of the information, however, has required some change. First of all, since various forms of property are treated in various ways, it was necessary to preface a chapter discussing these differences. The epiclerate, although technically perhaps a form of acquisition (but really not), demanded a chapter for itself; exchange and disposition could not be discussed before discussing the *kyrieia*, the so-called 'guardianship' of Greek women;

and the dowry, although it technically (at least in Athens) was not the woman's property at all, also required a full chapter. If the structure no longer yields a tripartite division, I hope it will at least yield a comprehensible order.

The recent awakening of interest in the history of women may bring this book into the hands of people whose Greek is not on a level with their English, and for their convenience I have translated all quotations of sources, even where the text or meaning was uncertain. I rely upon their discretion to refrain from attempting any scholarly use of the sources I have quoted in translation without acquainting themselves with the original.

In the scholarly world I am much indebted to Professor G. W. Bowersock of Harvard for advising me, and to Mr G. E. M. de Ste Croix of Oxford for reading parts of earlier drafts and offering valuable suggestions and encouragement; a further kind of debt was defrayed with the assistance of the School of History of Tel Aviv University and the Classics Department of Swarthmore College, to whom I am grateful. I am further obliged to Professors Helen North and Martin Ostwald for introducing me to the study of the classics, and for their continued help since I left their care. As for personal debts, I owe this book directly to the education of my parents, the help of my wife, and the encouragement of both. It is one of my smallest debts to them.

Contents

．．

Introduction

∙ ∙
∙

History is the invention of men. Most of the characters in the history
books are male, not simply because it is men who write the books, but
because the interests of history – politics, warfare, law, commerce –
have in most times and places been the domain of men. The literature
through which we study history was written largely (and for Greece,
overwhelmingly) by men. Lastly, the desire to perpetuate the memory
of the past, and the corresponding desire to have one's own memory
perpetuated, has tended in the past to characterize men more than
women. Women, engaged largely (though never exclusively) in the
production and training of the next generation, seem to have been less
anxious lest their children forget them. They do not seem to have felt
the need to have their own names and deeds inscribed in public places,
or remembered by the entire populace, though they may have nurtured
such hopes for their sons.

There were, of course, exceptions. There was Sappho, and there was
the Olympic victress Cynisca, and there were others, including those who,
like Xanthippe and Aspasia, owe their fame to the men with whom they
were connected. But it would be possible to write a history of Greece
with only passing intimations of the fact that there are two sexes; and
indeed, much history has been and will continue to be written thus. A
political history could not be written otherwise. Social, cultural, and
economic history, on the other hand, can hardly ignore women, who
constitute half of society. It is easy to follow the lead of our sources
and say what women did not do: they did not vote, did not, if they were
respectable, attend the men's drinking-parties, did not (if they could afford enough servants) go out in public unaccompanied. With the women
out of the way, we are then free to describe the assemblies, the drinking-
parties, and the market, about which the sources have so much more to
say. It is much more difficult, because it rarely interested the men who
wrote history or literature, to determine what, indeed, the women *did*
do; but until we know this, our view of ancient Athens, or ancient
Greece, will be lopsided and false.

I propose to deal with a part of the question only, and to investigate
women's relationship to property and possessions, both real and movable:
how they acquired them, how much they could acquire, and what dealings, direct or indirect, they had with them. The questions are not nuga-
tory, for there were, as we shall see, rich women and poor women,

women who dominated their families' economic lives and women who were excluded from them. I shall discuss only the place of women in what we now call 'economics', the transactions taking place in the society at large; I shall not discuss, but shall take for granted, their place in the household economy (what the Greeks meant by the word 'economics'), which was a position of importance both to themselves and to their families. Nevertheless, the reader should keep in mind throughout that the functions performed by women within the family – production of clothing, preparation of food, and production and care of children – were the major preoccupation of women in Greece, as indeed in most societies until the industrial revolution relieved them of the first; and that they formed then, as they form today, the economic basis for all the society's activities.

I have restricted my study to mainland Greece and the Aegean islands, from the earliest alphabetic inscriptions to the fall of Corinth in the year 146 before the Christian era, preferring to treat Greek culture on its home territory before attempting to explain its fate in other lands.[1] I have excluded the Hellenistic queens and slaves and prostitutes; each of these had a very different economic status from that of the ordinary free Greek woman, and each must be considered separately.[2]

I did not limit my study to women's 'ownership' of property, because the meaning of this term varied so greatly from place to place that any attempt at a uniform definition would have excluded a good deal of relevant material, or else run roughshod over the definitions that the Greeks themselves understood. In some places, as the book will make clear, women owned property and were free to dispose of it; in others, their ownership was so restricted as to allow them little discretion in its management or disposal. In yet other places, similar property may not have been considered 'theirs' at all – but legal restrictions on the person who *did* own it made sure it stayed with the woman, and sometimes even gave her a measure of real control over it. I have included all of these categories within the scope of the work; but I have generally referred to property as 'belonging to' a woman only if the local laws, as far as I can determine, considered it hers – whatever other restrictions they may have placed on it.

My work has been based on a survey of both literary and epigraphic evidence; I have attempted to find every literary passage or inscription that could shed light on the topic, and while I should be surprised if nothing had escaped me, I hope not to have missed anything of such importance as to affect materially the value of the study or its conclusions.

As any writer of social or economic history knows, the sources, while far from barren, are not cooperative. They come from different places and different times; they are of widely various sorts. We know, at least partially, what the law was in Gortyn, on Crete, in the sixth century; we know what percentage of the land in Laconia belonged to women in the fourth century; we have the speeches of lawyers from Athenian courts of the same time; we have temple-accounts from Delos from a somewhat later period; we have manumissions of Delphi from a period later still. Only in rare cases, however, do we have comparable documents from the same place at different times, or the same time at different places, or even two different sorts of document from the same place and time. Whatever differences we find may therefore be attributed to geographical factors, to historical factors, or to the accidents of preservation. To find the truth behind such documents — and to avoid falsehood when there are so many easy explanations — is difficult and uncertain; and the reader is cautioned against presuming my conclusions to be the only ones possible.

One particular inconvenience must be mentioned. The manumission documents from Delphi, Phocis, Aetolia, Boeotia, and Thessaly date from about 200 until well into the Roman period. The limit set for my study cuts a rather arbitrary line through these documents, including the earlier and excluding the later members of what is essentially a continuous series. Difficulties of precise dating, furthermore, have made careful chronological separation impossible. I have nevertheless maintained the separation as best I could, rather than be drawn further outside my area.

The reader may also be warned against the statistics drawn from tabulation of inscriptions. My subject matter has required that I be very sceptical about restorations. I have usually counted only those names whose sex was guaranteed independently of the subject of study: to presume that every *talasiourgos* was a woman would be reasonable in normal circumstances, but is inadmissible when the inquiry is itself asking what jobs women performed. I had to make many delicate judgments, and I cannot guarantee that another man's count would tally precisely with mine. In no case, however, is the room for variation sufficient to alter the conclusions drawn.

1

Types of Property

• •

In Athenian law, two concepts of ownership competed with each other. According to one, property belonged to the household, and the head of the family controlled it only by virtue of his position within the home: he was called the *kyrios* of his lands just as he was the *kyrios* of his wife and children. His rights over his property were restricted accordingly: he could neither make a will nor adopt a son if he would thereby remove the inheritance from his legitimate sons,[1] and the dowry which was given to him with his wife left the family again in case of divorce. But as early as the time of Solon we see property being treated, at least partially, as if it were 'a man's own':[2] he may do anything he pleases with it during his lifetime,[3] and he is allowed to make a will if there are no sons. In the courts of the fourth century, orators regularly speak of property as belonging to so-and-so, and deal with the law as if the property were wholly private; but the terms of the law themselves continued, in the main, to reflect the old concept.

In so far as the first, 'family' concept of ownership held sway, property could never legally belong to a woman unless she were *kyria* of a family. There is no evidence that such a thing was possible at Athens; the only mention of such women in the literature[4] is rhetorical and self-contradictory. It is true that, since the husband's rights to the property stemmed from his family position, they depended on the maintenance of the family; in certain cases — a woman's dowry and the estate of a man who left only daughters — this fact attached the property to the woman in a way which gave her considerable *de facto* rights over it. But she did not thereby become a legal owner. Was she ever a legal owner in Athens? Was she so elsewhere in Greece, where the *oikos*, the restricted family, did not occupy the same position of importance? The answer, as we shall see, depends on what sort of property we are speaking of, how much we restrict ourselves to the terms of the law — and how much the Greeks bound themselves to those terms.

Land. There is no property as secure as land. It is very difficult to steal; it produces an income, under proper management, year after year; houses can be built on it, or places of business established. A person who has unrestricted title to a sizeable plot of free land has an economic independence that money alone can rarely give. For these reasons, land tenure is often more closely regulated, and more restricted, than the tenure of other forms of property. If there was anything that a woman could not own, we should expect it to be land; and the evidence indicates that at Athens, at least, this was the case, with exceptions that are more apparent than real.

In the endless litigation of Demosthenes and Isaeus, not a single mention occurs of a woman who is *kyria* of land: Stratocles' daughter, when she was adopted by Theophon, became heiress to a field worth two talents,[5] but Stratocles was its *kyrios* during her minority,[6] and it must have passed to her husband on her marriage. The younger Phylomache was at one time heiress of Hagnias' estate,[7] but her husband, who was her *kyrios*,[8] presumably became *kyrios* of the estate as well.

In the *hekatoste* inscriptions of Athens, recording payments of tax on sales of land by organizations, clans, and demes, we find forty-three men among the buyers, but no women at all.[9] The *poletai,* whose responsibility it was to sell confiscated property and to lease the mines at Laureion, mention in their inscriptions eighty-eight men as buyers or previous owners of confiscated estates, as owners of estates with mines underground, and as owners of neighbouring fields and houses.[10] Here, indeed, four women are mentioned, but only obliquely. Two are identified by their husbands' names:

> : In Nape among the lands of Charmylus' wife, next to which :
> the land of Alypetus' wife, on the north Teleson of Sounion : on
> the east : land of Teleson of Sounion, on the west Epicrates of
> Pallene : Lessee : Epicles of Sphettus : 20 drachmas :[11]

I doubt whether either of the wives mentioned here was direct owner of the land. Charmylus was dead, and his estate presumably in the hands of his children's guardians;[12] his widow, who is referred to under his name, cannot have inherited from him – his children were his heirs – and the land must have been mortgaged as security for her dowry: it was apparently still in the hands of the guardians, awaiting either the return of the dowry to her father's family or her remarriage.[13] Alypetus, on the other hand, seems to have been alive;[14] but it is quite possible that this land, too, was in fact his, mortgaged for his wife's dowry. It may have been mentioned in her name to distinguish it from his other land in Nape. Two more women are mentioned: '(Ae)schylus' daughter',[15] if she was a landowner, was probably an orphan awaiting adjudication as an *epikleros*[16] (so that her property, too, will have been in the hands of guardians), and 'Boutes' daughter'[17] may not have been a landowner at all.

The absence of women is just as pronounced in those inscriptions that describe charges on real property. The inscriptions of *prasis epi lysei,* a form of fictitious 'sale' which amounted, in effect, to a loan secured by the land (the 'seller' accepted the money immediately, but had the right to 'repurchase' the property within a fixed period – and in the meantime, it remained in his possession), mention the names of seventy-four creditors who accepted real security: all are men.[18] Six formulae of land lease have come down to us with the names of the lessees: all are men.[19] Women do, indeed, appear on the mortgage-stones of Attica, but only to indicate that the land in question is security for their dowries – that is, that it guarantees payment of a debt from their husbands to their former families in case of divorce.[20]

Such was the situation in Athens: the inscriptions of Delos present a similar picture. The tenants of some eighteen houses and twenty-one estates in the possession of the sanctuary are recorded over a period of a hundred and sixty years, and not one is a woman.[21] Here, however, the exceptions are more significant, for one woman does pay interest for land (apparently land by which the previous owner had secured a loan),[22] and a house is referred to as 'the house that used to be Gorgo's'.[23] However exceptional these women may be, the first, at least, looks very much like an outright owner. A man was her *kyrios*, and under Athenian law, would have been *kyrios* of the land. The overwhelming male control of property suggests that the same held for Delian law, but there is a hint here that the *de facto* situation no longer matched the law completely.

Our evidence from other parts of Greece is quite different. Most striking is the case of Lacedaemon, where, as Aristotle complains, almost two-fifths of all land belonged to women.[24] At Gortyn, although the right to inherit certain categories of real property and cattle was restricted, in the normal case, to males,[25] it seems clear that women could own landed property as well as movables.[26] There is, moreover, some indication that they commonly did so, for women landowners were taken into account in the legislation: a divorced woman received 'half of the produce, if it be from her own property', a provision which apparently refers to agricultural produce.[27] There is no indication of just how much land women owned, but the common, and reasonable, assumption is that it must have been a good deal.

The property confiscated at Delphi in 191 by order of the consul M'. Acilius included four tracts of land (out of twenty-four) and five houses (out of forty-six) belonging to women.[28] At Larissa in Thessaly, after a period of wars and depopulation, some third of the landholders seem to have been women.[29] A register of land sales from Ceos, dating from the third or fourth century, includes a number of women;[30] in the records from third- or second-century Tenos, women are quite as common as men.[31] A few individual owners, from various localities, are also known to us: Arete, daughter of Aristandros, dedicated half a garden, 'which she had bought from the Aegosthenitae for a thousand drachmas', in Megara in the third century;[32] Epicteta of Thera speaks of 'the estates in my possession which I myself have bought',[33] and a letter of Ptolemy Euergetes mentions 'the lands which Timacrita used to own'[34] in the same place. A grant of citizenship to a woman in Crannon (in Thessaly) includes *enktesis*, the right to own land in Crannon.[35] Aristotle himself, according to Diogenes Laertius, left his mistress a choice of houses, one in Chalcis or his ancestral home in Stagiri.[36] Not even in Lacedaemon, we may note, did the women own nearly as much land as the men, and for most of the cities of Greece there is no evidence at all; but there were clearly very many places where women held much more real estate than they did at Athens, and they seem to have held it in their own name.

This is a pattern that will repeat itself; for not everywhere was the family as strongly idealized and institutionalized as at Athens. In Sparta and Crete, the presence of the other, conflicting institutions (the communal life for which these places were famous) seriously weakened the hold of the family on its members, and the law reflected the difference. In northern Greece, the law appears not to have followed the Athenian model, and we may presume that there, too, there were corresponding social differences. In these circumstances, it is well to keep in mind that the entire legal conception may have been different. For Gortyn, at least, it is certain that the property law conceived of each member of the family as an independent member of society, with his own rights and hence his own property; the family itself was an aggregate of these members, not a single unit whose rights and responsibilities applied to the family as a whole. In law, such a family is not simply a weaker version of the Athenian family; it is an entirely different institution. But the difference in practice, as we shall now see, was not as thorough as we might have expected.

Slaves. We find no signs of doubt between husband and wife as to the ownership of land (though we ourselves are often enough perplexed); but in other areas, ownership is likely to have been more ambiguous, at least as long as the marriage lasted. We shall occasionally find, as we look at non-real property, that the legal question of ownership wears a different aspect from that of ability to use, or even to dispose of the item.

Our most abundant evidence for the ownership of slaves comes from the numerous manumission-inscriptions of the late third and second centuries. These inscriptions, found throughout the mainland of Greece, leave no doubt as to the capacity of the Hellenistic woman to free a slave — and, by implication, to own him. The largest collection of these inscriptions is that found at Delphi: of the 491 manumittors identifiable in inscriptions before 150 B.C.E., 368 are men and 123 women.[37] The inscriptions from the rest of Greece show a similar picture: 516 men and 166 women.[38] The competence of the manumittors, however, seems to vary: while most of the inscriptions record manumission by a single person or a set of partners, a number record the presence of third parties 'present' or 'agreeing' (*parontes, syneudokeontes,* or *syneuaristeontes*). The significance of each of these terms need not concern us now; for the moment it will suffice to note that there were places where the woman was able to free the slave without requiring either the explicit approval or even the presence of a man.[39] In inscriptions of freedmen (who used, in Greece as in Rome, their former master's name in place of a patronymic) we find some who call themselves the freedmen of their former mistress, but these are not as common as the manumission-inscriptions would have led us to believe.[40]

Whether a slave was freed by his master, his mistress with the approval of his master, or his master and mistress jointly, seems to have depended upon different factors in different cases. It is unlikely that all the manumissions by husband and wife acting together deal with slaves who were bought jointly; in fact we have, to my knowledge, no record of anything in Greece ever having been sold to a couple — a point perhaps worth noting: we have places where the property was owned by the family's *kyrios* and places where each member owned his own property, but I know of no indication that there was any place in mainland Greece where the members of the family were considered equal partners in the property, as they are in many places today, though such relationship — guaranteed by contract — does appear in the papyri of Egypt.[41] The slaves manumitted jointly in the inscriptions were probably bought by the husband (perhaps in some cases by the wife), or born to a slave who had been so acquired, but served them both; when the time came to liberate them, both master and mistress performed the mamumission. In other cases, however, a slave who serves a woman is freed by a man,[42] or one who serves both husband and wife is freed by the husband only;[43] here it would seem that manumission is performed by the husband either because he acquired the slave originally, or in his capacity as master of the household, regardless of the slave's duties.[44] This variation in the manumittor does not seem to be temporal or geographical; it probably reflects the personal condition of the slave and the household that owned him. In general, it was to the slave's advantage to have all possible claimants to him agree to the manumission, and we do find inscriptions where an entire family takes part, in one role or another, in the transaction;[45] but in most cases the word — and the claim — of the master of the house will have been strong enough to ensure his freedom. For other slaves, the relationship with one member of the household was close enough to exclude the likelihood of other claims, so that a woman's personal attendant was not afraid of being claimed by her mistress' husband once her mistress freed her. Surely, too, some husbands insisted more than others on their rights as head of the household. It is not likely that all these manumittors would have been able to vindicate their title in case of divorce;[46] the law-courts presumably used a more consistent test of ownership than the inscriptions do. Nevertheless, we could hardly have had this number of women manumitting were there any serious legal bar to a woman's holding slaves.

All this evidence, however, bears only upon the later Hellenistic period, and none of it comes from Athens; a point that encourages some caution, since we have already seen that, in the matter of land ownership, Athenian women were more restricted than their sisters elsewhere. There are, however, some indications. Nicarete, a freedwoman, could purchase slaves and sell them in Corinth at the beginning of the fourth century,[47] and Neaera, herself a freedwoman, had her title to slaves that she had purchased confirmed by a group of Athenian arbiters.[48] Theodote, a *hetaera* (as, for that matter, was Neaera; Nicarete was a madam), owned neither field nor house nor factory, but she had 'many beautiful serving maids', as did her mother.[49] Archippe, the wife of the banker Pasio, received maids — presumably women who had always served her — in her husband's will.[50] But the title of an Athenian woman to her slaves does not seem to have been as strong as that of the women in the northern manumissions. The records of the 'manumission bowls' dedicated by freedmen, records which survive from the end of the fourth century, mention 194 manumittors whose sex is certain and all are men.[51] These dedications, which record the outcome of what was at least formally a judicial procedure,[52] must reflect the legal disabilities of women in Athenian courts; they cannot be considered as a proof that no women owned slaves. In at least one case of a man and a woman pressing a claim to a slave, the slave did not become the possession of either, nor, as far as can be told, did the case ever reach court.[53] But Theophrastus, a Lesbian who lived in Athens, presumes that a lady who had brought a large dowry could still be dependent upon her husband for her personal attendants;[54] and it is probable that the household slaves remained legally attached to the household and its *kyrios*, not to the mistress whom they served. Whatever the legal restrictions, however, it is clear that a young girl's personal attendants might in fact accompany her throughout her life, and surely some did so.[55]

Movables. If legal rights to slaves are occasionally unclear, legal rights to movables are virtually impossible to determine in the absence of a court case. Regardless of whose money is spent on a dress, it is the wife who will call it hers; and if she should choose to dedicate it to a god or give it away to a friend, her husband isn't likely to prevent her — though he may raise difficulties about replacing it. For this reason most of our information is useless as regards establishment of legal title: dedications, and non-legal references in the literature, can tell us only what we should have assumed in any case, that a woman had practical title to her clothing and jewelry. Movables that are not sex-linked, on the other hand — furniture, food, pots and pans — are shared as long as the marriage lasts. What happened to them when the marriage dissolved? We must rely on indirect evidence, all of it Athenian.

We may note at the outset that virtually all the movables 'owned' by women in the Attic orators fall under the category of *himatia kai chrysia*, 'clothing and jewelry'. Zobia, a metic, is able to provide Aristogeiton with 'a little tunic and a cloak', in addition to eight drachmas, to support him in his flight.[56] Neaera removes from Phrynio's house *himatia kai chrysia* and two slaves; the arbitrators permit her to keep some of what she has taken.[57] The Thirty Tyrants take from Polemarchus' wife 'gold earrings, which had been in her possession when she first entered (Polemarchus') household'.[58] The only item other than clothing and jewelry that we hear of belonging to a citizen woman is a *phiale* of Polyeuctus' wife's, which his daughter and son-in-law give as security on a loan.[59]

In two places furniture is mentioned: Socrates marvels not only at Theodote's clothing and servants, but notes 'that the house was generously furnished in other respects as well'.[60] Theodote is, of course, a *hetaera*, with no husband to provide (or to claim) house or furnishings; but it is clear from her case that the possession of movables by a woman was not of itself illegal or impossible. Another woman claims the furniture of her house, 'saying that it was hers, having been assessed as part of her dowry'[61] — a statement which makes it clear that the furniture was not hers in any legal sense.[62]

Now, 'clothing and jewelry' are not collocated by accident; they are a technical term for the personal accoutrements brought along by the bride into the husband's house. Sometimes they were included in the dowry, sometimes not; in the former case they had to be returned to the bride's family in case of divorce or childless death, in the latter — technically — not. But a wife remembered what was part of her trousseau. Polemarchus' wife's earrings were those that she had had when she first entered the household, and Lysias is careful to mention it,[63] not merely as an artistic touch, recalling the wedding in the narration of Polemarchus' death, but also to indicate that the earrings were really his wife's, not a gift by which he was trying to protect his property from confiscation. Legally, however, the Thirty Tyrants had a good claim in treating them as his, as we see from Isaeus and from Demosthenes.

The speaker of Isaeus 2 attempts to prove that his mother's divorce from Menecles was amicable: 'Menecles returned her dowry . . . and the clothing which had been in her possession when she married him, and the jewelry, whatever there was, he gave to her'.[64] He 'returned' her dowry (to her legal *kyrios*, not to her), but simply 'gave her' her garments and jewelry, although he had received both at the time of the wedding. Again in the will of Pasio: 'I give my wife Archippe to Phormio, and I give along with Archippe as a dowry the talent owed to me at Peparethus, and the talent (owed to me) here, an apartment house worth a hundred minae, maids, and the jewelry, and whatever else she has in (my house), all of these I give to Archippe'.[65] It is not clear in this case where the dowry ends and the gift to Archippe begins, but it is certain that *epididōmi*, the normal expression for giving a dowry 'along with' a woman as used in the beginning of the passage, cannot be equivalent to *Archippēi didōmi*, 'I give to Archippe' at the end.[66] The reason for the difference in terminology is that the dowry belonged to the husband only as long as the wife did, that is, for the duration of the marriage, whereas the trousseau, and anything else not assessed as part of the dowry, belonged to him permanently and could not be recovered in case of death or divorce. The 'assessment' of the items included in the dowry established the cash value that was returnable; nothing more could be claimed, as Isaeus states expressly: 'If a person should give something without assessing it (in the total value of the dowry), then if the wife should divorce the husband or if the husband should divorce the wife, as far as the law is concerned, the giver cannot exact payment of anything which he gave without assessing it as part of the dowry'.[67]

This was the case *heneka tou nomou*,[68] as far as the law was concerned. But in point of fact, the clothing and jewelry probably remained with the woman in any event. At the conclusion of a happy marriage, as the two above are alleged to have been, they would be presented to the wife; if the divorce was not amicable, her new *kyrios* would have to pay for them, but she would take them anyway, as Spudias' wife had when leaving her previous husband: 'Spudias', complains his rival at law, ' . . . received his wife from Leocrates while she was in possession of the jewelry and clothing (*echousan ta chrysia kai ta himatia*), for which Polyeuctus had paid over to Leocrates (at the time of the divorce, when she returned to Polyeuctus' household) more than a thousand drachmas'.[69] There is no evidence of a husband actually keeping the trousseau itself, although he surely had a legal right to do so.[70]

The contrast between the legal and the actual status of the trousseau illustrates the normal rights of a married woman to movables. On the one hand, her legal claim was very limited: in case of divorce or childless death, the husband or his heirs had to restore her dowry and nothing else. We know of no legal procedure by which other possessions of the wife's could be recovered from the husband, nor do we know of any such claim that was ever made. Even the property that she had owned before the wedding was not legally hers after the marriage, but her husband's; this may well have been equally true of any property that she had obtained while in his household. On the other hand, there was in actuality little likelihood that she would be parted from her personal belongings, whatever happened to her, and if she took them with her illegally, it was the responsibility of her *kyrios* to pay for them, rather than her responsibility to return them. When, however, we begin to deal with objects that might be of value to her husband, such as furniture, her legal disabilities will have carried more weight; and for this reason we rarely find anything other than clothing and jewelry in the possession of married women, though furniture might be included in the dowry. Once the marriage was terminated, the woman passed to another *oikos*, separating her property from her husband's, and so the return of the trousseau (which in effect meant the renunciation of claims against her new *kyrios*) could take place by direct gift to her.

The real, as opposed to the legal, situation is best illustrated by a relationship that was not a marriage at all. Neaera was a freedwoman who had been living with Phrynio, and when she left him, she took with her 'the clothing and jewelry (*himatia kai chrysia* again) from her house (i.e., what she had had before entering into the relationship with Phrynio) and whatever had been furnished by him to her for personal use, and two maids, Thratta and Coccaline'.[71] She was behaving as a wife would have, packing up and leaving. Phrynio, on the other hand, claimed — as a husband could have — that she had no right to remove anything, including personal effects, from his *oikos*. (He of course had no dowry to return.) The matter was submitted to arbitrators, who decided that she could keep those clothes, jewels, and servants 'which had been bought for the woman herself'.[72] There was nothing arbitrary about this compromise; it was based on a recognition that, since there had never been a marriage, Neaera's property had remained independent of Phrynio's *oikos* — so he had no right to anything he had bought as a gift for her. On the other hand, whatever else he had bought — since she had no one ready to repay him, as her *kyrios* would have done had she been his citizen wife — she had to return to him. In a similar situation in Menander's *Samia*, Demeas tells Chrysis as he expels her from his house: 'You have all of your own things; I'll give you the maids as well, Chrysis. Get out of my house'.[73] 'Her own' property is already hers; and Demeas — more generous than Phrynio, or more anxious to get rid of his *hetaera* — adds her maids as a gift.[74]

In Athens, then, a woman had the *de facto* ability to own movables, but a married woman had no legal right to take them with her when she left the household; and as a result of this, few respectable women accumulated much besides personal effects. Free *hetaerae*, of course, since they did not marry, might own considerable possessions, as Theodote did; but in this as in other matters they were exceptional.

Outside of Athens, where our literary sources do not help us, we have less evidence but less of a problem, as it is to be presumed that in any place where women could hold land, they could hold movables, and that wherever they could have money independent of their husbands', they could use it to buy movables. Certainly Cynisca, the queen of Sparta at the beginning of the fourth century, owned the horses that won her Olympic victory,[75] and the dedications from a temple at Oropus indicate that women on the very borders of Attica in the mid-third century were not limited to trinkets.[76]

Money. There was no place in Greece, as far as we know, where women could not have money at all; and there is epigraphical evidence to suggest that married women in much of Greece had money which they considered theirs. The property of free Gortynian women seems to have remained theirs whether they were married or single; presumably money was included.[77] Nicareta of Thespiae was married when she lent 17,585 drachmas and two obols to the town of Orchomenos at the end of the third century,[78] and two more inscriptions — one from Opuntian Locris in the second century,[79] one from Corcyra[80] — mention joint gifts by husband and wife of respectable sums of money.[81] In the case of Nicareta, at least, we may be reasonably certain that the money was legally hers: her husband was present as *kyrios* at all the transactions, and could have managed the affair himself had the money belonged to him. At Delos, from the late third century onward, married women begin appearing frequently as debtors, with their husbands present as *kyrioi* at the contracting of the loans.[82]

In addition to these cases of married women, we have numerous examples of unmarried women, or of women whose marital status is unknown to us, in apparent control of large sums of money. The widow Agasigratis of Calauria toward the end of the third century left behind at least three hundred drachmas as a religious dedication — hardly a fortune, but not mere pin-money.[83] Epicteta of Thera, another widow, was able to endow a cult of her family for three thousand drachmas;[84] Argea of Thera had five hundred to give.[85] Also notable is the epigram of Philopoemen's granddaughter:

> For a sturdy wall around the temple she built
> for the god, and a house for the public guests;
> and if a woman has traded her wealth for a good reputation,
> no wonder; ancestral valour remains in one's children,[86]

where the last two lines indicate that she has donated her own money, not simply supervised the improvements. And then there are the athletic victresses: the Lacedaemonians Cynisca and Euryleonis, Olympic victresses (the former as early, perhaps, as 396);[87] Aristoclea of Larisa,[88] and the daughters of Polycrates of Argos, Panathenaic victresses in the early second century.[89] At last, just before the fall of Corinth, we find women being taxed: 'For,' says Polybius, 'when (Diaeus) saw that poverty had a strong grip on the local governments because of the recent war against Sparta, he required the rich — not only the men, but the women as well — to make pledges and to contribute individually'.[90]

We know from epigraphical evidence that for more than thirty-five years it had been customary in Greece to collect contributions from men in the name of the women and children of their families; [91] so it seems reasonable to presume that Diaeus' innovation consisted of requiring direct contributions from the women. To Diaeus, a man in desperate circumstances, the women of Achaea were financially independent individuals who could be tapped as a resource for the war.

None of the women mentioned were Athenians; and there is no reason to doubt that the legal conception which excluded Athenian women from property ownership applied, in principle, to money as well. But in considering the Athenian situation, it will be necessary to keep in mind the limits of the law. The law does not regulate the normal affairs of a married couple: who makes monetary decisions, who pays the grocer, who has the key to the storeroom, are questions whose answers depend on the temperaments of the partners, on the particular matter at hand, on habit, on custom — but only very indirectly on the law-courts. What Athenian law *did* regulate — besides the acquisition and disposal of money, with which we shall deal in the coming chapters — was the distribution of property when the marriage was dissolved by death or by divorce. It did so on the basis of certain legal presumptions about the nature of marriage; but we should not be surprised when the day-to-day reality does not match the legal concept.

Now, if we were to describe the legal situation loosely, we should say that a married woman's property belonged to her husband, and indeed, when the courts deal with the question after the marriage has been dissolved, it appears that way. But as long as the marriage lasted, the property belonged to the family, and the husband's legal rights derived not from private ownership, but from his position as *kyrios* of the *oikos*. Thus the wife could manage as much, or as little, of the family finances as the head of the family would allow; and while such arrangements had no effect on anything as heavily formalized as land title, we occasionally find married women managing sums of money far beyond their legal capacity. Aphobus claimed that Demosthenes' father had left four talents hidden in the care of his mother, as a trust-fund for the young Demosthenes. [92] The claim may or may not have been true, but it was not inconceivable. When Polyeuctus died, it was one of his married daughters who paid the funeral expenses; but it was her husband ` who went to court to force the other daughter's husband to pay her share. [93] Archippe, after her first husband Pasio's death, gave two thousand drachmas to her children by her second husband Phormio; the legal rights of the case are not at all clear — it was successfully challenged by Pasio's son Apollodorus [94] — but she clearly had the money in fact, if not in law.

Archippe was an exceptionally rich woman; but it appears to have been quite common for Athenian wives to manage the household budget. Lysistrata mentions the fact in her argument with the Probulus:

LYS. . . . for they are absolutely not going to take down this money! PROB. But what are you going to do? LYS. Is *that* your question? We're going to manage it (*tamieusomen auto*). PROB. *You* are going to manage the money? LYS. And why do you find that so awful? Don't we have complete management of your household money, too? PROB. But it's not the same. LYS. How isn't it the same? PROB. With this money the war must be fought. LYS. But the war must not be fought in the first place![95]

Plato describes the Athenian custom as 'piling up whatever one gathers into some one house, (where) we give all the money over to the women to manage'.[96]

In some families, on the other hand, the pantry seems to have been kept locked, as another Aristophanic woman complains: 'the things we used to be able to manage ourselves, and to sneak a little bit without getting caught – cereal, oil, wine – that isn't possible any more either. Now the men have keys that they carry around themselves, secret, nasty Spartan doodads, with three teeth.'[97]

Also instructive is a passage from the *Samia* in which we see the woman (in this case a mistress rather than a wife) in charge of the pantry – but it is the man's slave who is telling her what to do with it: 'Chrysis, give the cook whatever he asks for, and see to it that the old lady doesn't get at the jugs, for the gods' sake'.[98]

Xenophon in the *Oeconomicus* recommended turning all the affairs of the house over to the wife, but he made no pretence of describing the normal situation. Presumably the monetary activity of the wife varied greatly from family to family. At one extreme were the husbands who put 'Laconian locks' on their pantries (if there were such; even Xenophon's foil, Critobulus, seems to have been more trusting – 'Is there anyone else to whom you turn over more affairs of importance than to your wife?' asks Socrates, and Critobulus answers, 'Nobody'),[99] and at the other – among families that had a *kyrios* – houses like that of Archippe, or of Xenophon's hero Ischomachus, who could say that he hardly spent his time at home, since he trusted his wife to run the house.[100] Beyond this were families whose master was away, or had recently died. Here the woman might be left in virtual charge of all the family's affairs, as Polyeuctus' wife seems to have been after his death. She made loans to both her daughters, and one of the daughters paid the funeral expenses. In this family women seem regularly to have dealt with the family's money: we see Spudias' wife being sent to represent Spudias at the making of Polyeuctus' will, and Polyeuctus' daughters identifying the seals on his wife's papers.[101] In a situation similar to that of Polyeuctus' widow was the Troezenian mother of the sixth century or earlier who set up her son's funeral monument, 'since there were no children in the house' [102] to attend to it. Apollodorus complains of the bad state his affairs were in when he served as trierarch, and his wife and mother had to manage at home.[103] These are the sorts of families of whom Aeschines speaks, 'whose fathers had died, and the mothers managed their property'.[104]

The law, however, did not presume that a woman was likely to own money. Liturgies, whatever they may have been in a woman's case,[105] were distributed on the basis of the family's, that is, the husband's, wealth, and paid for by him. Laws dealing with women's crimes were not enforced by fines: an adulteress, for example, was forbidden to wear jewelry or to attend public rites, but she was not fined. If she disobeyed the law, she could have her clothing torn, her jewelry stripped off, and herself whipped, but still she was not fined.[106] The male citizen who married a foreign woman was fined a thousand drachmas; the female citizen who married a foreign man was not fined at all.[107] The property from which an Athenian woman lived, and which she might even manage, belonged not to her but to her family. It was only her person, and her personal effects, that the law could attack.[108]

2

Acquisition

..

We have seen in the previous chapter that the Athenian legal structure, with its refusal to see a woman as *kyria* of property, was not the only factor determining the actual use that Athenian women made of their possessions. There were exceptions to the legal rule, exceptions that became more significant as we came to deal with less permanent property. For all that, the law was not a fiction. Not only did it determine much of the economic procedure — the exceptions, after all, could occur only as long as the *kyrios* permitted them — but it reflected reality more or less faithfully. If the law could afford to treat Athenian women as having no property, it was because they had, in fact, no real way of acquiring it. When women take an important role in the acquisition of property, pressure is generated for them to have more direct ability to dispose of it, as the experience of Western societies will attest; in Athens they had no such role. But in this and in subsequent chapters, as we examine the various dealings that women had with property, we shall see that in Athens, at least, direct ownership — more correctly, the lack of direct ownership — was only part of the story of women's property.

Now, it is not entirely true that one must acquire property before one can exchange or dispose of it. Leaving aside the activities of the speculator and the swindler, we will still find areas where property is less than personal, and what is acquired by one may be disposed of by another. This is true, to a greater or a lesser extent, of every family's possessions, and it is difficult to trace every transaction between husband and wife, or to evaluate the economic meaning of such transactions. A man brings home money; his wife buys food; his cook prepares the food; all three eat the food, along with children and perhaps others who have had no part at all in any of the business. We will make our task much simpler if we say: the family acquired money, bought food, and consumed it. When dealing with a family that has been dead for more than two millennia, we will be very lucky to be able to say that much.

In studying women, it will be well to bear this in mind. If the entire family has no means of acquiring property, it is in danger of starvation; if the woman has no means of acquiring property, she is dependent upon her husband. She may still be comfortable, even pampered. Thus when we examine the ability of women to acquire property on their

own, we are examining not their capacity to survive, but their capacity
to survive independently. Independence, however, was not the normal
condition of Greek women, and in most women's life the dowry, which
we shall discuss later, was a more important matter than any that will
be treated in this chapter.

We are considering, for the moment, only means of original acquisition, that is, means of acquiring property without giving something
else in return. Forms of exchange will be dealt with in chapter 5.

Production and services. The productive activity of a family's women
may be designed either for internal or for external consumption. In the
first case — that of a woman who makes her family's clothes, for example — it decreases the amount of capital required, since the family
need buy only raw materials; in the second — that of a professional
seamstress — it increases the amount of capital available to the family.

These two modes of production are obviously similar in their effects,
but they are not identical. The second method is today the more
profitable, for a woman can produce much more than her family needs,
and so earn more money than she could have saved by staying at home.
This is particularly true after the industrial revolution made hand-sewn,
let alone hand-woven, clothing an expensive luxury; but it was clearly
the case in Greece as well, for the sale of a woman's produce (or of her
labour) was the refuge of women in need of money. Euxitheus argues
that his mother's employment as a wet nurse, though a sign of poverty,
does not impugn her citizenship: 'for, as I've heard, many citizen women
became wet nurses, weavers, and harvest-hands because of the hard
times that the city was then going through — and many women who
were poor then are rich now'.[1] A poor Aristophanic widow depends
upon her income from plaiting myrtle-wreaths: 'For my husband died
on me in Cyprus leaving me five little children, whom I barely managed
to feed by plaiting wreaths in the myrtle-market. Now at first I managed to feed them half-badly ...'[2] and the poverty of Micyllus, in a
fragment of Crates of Thebes, is emphasized by the fact that his wife
helps him in his work: 'and I watched Micyllus combing wool, and his
wife combing with him, trying to escape starvation in baleful respectability'.[3]

The wealthier women did nothing of the sort. Ischomachus urged his
wife to be energetic and manage her servants, rather than sit idle all day:
'It seemed to me,' he says, 'that this would give her both something to
do and a chance to walk around. I said that mixing and kneading dough
was also good exercise, and shaking out and arranging the clothes and
the bedding. I said that if she got this kind of exercise she would improve both her health and her appetite, and improve her complexion in
reality'[4] (i.e., as opposed to using make-up). Even for its cosmetic

value — and even to Ischomachus, whom Xenophon presents as a model of good management for the responsibility he grants his wife — a wealthy woman's work was neither difficult nor profitable. Only economic necessity ever made a woman do work for external consumption.[5]

A good example of such necessity is given by a chapter of Xenophon's *Memorabilia*.[6] During the rule of the Thirty Tyrants, Aristarchus' house has become a refuge for his sisters, nieces, and cousins — he now has fourteen free people living with him — and his income from his real estate has been cut off. 'Now, Socrates,' he complains, 'it is hard to ignore one's relatives as they are ruined, but it's impossible to feed so many people in times like these.' Still, he has not considered putting the women to work, and Socrates has to persuade him that to do so would be proper for free women.

It was not the work that was shameful, but the compulsion. Aristarchus' relatives all knew how to prepare food and clothing, and we must presume that they had actually done so on occasion.[7] Ischomachus' wife knew how to weave.[8] Perhaps they might occasionally have made something for sale. Other women did; the woman who complains of Euripides that he has taught the men all the women's tricks, 'so that if some woman should ever plait a garland, her husband thinks she has a lover'[9] obviously has in mind neither a professional garland-plaiter like the widow mentioned above nor a housewife making a garland for her husband. Such also must be the woman of the *Frogs* who is working on a single garment, which she plans to sell herself.[10] We do not know how high up on the social ladder such activity might extend; it is possible that even a rich woman might sell her products, or have them sold. But she would not work full-time in the hope of earning her keep; such labour was worthy only of a slave.[11]

Among those women who did work professionally, it would seem that the vast majority were *talasiourgoi*, workers in wool. Every housewife was at least an amateur *talasiourgos*, though I doubt whether she would have called herself that; the produce of her industry is referred to in Gortynian law as *oti k'enupanei*, 'whatever she has woven within'.[12] In the *Odyssey* Penelope, of course, spends her time at the loom; Calypso is first seen weaving, as is Circe, and we remember the tribute to the Phaeacians: 'The Phaeacians were as far the most skilful of men in sailing a swift ship in the sea, as women are (the most skilful) craftsmen of the loom'.[13]

Of forty-two freedwomen whose trades are known to us from the Athenian manumission-inscriptions, thirty-one were *talasiourgoi*; the remainder are distributed among eight other occupations.[14] The meaning of this concentration can be appreciated if we look at the sixty-one men in the same inscriptions: six farm-hands, six retailers, five cobblers,

three cooks, and the remainder scattered through forty different categories, no more than two to a job. A male slave might be trained for
any employment that would pay; the women were used overwhelmingly
as weavers, and they continued as such when they were freed.

What was true of freedwomen is likely to have been true of citizens
and metics as well; these were even less likely to be trained as labourers, but they would know how to spin and weave. This would be their
most likely occupation, unless they could earn a living by helping their
husbands in a small business. We do, of course, find women in jobs
other than spinning and weaving. The inscriptions list two seams-
tresses,[15] two wet nurses[16] and one dry nurse,[17] three laundresses,[18]
and even a cobbler;[19] from other sources we know that women performed many tasks in the preparation of food.[20] A woman potter appears on a vase,[21] and an Athenian curse-tablet mentions a gilder who
apparently decorated the helmets that her husband made.[22] Midwifery
was the particular province of free women,[23] and small tradeswomen
appear frequently.[24] In short: many women worked for a living, but
they did so to escape poverty, not to become rich. They were chiefly,
though not exclusively, occupied by what the Greeks considered
'women's work'. They were able to support themselves, and even their
families; but while Cleon, and Pasio, and Callias, and other Athenians
could become wealthy by their businesses, we know of no woman who
ever did so.

Gifts. It is not likely that there was any legal force in the gifts given by
a man to a woman in his household; as long as he remained *kyrios*, he
was still 'master' of the property, and such things as he provided for
his dependants — chiefly food and clothing — will have been considered
a part of his responsibility for maintaining them, rather than free gifts.[25]
Gifts of large value, as of land or money, would have no purpose as
long as the family remained together, and we have no examples of such
gifts.[26]

The gifts given upon changes in the household — marriage, death, and
divorce — were formalized by custom and by law, but the precise form-
ulation differed from place to place. Thus the dowry was in some states
a gift to the woman, in others to her husband; a woman's inheritance
came to her sometimes by right, sometimes only by special gift of the
deceased, or not at all. Rather than separate out those localities where
these matters took the form of gifts, I have treated each of them in its
own place.

Inheritance by will. Greece in the classical period was first beginning to
accept the principle of free testamentary disposition, a principle based
on the idea of personal, rather than family, rights to property. The law

of Gortyn permitted no changes in the succession except by adoption, and even the provision of free choice in adopting a son was probably an innovation.[27] In Athens, the power to bequeath freely was first instituted by Solon,[28] but it was restricted to men without legitimate sons. In Sparta, a man was entirely free to leave his property to whomever he wished.[29] The trend was toward the Spartan, and away from the Gortynian, system. At the beginning of the fourth century a litigant could claim that 'while the Greeks differ on many other (points of law), on this (the right to make a will in the absence of descendants) they all agree'.[30] In the Hellenistic period, bequests became yet freer.[31]

In Athens, the restrictions were formidable. The law read, 'Whoever had not been adopted under terms forbidding renunciation or judicial challenge when Solon became archon, shall be permitted to bequeath his own property as he pleases, if there are no legitimate male children, (and) if he does not act by reason of insanity or old age or drugs or illness, or under the influence of a woman, behaving senselessly because of one of the above, or being constrained by force or by imprisonment'.[32] These provisions left sufficient room for virtually any will to be challenged (the Thirty Tyrants, according to Aristotle, eliminated some of the limiting clauses 'so as not to leave an opening for troublemakers'[33]), and in fact the courts tended to be hostile to litigants claiming rights under a will.[34] We must suppose that a will whose beneficiary was a woman would *ipso facto* be suspected of having been made 'under the influence of a woman'; but in spite of that we do know of such wills being made. In two of the three known cases, the wills were made for specific dangers – a military campaign[35] and an embassy[36] – from which the testators returned safely, so that the provisions were never fulfilled; in the third, the girl did in fact succeed to the estate – but the heir *ab intestato*, who was her natural father, controlled the estate for nine years during the girl's minority, a circumstance which may have blunted his eagerness to contest the will.[37] All of these wills were in fact testamentary adoptions, whereby the entire estate was left to the woman; we have no example of an estate being left to a woman who was not adopted by the testator. The adoption of women is attested for cities other than Athens, but no details are known.[38]

If it was uncommon to designate a woman as heir to one's entire estate, it was not at all uncommon to write a will in which the women of one's family were provided for. Apollodorus, in contesting Pasio's will, claimed that such provisions could be made only in the absence of legitimate sons;[39] but we have other cases to deny his claim. The father of Demosthenes, with a legitimate son, left a will giving a dowry of eighty minae to his wife, one of two talents to his daughter, and the usufruct of seventy minae to one of the three guardians he appointed;[40] in the suits Demosthenes later brought to recover the estate, he never contested his father's right to give away this money. Diodotus, going off to war, left a will with his brother Diogeiton, and commanded him 'if anything should happen to him, to give his wife away with a talent's dowry and to give (her) what was in the house (presumably her 'clothing and jewelry'), and (to give) a talent (as dowry) with his daughter. He also left his wife twenty minae and thirty Cyzicene staters'.[41] This will, too, seems to have gone unchallenged, although Diodotus' had two legitimate sons.[42] At Gortyn, where disposition by will was not authorized, a husband could nevertheless leave his wife up to a hundred staters without the consent of his heirs; it seems probable that the older law allowed even more generous settlements.[43] In view of these examples, Apollodorus' argument — which, as Wyse points out, even he did not offer for twenty years after his father's death[44] — has very properly been rejected by all scholars who have examined the question.[45] Even a man with sons, apparently, could bequeath sums of money to others (though a woman, of course, would not be 'another' unless, as in the cases just mentioned, she was being given in marriage to another family);[46] what he could not do was appoint a principal heir other than his sons.[47] In Sparta, and presumably in other cities as well, he could do even this; and we do know of one will from Erythrae in which a man's sons were replaced by his wife, who took responsibility for their welfare.[48]

The ability to make a will that did not exclude sons is likely to have worked to the benefit of women — wives and daughters — who were excluded from intestate inheritance, but in whose security the dying man was very interested. This is the case in the wills mentioned above of Pasio, Diodotus, and Demosthenes' father; it is the only case provided for in the Gortynian law. In Athens, the provision might take the form of a dowry given to a designated husband, or of a legacy bequeathed directly to the woman. Pasio's will provided for both, that of Demosthenes' father only for the first. The most interesting is that of Diodotus, which, rather than giving the dowries to a husband-elect, ordered his executor Diogeiton to do so; in this way, Diodotus was able to ensure the women's future (assuming Diogeiton's trustworthiness) in spite of the fact that he had not selected a husband for them. The items 'in the house', which were to be given directly to his wife, were the trousseau that would go along with her to her new husband; the twenty minae and thirty Cyzicene staters were, on the other hand, left directly to her in the will, without passing through Diogeiton's hands and without being dependent upon her marriage.[49] In the two sentences that describe this will, we find all the forms by which Athenian men provided for their wives and daughters after their death.

Intestate succession. Where the father did not, or could not, make a

will, or when the will was voided by the courts, the estate fell under
the rules of intestate succession. These rules varied in particulars from
place to place, but their essential structure was the same throughout
Greece. Inheritance rights were determined by family proximity,[50]
but a woman had no right of inheritance in the presence of an equally
close male. Thus, for example, a daughter inherited only in the absence
of sons; a sister, only in the absence of brothers; an aunt, only in the
absence of uncles. Granted this restriction, however, the rights of women were not abridged, and we have no record of any place in Greece
where the rights of an uncle, for example, had precedence over the
rights of a sister. Thus in Athens, a man's sons inherited; if there were
no sons, his daughter became an *epikleros*, with the attendant rules –
eventually her sons inherited; if there were no daughters, the paternal
relatives: brothers (or their children), then sisters, then uncles, then
aunts, then, perhaps, great-uncles and great-aunts.[51] If there were no
paternal relatives within this circle, maternal relatives came in the same
order: brothers, sisters, etc. Failing these, the estate reverted to the
nearest paternal relative – presumably according to the same rule.[52]

In other places the rules were similar. In Gortyn, the deceased's
daughters did in fact get a share – though not an equal share – in the
presence of sons; beyond that, the order (as far as the inscription states
it) was the same, with daughters (as *epikleroi*)[53] followed by brothers,
then sisters.[54] The fact that the sisters have no rights in presence of
brothers shows us that the limited inheritance of daughters was a special provision in their favour, and does not reflect a general equality or
near-equality of women in Gortynian inheritance. An inscription of
Naupactus on the occasion of a land division prescribes the order: sons,
then daughters, then brothers, and explicitly excludes the daughters
where there are sons to inherit.[55] In early fourth-century Aegina, a
paternal sister could claim an estate where the deceased had not left
children or brothers.[56] A private document from Tegea[57] and Plato's
Laws[58] point in the same direction, though in the latter the philo-
sopher's plan to have a male *and* female heir for each estate required
certain changes in the accepted pattern.

Two effects of this law must be noticed. Most obviously, although a
woman was legally competent to inherit, she was not guaranteed a
share. Every man was entitled to a share of his father's estate; but only
certain women – those without brothers – could ever expect to inherit
anything at all. The dowry was in some respects a compensation for
this: although it did not, as we shall see, belong to the woman in a
legal sense, it was a share of the patrimony, which was set aside for her
maintenance, and which every woman was likely to count on. In Gortyn, in fact, women *did* share in the inheritance: daughters received
one-half of a son's share of their father's inheritance, with the excep-

tion of certain forms of property (town houses; the contents of houses in the country, and the cattle — i.e., the essentials of the estate), which were divided exclusively among the sons. This phenomenon, unparalleled elsewhere and anomalous even in Gortyn, where sisters had no analogous rights, will be discussed later.

Another, perhaps less obvious point, is that since the woman's legal right to inherit was nowhere abridged, it was perfectly possible, even at Athens, for a woman to become the heiress of a very sizable estate. This being so, the absence of women from Athenian land records might seem surprising; but again, the reason is to be sought in the fact that they were not heads of households. When a woman inherited, even though all the records indicate that she inherited 'in her own right', her *kyrios* immediately became *kyrios* of the inheritance as well. He could dispose of it, and she could not; he was responsible for managing it, and she was not. Attic law recognized no other form of ownership;[59] the inheritance law, in which women were clearly capable heirs, was not stating who was to become *kyrios* of the property, but rather, into whose *oikos* it was to pass. It went without saying that the *kyrios* of that *oikos* became *kyrios* of the inheritance; and so whether a man or a woman inherited, it was always a man who became the legal owner.

3

The *Epikleros*

• •

Women, then, could inherit in certain circumstances; but they did not
become the legal – or the effective – owners of their property. Particularly thorny was the matter of the *epikleros, the daughter left without brothers at her father's death*. It would have seemed, on general
principles, that she should have been the heiress of the estate; there is
no hint in the law of any Greek city that would place a more distantly
related male before her or any other female. Nobody should have come
before a daughter except her brothers, and the *epikleros*, by definition,
had none.

But the matter was not as simple as that. In Athens, it was the *epikleros* herself who passed, along with the inheritance, to her father's
next-of-kin. This latter – the *anchisteus*, to use the Attic term –
claimed her along with her estate in the court of the archon; if he was
successful in his claim, the girl was betrothed to him, and the estate
passed to the children born of this union when they came of age. The
law was not peculiar to Athens; it recurred, in various forms, in other
cities, and may well have been true throughout Greece.[1] It put the
epikleros in a unique position both legally and socially, a position at
once more powerful and more helpless than that in which her dowered
neighbours found themselves.

Definition. The 'normal' case of an *epikleros* was the one we have mentioned, a daughter without brothers at her father's death. But in fact
the word was used with various meanings, of which the reader should
be aware at the outset. The different definitions are given concisely in
the Suda under the word *epikleros*: 'When a girl is orphaned of father
and mother and lacking brothers, and when she has property pertaining
to her, they call her an *epikleros*; similarly also a woman already married, when she is left along with the entire property, for they call property a *kleros*. A woman is also called an *epikleros* who is not yet married, but living with her father, inasmuch as all the property falls to her.
And they are called *epikleroi* even if there are two or even more.' The
first sentence of this entry corresponds approximately to the case we
mentioned above, except for the words 'and mother', which are incor-
rect; whether or not the girl's mother was alive had no effect on the
inheritance of her father's estate.[2] We may also note that the 'property
pertaining to her' might consist of an estate encumbered with debt.[3]

The extension of the definition to married women and to women who have sisters is supported by our sources;[4] the application of the term to 'potential' *epikleroi* whose fathers are still alive or not, but is likely enough.[5] The word seems also to have been used, on occasion, as if it were the feminine of *orphanos*, 'orphan'.[6] These last two uses have no legal significance. The statement of the scholiast on Aeschin. 1.95 ('A woman is called an *epikleros*, if her father on his deathbed leaves her to someone in marriage, saying that "I wish to give her to this man" ') is not borne out by any of the extant literature, and may be a misunderstanding of a passage in Aristophanes.[7]

A certain amount of legal uncertainty seems to heve existed — or to have been created — as to the precise definition of the term *epikleros*. None of the laws that have been preserved define the term, and some of the claims of speakers seem to have been legally disputable. Apollodorus, attempting to demonstrate that his mother was an *epikleros*, quoted a law on betrothal, which — he claimed — defined an *epikleros* as any woman without father, brother from the same father, or paternal grandfather; the effort he makes to demonstrate his mother's status shows that his opponent denied it,[8] and his opponent was certainly correct. The claim of the speaker of Isaeus 10 rests on the presumption that his mother became an *epikleros* when her minor brother died after his father; this claim is uncertain to us, and may have been denied by the archon.[9] The basic meaning of the word, however, is clear, and most women must have known whether or not they were *epikleroi*.

Ownership of the estate. The only legal restraints on the husband's *kyrieia* of his wife's property were those connected with her dowry, and her only protection against having her money spent by a profligate husband came from her male relatives. This was hardly direct control of her property, but it could, as we shall see when we come to discuss the dowry, be used to good advantage. The *epikleros* had no such leverage; she could not take her fortune and return to her former *kyrios*, for it was to him that she was married. The protection of her estate was therefore managed by removing it as soon as possible from the *anchisteus* and placing it in the hands of its heirs, who thereupon became responsible for their mother's maintenance, just as they would have been if they were in possession of her dowry. This law has been preserved for us: 'And if a person be born of an *epikleros*, as soon as he is two years past puberty, he is to have control of the possessions, and give an allowance of food to his mother'.[10] The law does not seem to distinguish the case of an *epikleros* married to the *anchisteus* from that of an *epikleros* married to an outsider; we do not know if any such distinction existed in practice.[11]

No law that has come down to us specifies who was to own the es-

tate of the *epikleros* until her children came of age, and it is certain
that no such law existed; for whenever the orators refer to the interim
state of the inheritance, it is always the law we have just quoted to
which appeal is made. The text of the law, of course, says nothing
about this problem; but its intention was clear enough to the Athenians,
who recognized it as denying to the husband of the *epikleros* the *kyrieia* (and here we must translate 'right of ownership') that a husband
normally exercised over his wife's goods. Thus the speaker of Isaeus 10
remarks, 'Nor, gentlemen, was it permissible for either Aristomenes or
Apollodorus, who had the right to claim my mother's hand by *epidikasia*, (to have had her estate without marrying her). For it would be
extraordinary to believe that, whereas if Apollodorus or Aristomenes
had married my mother, he would not have been able to become *kyrios*
of her possessions — according to the law which permits no one to become *kyrios* of the possessions of an *epikleros* except the children, who
have control of the possessions when they are two years past puberty —
but now that he has given her in marriage to another, it would be possible for him to have a son adopted as heir to her possessions!'[12] Similarly Ciron's grandson: 'For if my mother, Ciron's daughter, were alive,
and Ciron had died without making a will, and my opponent were his
brother, instead of being (merely) his nephew, he would be entitled to
marry the woman, but not entitled to her property; (her property
would rather belong to) the children born from him and from her, when
they were two years past puberty; for that is what the laws command'.[13]
In other passages it is stated directly that the estate belonged, during
the minority of the children, to the *epikleros* herself: 'For we believe
that the nearest of kin should marry her, but the possessions should
belong at first to the *epikleros*, and then, when the children are two
years past puberty, they should control them'.[14] Similar in intent is
the expression 'what had been left to my mother' in a fragment of
Hypereides dealing with the succession of an *epikleros*' son.[15]

We might accept these last citations and state that the *epikleros* herself controlled the estate during her sons' minority; but this control
must have been very passive, since her right to dispose of it legally was
limited to transactions of the value of a medimnus of barley. Nevertheless, the estate had to be managed by someone; if it included land, the
land had to be worked, and if it included a tenement, the rents had to
be collected. Now the *epikleros*' husband was surely *kyrios* of her person, and presumably, as every other husband at Athens, he managed
his wife's estate. If there were expenses involved in its management, he
must have been able to pay them out of the capital. But he was responsible to the heirs when they came of age, and if he had mishandled the
property he could be called to account. The difference between the
estate of an *epikleros* and the dowry of an ordinary wife was not that

the *epikleros* could exercise more legal control over her property, but that her husband could exercise less; and for this reason the sources never refer to her estate as if it belonged to him.[16] His position was analogous to that of an *epitropos*, the guardian of an orphan – so much so, in fact, that the estate was exempted from liturgies, as were those of orphans, during the children's minority.[17]

It appears to have been possible, though not required,[18] for the husband of the *epikleros* to have one of her sons adopted post-humously as a son of her father. Normally adoption conferred rights of inheritance; this was true of posthumous adoption as well.[19] Where there was an *epikleros*, however, the adoption had to be 'with' her, that is, the adopted son had to marry the girl.[20] Clearly this was out of the question when it was her own son who was being adopted; and the question has been raised, whether the adopted son now enjoyed exclusive rights to his grandfather's property. On the one hand, as Hruza pointed out,[21] he lost his rights to his father's estate by being adopted; on the other, we know of at least one case where the adopted son already had a brother who had achieved his majority, and it seems unlikely that this elder brother could have been required to relinquish the estate of which he was already *kyrios*.[22] Much has been said on both sides,[23] none of it entirely convincing. Where adoption did not take place, the *oikos* of the deceased became extinct, for its heirs – the children of the *epikleros* – belonged to their father's *oikos*, not their maternal grandfather's. The point is of some significance, for it shows that whatever the function of the epiclerate may have been at Athens, it was not a method of preserving the *oikoi*.

Marriage to an outsider. Not every *epikleros* was conveniently unmarried at her father's death. Even a father with no sons, when his daughter came of age, was obliged to arrange a marriage for her; and he did not necessarily marry her to his next-of-kin. There were certainly some cases, however, in which such a marriage could be dissolved by the *anchisteus* upon the father's death. 'Many men who were already married have had their own wives taken away from them'[24] says one litigant, and it is not the sort of statement that could be made if it were false. Another litigant alleges that his father had to give up his claim to his mother's estate because of threats from the *anchisteus* to take away the mother by *epidikasia*.[25] The prevalent view among modern scholars is that the marriage could be dissolved only so long as it had not produced a male heir; various attempts have been made to prove this, but none have been completely successful.[26] The best piece of evidence comes from the *Adelphoe* of Terence, where Micio teases his adopted son Aeschinus by pretending to represent the *anchisteus* of the girl Aeschinus has seduced and would like to marry.

MI. This girl is orphaned of her father; this friend of mine is her
next-of-kin: the laws require her to marry him. AE. I'm done for.
MI. What's wrong? AE. Nothing; it's all right; go on. MI. He's coming
to take her away with him, since he lives in Miletus. AE. Oh no! To
take the girl away with him? MI. That's right. AE. Excuse me – all
the way to Miletus? MI. Yes. AE. I don't feel well. What about them?
What do they say? MI. What would you expect of them? But it
doesn't matter. The mother made up a story that a child had been
born by some other man – and she doesn't name him; she says that
he comes first, and the girl shouldn't be given to my friend.[27]

The 'some other man' is, of course, Aeschinus; but what is significant
for us is that the law must be Athenian – it is hardly Roman – and the
mother can challenge the right of the *anchisteus* by claiming that the
girl has had a son. Micio later objects by questioning the legitimacy of
the marriage ('who betrothed her? who gave her away? whom did she
marry, and when?'), not by denying that the law is as the mother
implied.[28] Terence, a Roman playwright who adapted Athenian comedies, is not the best authority we have for Attic law; but in this case
there is little reason to doubt his word. In fact, where a son had been
born, the adjudication of the *epikleros* would serve little purpose, for
the deceased would already have his grandchild, and we have no reason
to believe that a potential son by the *anchisteus* was any more desirable;[29] before the son was born, on the other hand, the *anchisteus*
would probably have been able to dissolve the marriage by his authority as *kyrios* (for Greek marriage was in certain respects a conditional
agreement, dependent upon the birth of children) – whereupon the
girl would be liable to *epidikasia*, and he could claim her.[30]

The original marriage, then, would apparently subsist if it had produced a male heir;[31] it could also remain if there were no *anchisteus*,
or if the relatives chose not to challenge the marriage. Such seems to
have been the case with the daughters of Polyeuctus, whose marriages
remained after his death although there is no indication that their
husbands were his next-of-kin;[32] Meidylides attempted to marry his
daughter to the *anchisteus* during his lifetime, and married her to a
third party only when his brother 'said that he preferred not to marry,
and rather allowed the estate to remain undivided because of this,
living on his own in Salamis'.[33] The father might also ensure the future of the marriage by adopting his son-in-law; this possibility will be
considered later. Lastly, the *anchisteus* himself might give away the
epikleros to another man, preferring either to keep his own wife, or to
remain unmarried, or to avoid saddling himself with a debt-ridden
estate – or even, perhaps, to find a more suitable husband for the girl.[34]

The estate of an *epikleros* always passed to her children, whether by
the *anchisteus* or by an outsider. It could enter the *kyrieia* of the

anchisteus only if he married the girl; this is the meaning of the law of succession which begins, 'whoever dies without having made a will, if he leaves female children, with these; if not, the following are to be *kyrioi* of the property'. (There follows a list of possible heirs, beginning from the paternal brothers of the deceased.) [35] The words 'with these' — *syn tautēisin* — here mean, as they do in the law of adoption, [36] 'on condition of marrying them'; if the girl was given instead to an outsider, her husband assumed the management of her estate, and his children became *kyrioi* of it upon their majority, or perhaps on their mother's death. [37] The real and hypothetical applications of this rule are numerous. [38]

If the estate was worth anything at all, it was obviously to the financial advantage of the *anchisteus* to marry the girl and obtain her father's entire patrimony, rather than the smaller portion he could get by marrying a dowered woman of the same wealth. Occasionally the girl's husband, or another interested party, would make an arrangement to buy off the next-of-kin. The speaker of Isaeus 10 claims that his father allowed the next-of-kin unchallenged rights to the estate throughout his lifetime, for fear that his wife would be taken away from him. [39] Chaerestratus offers a similar bargain to Smicrines in Menander's *Aspis*,

> so take the entire estate, however much it is, become the *kyrios*, we give it to you; but let the girl get a husband appropriate to her age.

I will give along with her two talents' dowry out of my own pocket, but Smicrines refuses with foresight:

> By the gods, do you suppose that you're talking to Simple Simon? What are you saying? I should take the estate, but let the girl go to this other man so that, if a son should be born, he could sue me for having possession of his property? [40]

He is worried, of course, about exactly the kind of suit that the speaker of Isaeus 10 claimed to bring. It is possible that a similar agreement existed between Xenocles and Endius, whereby the former agreed not to contest the estate until the latter's death; the speech we have, delivered by Endius' brother and heir, makes much of Xenocles' delay, and takes it to imply that he knew his wife was not a true *epikleros*. [41] An interesting bargain was struck, according to Andocides, [42] between Callias and Leagrus in the matter of an *epikleros* who had been adjudged to the latter. Leagrus, in return for a sum of money, gave up his claim on the woman; this would then permit Callias' son to claim her — if Andocides, who was a nearer relation, could be kept away. Andocides advances this as Callias' reason for allegedly framing him on the charge of profaning the mysteries.

However that may be, it is interesting to see that the *anchisteus* could, in this case, be bought off for a fixed amount — presumably less

than the value of the estate. The explanation lies in the nature of the
estate: it consisted, according to Andocides, of two talents of assets-
on-hand and more than five talents of debt. Andocides tries to paint
this as a poor estate ('the household's affairs were doing badly', he
says), but the battle over it is an indication that considerable wealth
was involved; presumably as much was owed to the estate as by it, and
possibly much more. Callias, a man of fantastic wealth who was in the
process of losing it,[43] was casting about for a way to regain his fortune;
he was willing to gamble on his ability to collect the outstanding
wealth of the estate. Leagrus, for his part, was willing to accept a bird
in the hand; but the attempt apparently failed, for Callias' son married
another woman, the daughter of Alcibiades.[44]

Adopted sons. The law of Solon permitted a man with no sons to adopt
one. The adopted son thereupon became his heir, and was known by
the patronymic of his adoptive father; on the other hand, he lost his
claim to the inheritance of his natural father. If his adoptive father had
a daughter, the son was required to marry her.[45]

In effect, then, a father could prevent his daughter from becoming
adjudicable upon his death by adopting his son-in-law. This method,
however, was not always the best. The son-in-law might refuse, since
the adoption would exclude him from his own patrimony; and a man
with two daughters might not want to settle his estate on only one of
them.[46] Instructive is the case of Polyeuctus, who gave away his elder
daughter with a dowry of forty minae, and married the younger to her
maternal uncle, whom he adopted. He quarrelled with the uncle, dissolved the marriage, and married the younger daughter to Spudias, giving her a dowry of (apparently) thirty minae; arbitration was required
between Polyeuctus and his daughter's ex-husband to resolve the
economic problems arising from the divorce. In the eventual settlement, the adoption was cancelled,[47] and Polyeuctus' estate was
divided between his daughters at his death. His sons-in-law, in their
turn, quarrelled over the division of the estate: the dowry of forty
minae promised to the first included ten minae to be delivered by the
adopted son at Polyeuctus' death. Since, at Polyeuctus' death, the
adoption had been invalidated, the son-in-law tried to remove the ten
minae from the estate, but was resisted by Spudias; our speech is from
the court case that resulted.[48] It is quite possible that Spudias claimed
that the ten minae were to be the speaker's share in the inheritance,
which meant he had no more right to the extra compensation. In any
event, it is clear that Polyeuctus created a good deal of trouble for himself by adopting his daughter's first husband, and that he did not
improve the situation by failing to adopt her second.

The epikleros and the oikos. On the face of it the mandated marriage
of an orphan daughter with a near relative looks like a device to preserve
the deceased's *oikos*; and indeed, it has been claimed[49] that this was a
major purpose of the law, or even the major purpose. This may have
been the case elsewhere in Greece, where the details of the law differed from the Athenian; but it cannot have been its function at Athens.

Now, there is no doubt that the preservation of the *oikoi* was an
important goal of Athenian law;[50] and in fact, the law offered a means
for that, by the adoption of a son. If there was a daughter, the adopted
son had to marry her; if there was not, he became the sole heir. Either
way, he or his children remained in the household and continued its
existence after the death of the adopter. This was, in fact, the entire
purpose of adoption in Athens; it was not designed to provide parents
for orphans or to provide children for childless couples, but to perpetuate the *oikos*. Thus the adoptee was usually a relative of the adopter,
often an adult;[51] and adoption could take place even after the death of
the adopter, in which case his heirs would arrange the adoption, but
the adopted would still be considered the son of the deceased.[52]

The law of the *epikleros*, however, saved no *oikos* from extinction.
For there were in fact two *oikoi* involved: the immediate *oikos* of the
deceased — that is, his descendants — and that of his parents or grandparents, of which his collaterals were a part. The latter (as long as there
was a male next-of-kin to claim the *epikleros*) was in no more danger
of dying out than any other *oikos* with surviving males. It might be
argued, perhaps, that this larger *oikos* had an interest in seeing that no
share of the grandfather's inheritance passed to another family; but had
this been the intent of the law, it would have had to apply to all women
who inherit — which seems not to be the case, although it cannot be
proven — and maternal relatives would have had to be eliminated from
the succession, which, in Athens, was explicitly not the case.

The smaller *oikos*, on the other hand — that of the deceased — had
only daughters; what we should require would not be that their children
be gotten by members of the larger *oikos* (which does not lack for
heirs), but rather that these children, by whatever father, remain in the
smaller *oikos*. We need, in short, a system whereby the deceased would
be considered father to his daughter's children, or to some of them;
that is, a system of automatic adoption. We have not a shred of evidence
for such a system in Athens, or in Gortyn, or anywhere in Greece. In
Athens, indeed, we know the contrary to have been true, for the
younger Eubulides, whose mother was an *epikleros*, was a member of
his father's *oikos* until given in posthumous adoption into his grandfather's.[53] There was nothing automatic about his entry into his
grandfather's household; this entry was accomplished by the appro-

priate vehicle, adoption, and the epiclerate had nothing to do with it.
The adoption was neither compulsory when the law of the *epikleros*
applied[54] nor precluded when it did not.[55] The *oikos* which survived
was the one whose *kyrios* saw to it that a son was born or adopted, and
if nobody took care of this, the presence of an *epikleros* would not
save it.

Rich epikleroi. A rich *epikleros* was a prize, and suitors flocked around
her. Protomachus divorced his wife in order to marry one,[56] and Timo-
crates seems to have done the same.[57] Androcles was so eager to gain
Euctemon's estate that he claimed the hand of his daughter as an *epikleros* at the same time as he advanced two boys as being legitimate
sons of Euctemon.[58] Andocides accused Callias of plotting 'to have me
killed without trial or exiled, bribe Leagrus, and marry Epilycus'
daughter'.[59] Aristotle, describing how civil wars arise 'not over small
issues, but out of small incidents' (*ou peri mikrōn all' ek mikrōn*).[60]
mentions even bloodier competitions: 'and in the case of Mytilene, it
was the beginning of many troubles when a conflict arose concerning
epikleroi, culminating in the war against Athens in which Paches cap-
tured their city. For when Timophanes, one of the rich men (of Mytilene), left two daughters, Dexandrus – who had been forced out of the
picture and failed to get either of them for his sons – began the civil
disturbance and egged on the Athenians, whose *proxenos* he was. And
in Phocis, too, when there was a conflict about an *epikleros* concerning
Mnaseas the father of Mnason and Euthycrates the father of Onomarchos,
that conflict was the beginning of the Sacred War against Phocis.'[61]
Neither of these stories is attested elsewhere, and they may be apocry-
phal; but they do indicate how serious could be the competition for a
rich woman's hand.

Epidikasia. It was the duty of the archon to decide such disputes, as it
was his duty to decide inheritance cases in general; the polemarch had
jurisdiction over metic *epikleroi.*[62] The *anchisteus* had no right to marry
the girl until the archon adjudged her to him.[63] Any claimant to the
rights of next-of-kin had to put in a claim with the archon; the claim
was publicized, and other claimants invited to apply.[64] The woman was
awarded to the nearest relative who appeared; the order was apparently
the same as that in the normal inheritance law, which appears to have
specified (a) paternal brothers of the deceased, or their legitimate
children; (b) paternal sisters, or their legitimate children; (c) paternal
uncles, or their legitimate children; (d) paternal aunts, or their legitimate children – in these last two categories the limit 'as far as cousins'
children' (*mechri anepsiōn paidōn*) may mean that representation did
not pass on indefinitely;[65] (e) maternal relatives, in the same order as

the above, also 'as far as cousins' children'; (f) more distant paternal relatives *ad infinitum*.[66] In the adjudication of an *epikleros,* of course, only males could be considered; but it seems clear that in Athens, unlike Gortyn, the claim to an *epikleros* could be inherited through females, so that a sister's son, for example, would be an eligible claimant. [67]

Athenian inheritance law did not recognize primogeniture, but prescribed equal division *per stirpes*[68] among members of each of the groups mentioned above. Since the Athenians were monandrous, this was impossible in the case of the *epikleros,* and the girl, with such rights to her fortune as her husband had, belonged to the oldest member of the nearest class of relations.[69]

Since the archon was called upon to judge only among those candidates who presented themselves, there was always the possibility that a nearer one existed. The announcement of the herald, inviting any claimant to apply was an effort to make sure that all possible claimants appeared; *epheboi* — young men undergoing military training, who normally could neither sue nor be sued — were granted special leave to appear in court to claim their inheritance or their rights to an *epikleros.*[70] If in spite of this a nearer relative appeared later, he could challenge the adjudication and have it revoked in his favour;[71] but his opponent might argue that his delay in claiming demonstrated the weakness of his case.[72]

Except for the rule of primogeniture, the entire procedure of *epidikasia* was the same for any estate, whether or not it included an *epikleros.* This is not quite to say that the *epikleros* was 'merely a piece of property', but rather that the right to the *epikleros* and the right to the estate were, in Athenian law, functions of the same thing: proximity of relation to the deceased. The purpose of the *epidikasia* was to establish who the nearest relative was; he then became *kyrios* of the deceased's *oikos,* a position which made him both owner of the property and *kyrios* of the women.

If the women were not *epikleroi* — if, for example, a man inherited his brother's estate, and became thereby *kyrios* of his unmarried sister — then the heir's responsibility was the same as that of any *kyrios*: to find her a husband, if she was of marriageable age, and provide a suitable dowry. But if there was an *epikleros* in the *oikos* under adjudication, the law was just the opposite: her new *kyrios* was not to marry her off to another, but to take her for his own wife. The law, in fact, equated the adjudication of an *epikleros* with the betrothal (*engyē*)[73] of other women: 'Any woman whom a father or paternal brother or grandfather on the father's side betroths lawfully to be a wife — children born from her are to be legitimate. If there be none of the above, if she be an *epikleros,* the *kyrios* is to marry her, and if not, that person will be *kyrios* to whom he shall turn her over.'[74] Now, it was the hallmark of a lawful marriage that children born from it were legitimate; thus the first phrase, legitimizing the children of a betrothed wife, legitimizes marriage by betrothal, and the second phrase, legitimizing the marriage of an *epikleros* with her *kyrios,* legitimizes the children of such a marriage. No further betrothal was necessary.[75]

The *kyrios* of another woman could give her in marriage but not marry her; conversely, the *epikleros'* next-of-kin could marry her himself, but not — as long as there were other claimants — give her in marriage. This is hinted at by Aristotle, who complains that in Sparta 'whoever is left as heir gives her (the *epikleros*) to whomever he wishes'[76] — a complaint which implies that such was not the case at Athens, since Aristotle is describing the causes of Spartan weakness in his day. But a clearer indication is given by the case already mentioned of Andocides and Leagrus, in which Callias, having bought off Leagrus (the nearest relative) then had to dispose of Andocides in order to get the girl for his son.[77] Had it been legal, it would surely have been much simpler to have had Leagrus agree to claim the girl, and then give her in marriage to Callias' son; but Leagrus apparently had no such option. He could fail to put in a claim for the *epikleros*, in which case Andocides would succeed in his claim; or he could claim her, in which case he would go out of court with the girl already legally betrothed to him. Only in the case of a poor *epikleros*, whom nobody was willing to claim, did the law provide for the next-of-kin to offer her in marriage to another.

Since the benevolence of the Athenian people was a myth dear to their own hearts, judges might perhaps have listened to the argument of a claimant like Chaerestratus, who wished the court to declare his aunt an *epikleros* for — he assured them — her own good: 'Now, you must consider this . . . whether Philoctemon's sister, who was married to Chaereas and is now widowed, ought to be turned over to these men (sc. her alleged brothers, whose legitimacy Chaerestratus is contesting) to be given in marriage to whomever they please or left to grow old unmarried, or whether, being legitimate, she ought to be adjudicated in marriage to whomever seems best to you.'[78] Chaerestratus, of course, is her next-of-kin. Aristophanes shows less innocence when Philocleon describes the procedure in the *Wasps*: 'And if a father dies leaving his daughter to someone as an *epikleros*, we tell the will to go cry its head off along with the case so solemnly placed on its seals, and we give her to whomever persuades us with his pleading. And we can't be held accountable, unlike all the other offices'.[79]

The married epikleros. Where the estate was rich, the system of *epidikasia* was hardly likely to produce a love-match. The most immediate problem caused by the rules themselves was the danger of a young *epikleros* being claimed by a much older man. One law, reported by Plutarch, required that the husband of an *epikleros* sleep with her three times a month, and this will have eliminated some from the competition; another, ostensibly Solonian, mentioned in the same passage, permits the court to dissolve her marriage and choose a more reasonable mate, if the man to whom she has been adjudicated is unable to perform his marital functions.[80] But the young *epikleros* and her old husband were surely not unknown at Athens: Isaeus mentions a girl, still a minor at her father's death, who was eventually married by her guardian,[81] and age is one of the considerations urged unsuccessfully on Smicrines in the *Aspis* to get him to withdraw his claim.[82] Plato's *Laws* provided for judgement by the magistrate as to the pair's suitability, 'examining the males when they are naked, and the females stripped to the navel'; [83] the law of Gortyn included the most obvious safeguard, for there the woman could refuse the match.[84] It is probable that popular scorn, along with the legal minimum of marital rights, discouraged many people from applying for *epikleroi*; but a middle-aged man was surely eligible to compete for a pubescent girl, and surely many did.

As for control of her money, the position of the *epikleros* differed from that of the dowered bride only in degree. Like the dowered bride, she was not *kyria* of the money, which her husband could use as he pleased — but since her estate was larger and her husband had usually been attracted by it more than by her, she was rather more exposed to his abuse. On the other hand, again like the dowered bride, she derived leverage from the fact that the husband who abused her sufficiently was open to very uncomfortable legal action — but since the law provided sterner penalties for *epiklērou kakōsis* (abuse of an *epikleros*) than for wasting a dowry,[85] the *epikleros* had a stronger hand. We find at least one case of alleged exploitation: 'as long as the estate of the *epikleros* whom Hegesandros — this man's lover — had married and the money which he brought back from the expedition under Timomachus lasted, they led a wanton and profligate existence . . . ',[86] but the men seem to have been equally wary of the opposite problem: 'Whoever sets his heart on marrying a rich *epikleros* is either paying the penalty of the gods' anger, or else wants to be miserable and be called lucky',[87] or again:

A. I've married a witch of an *epikleros*; hadn't I told you? B. Not about this. A. We've gotten ourselves an outright boss of the house and the fields and everything. B. Good God, how awful. A. As awful as can be. She's a pain to everybody, not just to me, much more so to my son, my daughter. B. You're describing a hopeless situation. A. Don't I know it![88]

Aristotle, after comparing the normal household of a man and wife to an 'aristocracy', finds the degenerate form in our case: 'Sometimes the wives rule, being *epikleroi*; then the rule is not according to merit, but by wealth and power, just as in oligarchies'.[89] The position of the *epikleros* seems to have differed little in this respect from that of the modern rich heiress: exposed to fortune-hunting and avarice, she also had considerable power to wield over the man who won her. What she did not have was any part in choosing that man — nor even the paternal benevolence that served the other women of Athens at the time of decision.

Poor epikleroi. Quite different was the state of the *epikleros* with a small inheritance. She had neither money to attract a mate, nor a father or brother who could try to collect a dowry. The situation was bad enough for the *polis* to have to force her relatives by law to marry her off. The law is preserved in a speech included in the Demosthenic corpus:

> Those *epikleroi* who are assessed in the thetic (i.e., poorest) class: if their nearest relative does not wish to marry them, he is to give them in marriage, along with a dowry of five hundred drachmas if he is a *pentakosiomedimnos* (the richest class), three hundred if he is a *hippeus* (the next class), a hundred fifty if he is a *zeugitēs* (the third class), in addition to her own property. And if there are more than one in the same proximity of relationship, each is to give proportionately to the *epikleros*. If there are more than one woman, it is not compulsory for each one[90] to give more than one in marriage, but each nearest relative in turn (*ton engutata aei*) shall either give her in marriage or marry her himself. If the nearest relative does not marry them or give them in marriage, the archon is to compel him either to marry her himself or to give her in marriage. If the archon should not compel him, he is to owe a thousand drachmas, which are to be consecrated ... Anyone who wishes may denounce before the archon the man who does not fulfil this.[91]

Along with the laws went a sense of obligation; the speaker of Isaeus 1 says to the jurors that if his cousin had been a poor *epikleros*, the laws 'and my sense of shame before you' would have forced him to marry her.[92] Nor should we forget the noble speech of Andocides to Leagrus, insincere though it be: 'This would be behaving like honourable men, to show our family ties to each other in such a circumstance. It is not right for us to choose other property or a man's fortune, if that would mean disdaining Epilycus' daughter. For if Epilycus were alive, or if he had died and left much property, we would have expected to marry his children, since we are the nearest relatives. Now, that would surely have been because of Epilycus or because of his property; but now it will be because of our honesty. So you claim the hand of one of them, and I the other.'[93] The fine sentiments are only slightly dimmed by the likelihood that the girl was, in fact, rich.

How often such noble feelings were aroused by a true pauper we do not know. In Athens the legally fixed dowry of five minae was apparently insufficient to attract a husband, and it had to be doubled.[94] In Thurii, too, where the law had been the same as the Athenian, it was finally necessary, according to Diodorus, to change it: henceforward the *anchisteus* was required to marry the *epikleros,* with no alternative of giving her away.[95] As barbaric as the custom of assigning a husband by inheritance law may seem to the modern mind, the plight of the penniless *epikleros* was bad enough to make it an act of charity. After all, anything — to a Greek — was better than spinsterhood.

Redress. The archon was the legal defender of citizen *epikleroi,* the polemarch of metics.[96] It was his duty to punish all the abuses to which *epikleroi* were subject: *kyrioi* who refused to marry the women or to give then in marriage; husbands or guardians who wasted their estates; husbands who failed to perform their marital duties; outsiders who occupied their property illegally.[97] The law that has been preserved seems, in fact, to give the archon power over all possible abuses: 'He is to take care of them, and he is not to permit anyone to do any injury towards them. And if anyone should commit any injury or do anything illegal, he is to have authority to impose a fine up to the limit of his powers'. He could also go to a heliastic court to demand a penalty larger than his own powers would allow.[98] It was, furthermore, the prerogative of any citizen to denounce a man to the archon for abuse of an *epikleros* and to prosecute without having to pay court fees, or to pay the usual fine if he did not receive a fifth of the judges' votes, or to have his eloquence trammelled by a limit on the length of his speech.[99] The laws gave the widest possible latitude to the prosecution, and we know of a case of a man being accused — and convicted, though our source complains that the trial was improper[100] — of *epiklērou kakōsis,* wronging an *epikleros,* for abusive behaviour towards the daughters of a man from whom he was collecting a debt.

The Athenian courts, then, were anything but insensitive to the exposed position of the *epikleros.* With their accustomed paternal attitude, they did all they could to protect her. To the modern mind it seems obvious that they could have solved her problems by granting her the right to dispose of her own hand; but to do so would have required allowing her to meet many suitors, to become acquainted with this one and with that, to go through various flirtations, and finally to settle on a husband of her choice. Such an idea was abhorrent to Athenian ideas of modesty and family; we, who have but a passing acquaintance with either, may perhaps hesitate before making the obvious judgment.

The function of the epiclerate. The legal position of the *epikleros* may strike the reader as bizarre, but that need not concern us at the descriptive level of history. Many facts about the Greeks seem bizarre, and surely many more would seem so if we understood them truly rather than fitting them willy-nilly into our twentieth-century expectations. What demands explanation, though, is the fact that her position was anomalous within Athenian law itself. If we look at the major principles governing her position, four stand out: (a) when a man dies and leaves daughters, his nearest collateral relative inherits the estate; (b) along with the estate, he inherits the daughters as well — or rather, each of the near collateral relatives inherits one daughter, and a corresponding proportion of the estate; (c) 'inheriting' the daughters is the legal equivalent of betrothal, and he must in fact consummate the marriage in order to retain possession of the estate; (d) when his sons by the daughter are two years past puberty, they take over the estate.

But of these four principles, only one is consistent with normal Athenian practice. (a) is not, for, as we have already seen, men did not normally inherit in the presence of more closely-related women; although the women could not become *kyriai* of the property in their own right, it entered their household in preference to that of the more distant male, and their *kyrios* became *kyrios* of the money. (c) surely was not the case; a woman's *kyrios* (other than the husband to whom she had been betrothed) generally had neither the obligation nor the right to marry her himself. (d) was just as exceptional; normally sons did not become *kyrioi* of any of their father's property until he either died or resigned his property to them. Only the second principle is in line with common practice, for the heir to an estate did indeed, in general, become *kyrios* of any women who belonged to it; but even here matters did not work quite in the normal way, because in the usual case (where the *kyrios* did not have to marry the woman to get the estate) a single heir would become *kyrios* of as many women as there were.

The law of the *epikleros,* then, can only have been a law specially designed for her case, since it was not the outcome of the general principles at work in the rest of the law. What prompted the Greeks to make such a rule? Or, if its origins are perhaps lost in an age of which we are too ignorant to make intelligent statements, why did they maintain it throughout the classical period?

Let us consider, for a moment, what the situation of the *epikleros* would have been if there had been no special laws concerning her — if the law had simply declared that daughters inherit in the absence of sons, and brothers in the absence of daughters, without making any further provisions in the matter.

She would, indeed, have been 'heiress', in the sense that the property would enter her household; but since she was not *kyria* of that household, the ultimate *kyrios* of the property would have been whoever was her own *kyrios*. If she was married, this would be her husband; if she was not, it would be her nearest relative — that is to say, the *anchisteus*.

Now in fact only the latter case need be considered, since if she was married and had children, she did not, apparently, become an *epikleros* at all; but as long as she had no children, the marriage was considered incomplete, and her father, at least, had the right to dissolve it. If, as seems reasonable, this right devolved upon the next-of-kin with her father's death, he would have been in a position to make himself *kyrios* of the *epikleros* by dissolving her marriage, even had there been no special legislation in her case.

If the property fell to the woman, then, it was her next-of-kin who became its *kyrios*; that is to say, of the four principles stated at the outset, (a), while it seems contrary to the spirit of the inheritance law, follows necessarily from the structure of the Greek family, and would follow even if the law had made the *epikleros* heiress in her own right.

So far, so good, then, and if it disturbs our imaginary heiress to see her uncle or cousin managing 'her' money, she is no worse off than every other woman of Athens, each of whom had her property managed by her *kyrios*. This is all fine if she is eight years old. But what if she is fourteen, and ready to get married?

When an orphan came of age he was entitled to his patrimony,[101] and a girl, whose marriage was the beginning of her majority, must have been entitled to the same; that is to say, her *kyrios* — whose job it was to marry her off — would presumably have had to deliver to the groom the estate to which she was, under the 'what-if' laws we are describing, heiress. But now the crunch comes: for the entire value of the estate stands as an inducement to her next-of-kin to put off the marriage. Next year will be plenty of time. Or maybe the year after that. Or the year after that. And so the girl will reach twenty-four, and thirty-four, and forty-four without getting married.

A modern mind may find the poor girl's situation touching, but it hardly seems to demand the drastic remedy that was applied. Surely she could go to court? It is highly unlikely that any court, at the period during which these laws grew up, would have interfered between a woman and her *kyrios*; even in classical Athens, it was still her *kyrios* who represented her in court, and the law did not expect another man to be more zealous in protecting her rights than her *kyrios*. When he himself was the problem, the courts could offer little help. Could the woman elope? To concubinage, perhaps, but never to marriage. Marriage in Athens was a contract between families, not individuals. Until the head of her *oikos* gave her in marriage into another *oikos*, she was not married, and her children were not legitimate; and these were matters of which the Greeks kept very careful record. It would surely seem, to a modern mind, that an exception could have been made, either to allow the woman to contract her own marriage, or to appear in court to force her *kyrios* to give her away; but the entire conception of marriage, of the family, and of woman's place within the family militated against this.

It would appear, then, that it was the orphan daughter herself whose situation would have been most compromised had the laws of the *epikleros* not obtained. The laws cannot have been designed to protect the rights of the next-of-kin; he, as the girl's *kyrios*, had all the rights he needed. They did not protect the dead man's *oikos*, as we have already seen. But they did assure that the girl was married. The same thing might perhaps have been achieved by permitting the next-of-kin to keep the estate, and to marry off the girl with a dowry; but the way chosen was more equitable, in that it ensured that the estate did indeed remain in the family of the *epikleros*, by mandating her marriage to the next-of-kin, and it further protected her rights by delivering it to the *kyrieia* of her sons as soon as they were of an age to manage it. A modern woman would surely prefer a free choice of husband to this 'equitable' solution; but here we are introducing an idea that was foreign to Athenian law, for in fact, no woman was entitled to choose her own husband. Other women's husbands were chosen by their fathers; they might indeed get more consideration from their fathers than the *epikleros* could get from the law, but they never had a free choice.

But if free choice was not important to the Athenians, seeing to it that the woman was married most definitely was. It was a matter of concern, even in the normal case, to the family as a whole, and even to friends and to the state. To permit a woman to grow old unmarried was, to the Athenians, one of the foulest things that could be done to her. Litigants pleaded for sympathy on the grounds that they needed dowries for their marriageable daughters;[102] they attacked their opponents by accusing them of causing women to remain old maids.[103] (One particularly notorious pleader combines the two by attacking his opponent for not dowering the pleader's daughters).[104] Lysias gives a vivid picture of the crimes of the Thirty Tyrants, when he says that they caused citizens exile, shameful death, loss of civil rights – and women to remain unmarried.[105] Even a husband on his deathbed – even one divorcing his wife, if the divorce was amicable – was likely to make arrangements for his wife to be remarried immediately to somebody else, 'so that she not be left a widow'.[106] Aristotle's will arranged not only a marriage for his daughter, but a substitute bridegroom in case the intended one should die before children were born.[107] In view of all this, we should hardly be surprised if the Greeks were willing to modify their inheritance law to prevent leaving the *epikleros'* marriage dependent upon the willingness of her next-of-kin to give up her estate; and the less so when we consider, that marriage to a near relative was still considered very desirable even in the classical period.[108]

That the marriage of the *epikleros* was conceived to be arranged for her benefit — *faute de mieux*, perhaps, but for her benefit — is shown in the case, already mentioned, of the law at Thurii. For here, where the law of a poor *epikleros* had been, as at Athens, optional (she might either be married by the next-of-kin or given away with a dowry to another), it was made obligatory, and the option of choosing a different husband forbidden, on the pleading of an *epikleros* herself, whose next-of-kin had not lived up to his responsibility.[109]

When Plato came to describe the best state he thought practical, he included in its constitution the law of the *epikleros*. 'But', he wrote, 'if a man should suffer some unexpected misfortune (i.e., die intestate) and leave females, let us forgive the lawmaker if he arranges the daughters' marriage with regard to two out of the three (relevant circumstances), nearness of relationship and preservation of the family estate; and as for the third matter which a father would have considered — choosing from among all the citizens, with an eye to character and personality, the one suited to be a son to himself and a husband to his daughter — this he will pass over, because it is impossible to consider'.[110] That Plato has the good of the family and the state uppermost in his mind — in the *Laws*, since no one may occupy two *kleroi*, the children will indeed remain in the household of the *epikleros'* father — is entirely consistent with the rest of his political philosophy; but it is also worth noting that he considers the law to be an answer to the question: how shall we arrange this girl's marriage?

Epikleroi outside of Athens. The form that was taken by the laws and institutions surrounding the *epikleros* at Athens was, as we have seen, dictated by the nature of the Athenian family and of the *kyrieia* exercised by the head of the family over its members. In places where the family structure was different, we should expect to find differences in the epiclerate; but we must also remember that the same institution may serve different functions in different places, and that its best-attested manifestation is not necessarily the original one, nor the most widespread.

From most of Greece we have only isolated tidbits. A Tegean law of the time of Alexander provided for returning exiles with a passage limiting inheritance claims: 'The returning exiles are to receive back the paternal inheritance from which they were exiled, and the maternal inheritance of a mother who had been unmarried and in possession of the property, and had not had a brother; and if it happened that after a woman had

been given in marriage, both her brother and his line died, such property
is also to be considered a maternal inheritance, but no farther.' [111] Each
exile could claim only his father's estate, or one of which his mother had
been, or had become, *epikleros.* The limitation to the children of *epikleroi* who were unmarried, or of women who became *epikleroi* in exile,
is puzzling: why should not the children of an *epikleros* who was married at the time of the exile inherit as well? I suspect that they did
inherit the estates, as part of their *paternal* inheritance: that is, their
fathers had already been legally possessed of the estates at the time of
the exile, by virtue of their marriage to the *epikleroi.* If the husband of
the *epikleros* was indeed the legal *kyrios* of her property, with a title
strong enough to ensure his sons' succession, then he was better treated
in Tegea than anywhere else we know of; but other explanations may
perhaps be possible. It should be noted that nothing in the inscription
informs us whether these women were normally married to their next-
of-kin or to outsiders.

Laws from Naupactus[112] and of Thermus[113] indicate that women in
those places, as in the rest of Greece, had the right to inherit in the absence of males. Daughters are explicitly mentioned in the Naupactus
law, and very probably appeared in the Thermus law, of which only a
small fragment survives; but we cannot say in either case which of the
rules of the epiclerate may have operated. The will of Epicteta of Thera
includes in the list of her relatives a man named 'Antisthenes son of
Isocles, but by adoption son of Grinnus'[114] — apparently an adoptive
brother. In Athens, the existence of an adoptive brother would imply
that her father had left no sons; the adoption would have entailed the
responsibility of marrying his daughter. Antisthenes was not Epicteta's
husband, but there are a number of other possibilities. He may have
been married to a sister of Epicteta's; or the law of Thera may not have
compelled him to marry her in order to get a portion of the estate; or
his adoption may have been limited to a ritual significance, most likely
the responsibility for carrying on the cult at Grinnus' tomb. Only the
first of these three possibilities would be definitely consistent with Attic
law, but that does not mean much; according to Attic law Epicteta
probably could not have made a will at all. At any event the right of
women to inherit at Thera is certain, for Epicteta is in control of the
money of her husband and of her sons (all of whom died before the
time of the will), and her daughter — her only remaining child — is heiress of her estate.

About Lacedaemon we know slightly more. The existence of an epiclerate is attested by Herodotus: 'The kings are the sole judges of these
cases only: concerning a maid who is a *patrouchos,* to whom she is
awarded in marriage, if her father has not betrothed her . . .'[115] The
kings of Sparta, then, performed the function of *epidikasia* — but they

did so only if the father had not betrothed the woman to another man. That they were governed by the rules of kinship is suggested by the marriage of Gorgo, Cleomenes' only daughter, to his heir Leonidas,[116] though royal marriages are not good evidence for normal practice. The later testimony, from Aristotle and Plutarch, is less direct. Aristotle criticizes Sparta for permitting free testamentary disposition, and adds, 'Now it is possible to give an *epikleros* to whomever one pleases; and if a man should die intestate, whoever is left as heir gives her to whomever he wishes'.[117] This, as we have seen, was not the case in Athens. It would seem from Aristotle's phrasing that the *anchisteus* in such a case remained heir, presumably giving the girl a dowry; but the opposite is suggested by Plutarch's remark that Leonidas, a century later, did not want to let Agiatis marry anyone but his son Cleomenes because she was 'the *epikleros* of a large estate'.[118] The importance of a rich *epikleros* in Sparta, if Plutarch is correct, can be gauged by the fact that Leonidas was the king.

Our information about *patroiokoi*, as they are called at Gortyn, is relatively abundant, filling two columns of the Gortynian Code. Here the institution was significantly different from the Athenian epiclerate; the rules of Gortyn show concern for the family and for the tribe, and for the woman's freedom as opposed to her protection.

We may begin, though the law does not, with the definition: '(A woman) is to be a *patroiokos* if there is no father nor brother from the same father'.[119] She was, as at Athens, to be married to her next-of-kin — but the only eligible relatives were (a) her paternal uncles, or (b) their sons.[120] This restriction is designed, of course, to prevent the estate of the father from leaving the grandfather's family; if the father had had no brothers, there was considered to be no claimant (*epiballon*), and the girl was free to marry whomever she pleased of her own tribe.[121] Children of aunts, or relatives on the maternal side, had no claim at all, since they belonged to different *oikoi*; nor did paternal relatives more distant than first cousins have any claim.

This point is of great importance, for it shows us at the outset that we are dealing with an institution different in structure from the Athenian. The law of the *patroiokos* was not regulated by simple inheritance law; in Gortyn, as at Athens, sisters and their descendants had a place in the inheritance after brothers and their descendants, but here that did not give them any rights in the adjudication of a *patroiokos*. The Gortynian epiclerate was indeed what the Athenian was not, a law by which the larger *oikos* — descendants of the dead man's father — took care of the smaller *oikos*, in which now only a daughter remained. If the larger *oikos* was itself empty, then the law did not apply.

We have no way of knowing whether the new son was considered to belong to the deceased's *oikos*; indeed, we have no way of knowing whether such a concept would apply at all in Gortyn, since, as we shall see, the *oikos* in Gortyn did not occupy the place in property law that it did in Athens. It is unlikely that the Gortynian situation represents a new development; more likely it is the Athenian case that was an innovation, having assimilated the law regulating the *epikleros* to the general inheritance law. In Athens, where the overriding concern was to ensure the *epikleros'* marriage, the law could not allow a situation in which there was no claimant at all.

If the *epiballon* chose not to marry her, or if there was none, the entire estate belonged to the girl, and passed with her, as at Athens, into the house of her husband.[122] If, on the other hand, she refused to marry the *epiballon* — something which the Athenian woman could not do — she received the town-house and its contents (if there was one in the estate), and the rest of the property was divided between her and the *epiballon*.[123] The inequality is to be noted: in Gortyn the property was explicitly hers, as it could not be at Athens, and the *epiballon* could claim only part of the property, and that only if she refused to marry him. If, as is likely, her ability to do so was an innovation, the *epiballon's* claim here may simply be an indemnity for the monetary loss caused him.

In this situation, it was obviously to the advantage of each party to force the other to refuse the match: the *epiballon*, in particular, could simply protest his willingness to marry her without actually doing so, and thereby prevent her from marrying anybody else unless she was willing to give up half the estate. It must have been against this possibility that the law established a time limit on the *epiballon's* rights. If he had been a minor, entitled to support from the estate, he is deprived of this from the time he reaches puberty[124] until he marries the girl; when he comes of legal age, if he still refuses to marry her, her relatives complain to the judge — even in Gortyn it was not the girl herself who would appear in court — and the judge orders him to marry her within two months. If he still fails to do so, the *patroiokos* goes to the next-of-kin after him, if there is one, and when all the *epiballontes* have been exhausted, she is free to marry an outsider.[125]

If the woman became a *patroiokos* when she was already married, she might choose to maintain her marriage or to dissolve it.[126] If she chose the latter, the *epiballon* might claim her only if she had no children; once she had children, she divided the estate — with whom is not clear[127] — and could marry whomever she pleased within her tribe. Similarly, if her husband died and left her no children, the next *epiballon* might marry her, but if she had children, she was free to marry whomever she pleased within the tribe.[128] This distinction between the woman who had borne children and the one who had not was very probably in effect at Athens; there, however, she could be claimed in the middle of her marriage, and so neither her husband's death nor her own wishes would affect the situation.

As long as the *patroiokos* was a minor, her paternal relatives managed the estate and received half the income. If there was no *epiballon* – in which case the paternal relatives would have less interest in the property – the girl herself was in charge of it, and was cared for by her mother or maternal relatives; a later innovation provided for her paternal and maternal relatives to manage the estate, and receive half the income.[129] Merriam[130] rightly compared this to the law of Charondas, whereby the property of orphans was managed by paternal kinsmen, the orphans themselves by maternal kinsmen – an arrangement praised by Diodorus because it put in charge of the money those who, as possible heirs, would take the best care of it, and in charge of the children those who, not being heirs, could not gain by the children's death.[131] In Athens – despite a law attributed to Solon 'that no one is to be a guardian, to whom the estate devolves in case of the orphans' death'[132] – the *anchisteus* seems also to have been eligible to act as guardian.[133] In the case where, in Gortyn, the *epiballon* was a minor, the *patroiokos* – if she was willing to wait for his majority – received the house (if there was one), and the *epiballon* received half the income.[134] Who, in this case, managed the property, is not mentioned.[135]

In Gortyn as in Athens, special measures were prescribed to help the impoverished *patroiokos* find a husband. She – or her paternal and maternal relatives – could sell or mortgage property to pay off the estate's debts.[136] That an unmarried girl could sell or mortgage property is not attested for any case anywhere else in Greece; that relatives of a property owner could sell the property, even during the owner's minority, contradicts an important principle of the Code, and is obviously designed to make the indebted *patroiokos* more marriageable. In a later enactment, the heirs were entitled to refuse the estate entirely if it was burdened with debt; it is not expressly stated whether this applied to *patroiokoi* as well.[137] Also, I believe, directed at the poor heiress is the law applying when she can find no husband: 'If there should be no claimants for the *patroiokos* as prescribed, she is to have the property and marry whomever she wishes of her tribe. If no one of her tribe wishes to marry her, the *patroiokos*' maternal relatives are to announce throughout the tribe that 'Doesn't anyone want to marry her?' And if anyone marries her, he is to do so within thirty days of their announcement; if not, she is to marry whomever she can.'[138] No *patroiokos* could marry out of her tribe, and if she could find a mate within it – a regulation which may be based on a geographic division of the land, or at least the city, by tribes[139] – but when the choice lay between the tribe's prerogatives and a woman's marriage, the Gortynians chose as the Athenians did. The woman was to marry 'whomever she can', and not to grow old a spinster.

It is certain that the Gortynian epiclerate came from the same roots as the Athenian; but its structure has been modified radically by two main principles that dominate the Gortynian law, namely, that each member of the family is an independent property owner, and that a woman may decide whom she wishes to marry. Behind these two principles, it might be possible to claim that the Gortynian rules had once been, like the Athenian, a paternalistic system designed to ensure the marriage of the *patroiokos*. It might be posssible; but it is surely a simpler hypothesis to believe that it was what it looks like, a rule designed to keep the estate — with its property and, presumably, its sacred rites — within the larger family. The Gortynian law is surely concerned with keeping property within the tribe, and a similar concern with the extended family is in line with its general tenor. If so, we have in the epiclerate an interesting case in which the same institution, arising from the same roots, has come to serve different purposes in different societies. Which of these two was the original purpose — or if, perhaps, the original purpose was not quite like either of them — is a matter of speculation, in which the reader is free to indulge, if he pleases.

4

Economic Authority of the *Kyrios*

• •

Transactions 'with her kyrios'. Where property belonged to the family,
it was the head of the family who had ultimate control over it, for the
maintenance of the family's income implies ability to manage the estate;
if the family's lands could be sold or given away by the wife, the husband
might at any time be deprived of the means to feed his household. In
most of Greece, control of property was assured to the *kyrios* by the rule
that the transactions of other members of the family were valid only
with his approval. This applied to all dependent members of his household, including his wife, his unmarried daughters, his minor sons, his
elderly parents, and any other relatives (sisters, nieces, grandparents)
who might be living with him. It did *not* apply, in the historical period
(if it ever had), to adult males of sound mind, who were considered by
the law to be their own *kyrioi*; thus we find, for example, father and son
contributing independently to the same fund,[1] with neither requiring
the other's agreement. When adult males lived in the same household,
they did so as partners; this was often the case with brothers,[2] and we
have two examples — both from Athens — of a father and son who seem
to have shared an undivided estate.[3]

Within a limited circle, the title of *kyrios* seems to have been well defined. At a woman's birth, her father was her *kyrios*; at his death, her
brothers. When she married, her husband assumed the economic responsibilities of the *kyrios*,[4] though he did not have the right to give her in
marriage to a third party (at least, not in his lifetime).[5] After her husband's
death or retirement, her sons became her *kyrioi*. Outside of these relatives, however, the law seems to have allowed more leeway. In Chaeronea,
the manumission inscriptions show us cases of all the relatives mentioned
acting as *kyrioi*,[6] in addition to the *hierarchos*, who appears to have been
the *kyrios* of all *hieroi* and *hierai* of this particular cult, whether they
were married or not;[7] but beyond this circle we have four documents
where the woman is assisted simply by 'friends'. These 'friends' — who
may in fact have been more distant relatives[8] — did not have the same
authority as the nearer relatives; the former always appear in groups of
two or three, the latter, with one exception,[9] alone. It is possible that
these 'friends' sufficed to authorize the transaction even when the
woman had a father, brother, husband, or son who did not agree to it;
much more likely, the law simply permitted a woman who had no close
relatives to choose a group of men to ratify her actions. A fragment of a

law from Delphi appears to indicate that at Delphi, too, the law stipulated who was to be *kyrios* only when the woman had no close relatives:
'No loans are to be made to a woman or by a woman unless the husband
consents to each. And if a woman be a widow, her son is to ratify (the
loan) if he is of age, or else let her lend, with one man from among her
close relatives as a guarantor'.[10]

The text as quoted includes many conjectural additions, and may not
be entirely correct; but the remnants on the stone are sufficient to indicate that we are dealing with a regulation requiring the consent of a
kyrios to a woman's loans, and the indefinite phrase 'one man' shows
that beyond a certain point the law no longer prescribed which man was
to be *kyrios*. It is not impossible that the father may have been mentioned,
though it is more likely that a woman in her father's house would have
been subsumed under the rules for a minor (whatever they may have
been); there does not seem to be room for brothers or other relatives to
have been mentioned. That a similar leeway among more distant relatives applied in Athens is suggested by a passage of Menander in which a
younger uncle, too distant to claim his niece if she is an *epikleros*, is
nevertheless able to give her in a presumably legitimate marriage if she
is not.[11]

In those places where the agreement of the *kyrios* was required for all
transactions, a woman could do almost anything as long as she had his
approval; thus Nicareta of Thespiae and Epicteta of Thera were able to
dispose of quite considerable amounts, with the consent of their *kyrioi*.[12]
Whether or not their *kyrioi* could dispose of the women's property without the women's consent is not as clear, though it seems unlikely, for if
so the women's presence at these transactions would be unnecessary. If,
indeed, they could not do so, then the law of these places must have
recognized women as having property of their own — unlike Athenian
law — although it considered the property subject to the control of the
family's *kyrios*. One inscription of Chaeronea, in which a man and wife
manumit one slave, while another is freed only by the man,[13] would
seem to suggest that the man could not have freed both slaves on his own;
but we can hardly draw a firm conclusion from this, even for Chaeronea
alone — particularly in view of the vagueness which we have already
noted in legal title to slaves. Receipt of property, as long as nothing was
given in return, was completely untrammelled; no *kyrios* was required
for a woman to receive an inheritance, or a gift, or payment for services.[14]
Only exchange and disposal of property required the man's consent, since
only these might injure the family's holdings.

Not every city in Greece required the *kyrios'* consent to a woman's
transactions; as we have seen, it is very possible that there were places in
Greece where the family was conceived as an association of individuals,
in which case, indeed, there will have been no place for the economic

function of a *kyrios.* Our geographical information is unfortunately very
spotty, for this as for other problems. At Delphi, as we have seen, the
consent of a *kyrios* was at one time (the date of the law is between 390
and 360 before the Christian era) necessary for a woman to lend or borrow money. Later on, however, it is certain that a woman could at least
manumit a slave without a *kyrios*: of all the manumissions, from the
earliest − about 201-200 − to the end of our period, not one shows
a *kyrios,* even though the inscriptions do occasionally mention the 'agreement' of parties who were superfluous.[15] The same is true of Naupactus,
where, of the seven inscriptions in which women manumit, not one
mentions the presence or agreement of a man.[16] Other places are less
certain. Elatea (in Phocis) has left two documents in which women may
be manumitting without *kyrioi*, but the stones are not in a condition
that allows any certainty.[17] Also from Elatea is a decree of the people
whereby the city and a woman named Menecleia jointly free a slave 'who
used to be the servant of Lampron (Menecleia's father)'.[18] The reason
for the state's interference is unclear, but it seems likely that the woman
is not acting with a *kyrios.*[19]

   From Chaeronea, on the other hand, we have no fewer than twenty-
two manumissions in which a man, almost always a relative, is 'present'
at the act of a woman. Only one exception appears to be certain, and we
must presume this to be due to an omission in inscribing the stone.[20] It
is, as far as I know, the only example of such an omission; but we have
other stones in which the agreement of the *kyrios* is placed not in its
normal position, but at the end, and I suspect that these are cases where
the *kyrios* was neglected at first and added only by afterthought.[21] We
have no other large body of manumissions − those of Thessaly record
not the freeing of the slave, but the payment of a freedmen's tax, and
are in any event too concise to be conclusive − but those we have all
support the generalization that the agreement of the woman's *kyrios*
was required in Boeotia, but not in Phocis or Aetolia. The loan of Nicareta
indicates that a *kyrios* was similarly required for business transactions in
Boeotia;[22] we have no evidence as to whether or not a Phocian or Aeto-
lian woman could do other business without a *kyrios.*[23]

   Where manumissions fail, we must rely on isolated stones. At Tenos,[24]
Amorgos,[25] Cos,[26] Thera,[27] Delos,[28] and Rhodes[29] among the islands,
and at Olymus,[30] Mylasa,[31] and Erythrae[32] in Asia Minor, we find women
who act with their *kyrioi*; at Dodona we have one counter-example,[33]
and from Calauria in the Peloponnese comes a stone without a *kyrios* −
but this is perhaps a matter of accident, with only an excerpt of the will
being quoted.[34] These scattered stones may suggest a pattern, but they
certainly do not prove anything beyond the place and time from which
they come, and it may be best, for the present, to avoid generalizations
about these areas.

It may be assumed, *a priori*, that there was a lower limit to the type of transaction that required a *kyrios*, at least in practice. A woman is not likely to have needed a *kyrios* to buy ribbons, or even to sell them. For Delos, we have interesting confirmation of this in the records of the *hieropoioi*, who managed the temple property and submitted an annual accounting, which was inscribed on stone. Of the transactions involving women, seven have the women acting without *kyrioi*, dealing with sums from five to twenty-five drachmas; ten have the women acting with *kyrioi*, with sums from ten to more than eight hundred drachmas.[35] It would appear that at Delos, while there were certainly sums too small to require a *kyrios* and sums too large to be transferred without one, there was no clear legal minimum, so that within a certain intermediate area a woman might require a *kyrios* or not — probably depending at least partly on the demands of the party with whom she was dealing. Thus we find a woman paying, in the same inscription, a hundred and thirty drachmas with her *kyrios*, and later five drachmas without him;[36] another woman pays two identical payments of ten drachmas and half an obol, now with her *kyrios*, now without.[37]

The frequency with which women appear in the manumission-inscriptions and in the later accounts from Delos suggests that there was at this later period no impropriety attaching to a woman's dealing in business — that, in fact, an important social reason for the powers of the *kyrios* had disappeared. It is worth noting that at Naupactus, where women apparently did not need a *kyrios* for their transactions, a woman might even be head of a household — at least, so it seems from the participation of a woman who is apparently both mother and *orphanophylax* of the children in one manumission.[38] Much more noteworthy is an inscription of about the year 250 from Erythrae, in which a priesthood is bought by 'Astynous son of Euthynus and his guardian Nosso daughter of Simus and Nosso's *kyrios*, Theophron son of Demetrius; 200 (?) drachmas, sales-tax 10 drachmas, guarantor Theophron son of Demetrius'.[39] Here we find a woman as guardian (*epitropos*), even though her action must be approved by her *kyrios*. Now, a guardian is appointed to take the place of the family's head in managing its business; when a woman was considered naturally incapable of being the head of a family, she could not have been appointed anybody's guardian. The fact that we do find a woman with this function in Erythrae can only mean that the incapacity of women had degenerated into a legalism: a woman's actions were performed with a *kyrios*, but whoever appointed Nosso guardian of the children did not think that she was therefore incapable of managing the estate.

The same development is shown in a Boeotian inscription,[40] where an officious scribe has noted the husband's presence as *kyrios* at a manumission which he performed jointly with his wife: the presence of the *kyrios* is not being recorded to safeguard his rights (since his presence and agreement were obvious from his participation), but simply to fulfil the rule that a woman must have a *kyrios* ratify her actions. The Eu . . . who ratifies the agreement of Arcouse to her husband's loan in a fractured inscription of the Delian *hieropoioi*[41] is similarly none other than her husband himself, recorded through another excess of bureaucratic zeal. These two scribes were indeed careful to maintain the *kyrios'* position; but their misunderstanding is an indication that the reason for the law was no longer obvious.

The kyrios at Athens. The only Athenian law we know of dealing with the capacity of a woman to transact business is preserved for us by Isaeus: 'for the law explicitly provides that a child is not to be capable of performing a transaction, nor a woman beyond (the value of) a medimnus of barley'.[42] The same law is cited by a scholiast on Aristophanes[43] and by Dio Chrysostom;[44] the latter selects it as an example of distrust and mentions that it applied 'among the Athenians', which seems to suggest that we are dealing with a regulation more restrictive than the common Greek rule.

The language of the law indicates that a woman could make transactions for less than the value of a medimnus, and there is nothing in either the law or the literature to suggest that she needed the approval of her *kyrios* to do so. A medimnus, according to Kuenen-Janssens, was about six days' food supply for an ordinary family; the law, then, appears intended to permit the woman to do her week's marketing, while preventing her from spending large amounts of a family fortune — that is, it divides economic transactions into two groups, those which fall into the wife's domain and those which are the exclusive prerogative of the *kyrios*.[45] Included in the wife's domain are small purchases and transactions of all kinds, not merely grocery-shopping.

The language of the law also seems, on simple reading, to forbid all transactions by a woman for larger sums. It mentions nothing about situations in which such transactions might be permitted, and we might have presumed that they would simply be invalid. Unfortunately, however, for this interpretation, we have many examples of women dealing with much larger amounts. We know from the orators of a woman who gave a gift of three hundred drachmas;[46] of another who lent her son-in-law eighteen hundred drachmas;[47] of a third who gave her children two thousand drachmas, though another son seems to have objected successfully after her death.[48] From inscriptions we know of a woman who sold seventy drachmas' worth of reeds for construction work, apparently in a single transaction.[49] The female cloak-seller whose tombstone is preserved was doing a poor business if she sold her cloaks for less than the value of a medimnus of barley,[50] and the woman who appears to

have been collector of an *eranos*-loan — a loan collected from a group of
friends, rather than borrowed from a single lender — must have solicited
contributions of more than six drachmas apiece.[51] But only one of these
transactions was challenged, as far as we know, and we are not told on
what grounds.

Two solutions to the problem have been proposed. The simplest solution supposed that the law had lapsed.[52] There is nothing unreasonable
about the proposal, but it is chronologically impossible. Isaeus was still
able to adduce the law in the seventies of the fourth century;[53] but
Aristophanes in the *Plutus* had produced an old woman complaining
about the waste of gifts which included four medimni of wheat — surely
worth more than a single medimnus of barley.[54] Even if we reject his
evidence (as we often must in matters of law), the arrangements made by
Philo's mother for her burial, involving the gift of three minae, date from
the beginning of the fourth century, if not earlier, and cannot be explained
by a hypothetical lapse or repeal of the law which Isaeus quoted decades
later.[55] Another explanation seems preferable.

Another explanation has, in fact, been preferred. The assumption has
been almost universal[56] that the law did not, as it seems to, forbid all
transactions above the specified sum, but merely transactions performed
without consent of the woman's *kyrios*. It has been presumed, therefore,
that the transactions mentioned were all performed with the consent of
the women's *kyrioi*, but that this consent was not recorded.

This hypothesis has the advantage of bringing Attic law into line with
the law of other Greek cities; but other than that it has little to recommend it. In point of fact, we have no example of an Athenian woman
transacting business with the official consent of her *kyrios*. The Attic
equivalent of the manumission-inscriptions, the 'manumission bowls'
dedicated by freedmen, do indeed list a minor with a *kyrios*,[57] but since
this is commemorating the result of a trial, the presence of the *kyrios* is
to be taken not as a validation of the manumission, but as an indication
that the minor was represented in court by his guardian. A stone from
the agora, as published by Fine, reads

> Boundary stone of a field and house
> mortgaged by *prasis epi lysei*
> for a dowry of twenty minae
> to M . . . . . . and her *kyrios*
> D . . . . . of Melite,[58]

but this, even if correctly restored (Fine expresses some hesitancy), cannot represent a transaction on the part of the woman. The land is being
offered to the woman and her *kyrios* as security for her dowry; but the
dowry had been given by the *kyrios*, not the woman, and it was to him,
not to her, that it had to be returned. The woman herself neither gave
nor received money, and her mention on the stone indicates merely that

it was her dowry that was in question. We have other stones on which the woman is named with her father;[59] in Fine's stone the *kyrios* is mentioned because, the girl's father being dead, another *kyrios* had given her in marriage.[60] We cannot infer anything about his economic powers.

The presumption, then, that the agreement of the *kyrios* added any legal strength to the transactions of an Athenian woman has no argument to support it except analogy. The context in which Isaeus quotes the law, in fact, tends rather to imply the opposite, for he uses it to assert that the speaker's uncle, who died a minor, could not have made a will: if the law prevented him only from making a will without the agreement of his *kyrios,* the speaker would have no case, for the hypothetical will, in favour of the son of the boy's guardian, would hardly have lacked the guardian's approval. If Isaeus is not misusing the law (as of course, he may be), we should conclude that a minor in Athens could not perform a transaction 'with his *kyrios*';[61] we must then suppose that the law meant one thing when it spoke of a minor and another when it spoke of a woman. This, too, is not impossible, but our hypothesis now requires us to believe that the law was inconsistent; that it was incomplete, in that it failed to mention that a woman could transact business with her *kyrios*; and that all our testimonies of women transacting business are either exceptional or incomplete, while the normal form of transaction was one that is nowhere attested. None of these, I repeat, is impossible, but some discomfort at accepting all of them may be understandable.

We will do better, I think, to remember what the law says, and who is protected by it. If a woman cannot make a transaction, then the transaction is void; that is, if it were to come into court, the court would award the property as if the transaction had not taken place. If, for example, a woman sells me a house, her *kyrios* may object that she was not competent to sell it; the house will then have to be returned to her. But I doubt whether I could have taken possession of the house, refused to pay, and defended myself in court on the grounds that her transaction was illegal; if the transaction was illegal, I have no business in the house at all. The law protects the *kyrios,* not the man who enters into contract with the woman.

Now, the law was a very old one, as is shown by its use of a measure of barley, rather than a sum of money, for the limit of a transaction. Attic society had changed since its passage, and we should not expect to find Athens of the fourth century reflecting the same situation as that which had produced the law. Athens in the early period had been much more dominated by family organization than it was in the fourth century; and we must presume that the tendency to think of property as family property — and therefore, as an asset in the hands of the *kyrios,* whether it had come to him from his own inheritance or his wife's — was even stronger in the earlier period, though it was certainly not dead at the time of the orators. The law Isaeus quoted was not, I believe, a quali- fication to the more common Greek law that a woman's actions required the consent of her *kyrios*, but an alternative to it. The common Greek law distinguished property acquired by a woman (which could be alien- ated, in all probability, only by her, with the consent of her *kyrios*) from that acquired by a man (which could be alienated only by him); the *kyrios* could protect himself against wasting of the family's resources by not agreeing to transactions of which he disapproved. The Athenian law, on the other hand, regarded all property, regardless of its source, as belong- ing to the family, and distributed the right to alienate it according to each member's function: the wife could manage the household finances as she pleased, which implied a free hand in small transactions – and I know of no reason to doubt that she could spend money that her hus- band had acquired as well as money that she had acquired; her manage- ment of domestic finances would require this – while management of larger transactions was reserved to the husband.

The existence of such a law, however, does not make it actually impos- sible for a woman to alienate property; it makes it possible for her *kyrios* to claim at law any property so alienated. It follows that the woman may in fact do as she pleases, as long as the other party is satisfied that the *kyrios* does not intend to challenge her action. The indication of consent by the *kyrios* was formalized in the rest of Greece as a transaction 'with her *kyrios*', but whether or not we choose to believe that such an act was legally valid in Athens, the fact is that it will have been hard for anyone to challenge. The *kyrios* was in no position to challenge an act to which he had already agreed; the second party was no better off; and challenge by an outsider would only result in returning the money to the woman and her *kyrios*.

The practical effect of this will be seen if we look at the most cele- brated case, the 1800 drachmas which Polyeuctus' wife lent her son-in- law Spudias. The loan was recorded in a contract witnessed by her brothers and left behind at her death, and the speaker demands that it be returned to the estate.[62] Scholars, always eager to reconcile contra- dictory texts, have presumed that the brothers were not in fact present as witnesses, but as *kyrioi*.[63] The speaker, according to this interpretation, means to say that the brothers were present then as *kyrioi*, and are pre- sent now as witnesses. There is, however, no great likelihood that her brothers were in fact her *kyrioi* – her sons-in-law would be more likely candidates – and in any event, the passage cannot mean what, by this interpretation, it must. 'There are papers', says the speaker, 'which she left when she died, and the woman's brothers (were) witnesses, being present at the entire proceeding and inquiring about each particular (*martyres d' hoi tēs gynaikos adelphoi parontes hapasi kai kath' hekaston eperōtōntes*), so that we would have no unpleasantness towards each other'.[64] 'Breviloquentia' cannot explain why the speaker said *martyres . . parontes* in place of *kyrioi . . . parontes* if what he meant was 'they were present as *kyrioi*', nor why he used the present participles instead of the aorist if his meaning was 'they are now witnesses, having then been present at everything and having asked about all the particulars'. It is more reasonable to presume that the speaker means what he says, for that story will suffice: the brothers, even if they were *kyrioi*, could not challenge a document they had witnessed; their presence would have made the document strong enough for them to rely on, at least in dealing with their relative (for he could not have challenged it — if the loan was improper, then he had no business taking the money, and would have to return it immediately anyway), and strong enough for the speaker to attempt to collect the debt in court, though we do not know if he succeeded. Similar are the gifts made by Archippe to her sons: her husband, Phormio, was not likely to object to them, and a challenge from anyone else would simply have returned the money to him.[65] Philo's mother must also have had the tacit approval of her son (if he was her *kyrios*) in leaving three minae to a friend for her burial, despite the fact that the speaker of Lysias 31 takes her action to be a disgrace to Philo.[66] On the other hand, the statement of Apollodorus that his mother was 'no longer *kyria* of her property . . . so as to give me as much as she wished'[67] can only mean that she was in fact incapable of giving away her property as long as her *kyrios,* Phormio, opposed it. These cases do provide evidence that women engaged in transactions above what the law of Isaeus 10 prescribed as their legal capacity; but they are not evidence of transactions 'with her *kyrios*', for they were not open to challenge by anyone who stood to benefit from their nullification, and so the question of their legality or illegality was moot. Women might, as we saw, make sales in the marketplace that were above their legal capacity, though such sales were not the rule; I doubt whether their husbands were always present (or summoned) for such transactions. A man who bought from a female cloak-seller no more expected her husband to run after him and attempt to void the sale than one who bought from another tradesman expected to be attacked with a claim that the goods were stolen. If in this respect the practice of the fourth century did not match precisely the intentions of a law that was probably some two centuries old or older, that is no cause for surprise. It is less surprising when we note that the women who transact business so freely are mostly of non-Athenian (that is, non-citizen) origin,[68] or else widows living in the house of relatives rather more distant than father or husband, and more likely, perhaps, to keep their property — their dowry, or whatever they had been able to salvage from their husband's household — separate from that of their *kyrios.*

If the woman was not legally competent to dispose of her property, then her *kyrios* probably was. In my opinion, everything we know about Athenian property law as it related to women supports this conclusion. The *epikleros* was in a sense an heiress, in that the estate always passed to the *oikos* of which she was a member; but the property was her husband's, and the only check upon her husband's ability to spend it was the danger of a lawsuit when her children came of age and took it over. We know that a woman at Athens was legally able to inherit from her brother, cousin, uncles, or — probably — nephew, and she could certainly inherit his lands as well; but all the farms and houses we know of in Attica appear to have been considered the property of men, unless they belonged to an *epikleros* awaiting adjudication, or were attached to a dowry. Indeed the dowry itself was clearly the husband's to dispose of, as long as the marriage lasted, although elsewhere, in Gortyn and probably in Sparta, the dowry was a gift to the wife personally. Along with the dowry came the girl's trousseau; it was indeed intended for her personal use, but it undoubtedly passed into the *kyrieia* of her husband, who could sue for its value if she removed it without his having 'returned' it to her. It is possible to argue that the trousseau had a special status, that it was a gift to the husband while other property remained the wife's to dispose of, with his consent. As we have seen, there rarely was any other property; and I doubt in any event whether a man who could dispose of the clothes on his wife's back could be restrained from disposing of the rest of her fortune as well.

In attempting to find a clear and direct indication, we are again stymied by the nature of our sources. Thrasyllus, the speaker of Isaeus 7, claims that land belonging to his (adoptive) aunts was sold by their husbands for five talents;[69] but since he is trying to show the irresponsible way in which his opponents have mishandled the estate, his words are to be taken with a grain of salt. Not much more can be squeezed out of the claim of Demosthenes that Aphobus would have become *kyrios* of four talents allegedly deposited with Demosthenes' mother, had he married her;[70] the implication is clearly that he could have spent them as he spent Demosthenes' money, but we are dealing here with buried treasure, not an outright gift to which his mother's title would have been clear.

We have no direct evidence for our presumption, and cannot consider the matter to be finally decided on the basis of inference. But what we do know seems to indicate that the Athenian man was *kyrios* of the property of all the members of his family, and free to do with it as he pleased. In point of fact, there were few cases in which his wife would have owned much property; her dowry was his, not hers, and the most common case of a woman inheriting was that of the *epikleros*, who was under the special protection of the law. There does not, however, seem to have been any particular protection for an heiress who was not an *epikleros,*[71] and it is hard to see by what means such an heiress could force the return of her inheritance in case of divorce. Whether the courts would have allowed a plea of *epiklērou kakōsis* in her case, or subsumed it under some other heading, or whether, perhaps, she may have had no legal recourse,[72] I do not know, nor is any such case preserved for us. Socially, at least, it is unlikely that the husband who deprived her of her inheritance would have been considered less of a scoundrel than the husband who abused the fortune of an *epikleros* or of a well-dowered wife.

The kyrios at Gortyn. Traces survive at Gortyn of the authority that was wielded in the rest of Greece by the *kyrios*. A father or brother,[73] or even a husband or son,[74] might give a woman a dowry, and the expression *patros dontos ē adelpiō* ('when she has been given by a father or a brother') in the Code[75] indicates that marriage in Gortyn still took the form of a gift from the previous *kyrios* to the husband. The right to decide whether or not to expose a child belonged in the first instance to its father or (if he was a serf) its father's master;[76] if the woman was an unmarried serf, her father's master (or her brothers' masters) made the decision.[77] It is possible that the fine for adultery was higher for a woman whose *kyrios* was a member of the inner group — that is, a father, brother, or husband — than for one whose *kyrios* was a more distant relative.[78]

Of the essential economic power of the *kyrios*, however — the requirement of his consent to transactions of the other members of the *oikos* — there is no trace. Or rather, there is a trace, for the Code specifically legislates against it:

> As long as the father lives, the father's property is not to be bought or taken on mortgage from a son; whatever he himself (i.e. the son) has acquired by purchase or inheritance he may alienate, if he pleases. Nor may the father (alienate) whatever his children themselves have acquired by purchase or inheritance. Nor may the husband alienate or pledge the property of his wife, nor a son the property of his mother. And if anyone buys or takes on mortgage or accepts on pledge otherwise than is prescribed, as of the time when these laws are inscribed, the property is to belong to the mother and to the wife, and the seller or mortgager or pledger is to pay double to the buyer or mortgagee or recipient of the pledge, and if there is any further penalty, its simple value; previous matters are not to be justiciable. But if the second party contends about the disputed item that it is not the mother's or the wife's, he is to bring an action in the appropriate place, before the judge in the place prescribed for each type of action.[79]

This is not simply a rule against selling other people's property — that could have been said in many fewer words; it is a law abolishing the econ-

omic power of the *kyrios*. To begin with the second part, the power of a
husband to dispose of his wife's goods – and in Gortyn, this included her
dowry – is not to exist; nor is the power of a son to dispose of his mother's
goods. These are not simply examples of women vulnerable to exploitation; they are women whose goods were, in other states, under the
kyrieia of the men named. These men are, in fact, the most common
kyrioi of adult women: they appear more often than anyone else in those
manumission-inscriptions which mention *kyrioi*, and they are the only
kyrioi prescribed by the law of Cadys at Delphi.[80] The amnesty for their
actions before the passing of this law can only mean that they had previously been prescribed as *kyrioi* at Gortyn as well, and that they had
been possessed of the right – as I have argued that Athenian men were –
to sell, mortgage, or pledge the property of their wives and mothers without the women's consent. Under the terms of the new law, any such sale,
mortgage, or pledge is invalid; the property alienated returns to the wife
or mother, and the good-faith purchaser is recompensed doubly as the
victim of fraud.[81]

In the first clause of the law, we find abolished an aspect of the power
of the *kyrios* with which we have not yet concerned ourselves: its transfer during the life of the *kyrios*. Under this system a man's sons, when
they reach a suitable age, become *kyrioi* of the household and assume its
management; they are then responsible for maintaining their parents. We
do not find such a system in full legal development anywhere in Greece;
it is a stage that antedates historical society. But we do find traces of it
in Athens and elsewhere, in houses like that of Euctemon, whose son
shared the estate until his death,[82] or Menander's Cnemon, who resigns
his property to Gorgias.[83] We find men whose sons are their *kyrioi* in the
manumission-inscriptions of Chaeronea,[84] and Aristotle speaks of 'retired
old men' who are 'not simply' citizens, but only citizens in a qualified
sense.[85] But in Gortyn, from the time of this law, no competent adult
was to be *kyrios* of the property of another. Henceforward a father's
control of his property does not terminate until his death; and his children are free to acquire property on their own, without having it pass into
the *kyrieia* of the father. Whether or not the children would manage their
property themselves probably depended upon their age.[86]

Also noteworthy is the beginning of the law on division of property:
'The father has authority over (the words *karteron emen* in the passage
would be rendered in Attic *kyrion einai*) the children and the division of
the property, and the mother over her own property'.[87] The difference
in expression between the mother's rights and the father's may indicate
an additional power that the father as head of the family – the right to
decide whether or not to raise a child seems like a good candidate – or
it may merely be a remnant of the old law, under which the father was
kyrios of the entire family and its money: when the law was changed, the

authority of his wife over her own property was added, and the children (presumably minor children are meant) were all that was left in the father's *kyrieia*. Under either interpretation, the difference of wording indicates an original difference in authority between man and wife; but the legal difference, at least, was dying an early death in Gortyn. We do not know why: whether the legislation was prompted by internal considerations, by a general movement that did not reach Athens, or by influence from the pre-Greek population which was still present in Crete, and in which women's position seems to have been more independent than, for example, an Athenian woman's was. But the Gortynian example did not become general; elsewhere, the power of the *kyrios* was to survive well into the Roman period.[88]

5

Exchange and Disposition

• •

Trade. The limitations on a woman's right to conduct transactions were reflected in the marketplace — or perhaps more correctly, the social norms that gave rise to those limitations also affected the role of women in the market. Our only information, unfortunately — but not surprisingly — comes from Athens; of the small retail trade of other cities we know next to nothing. In Athens, however, it is clear that tradeswomen were common enough. We hear of *kapēlides* and *pandokeutriai,* keepers of cafes where one could get a drink of wine and a meal.[1] Women are attested selling salt, groats, bread, figs, beans, gruel, and sesame; one seller of clothing and one of hats are known; also sellers of perfume, incense, garlands, and ribbons; a seller of reeds, and perhaps one of hemp.[2] Occasionally we can recognize a woman who is her husband's partner. Artemis the gilder, the wife of Dionysius the helmet-maker, worked in his shop, presumably decorating his helmets,[3] and one suspects that Midas and Soteris, the freedmen of Hipparchides, both of them sesame-sellers, may have been husband and wife.[4] Euxitheus and his mother seem to have worked together selling ribbons.[5] Some trades were even dominated by women: 'And furthermore, what could possess a man, to make him sit and sell perfume, under a parasol on high, fitted out for a meeting-place for teenagers to babble in all day long?'[6]

In spite of all this, there is little question that the *agora* was dominated by men. For certain trades women are completely unattested: armaments, books, and animals were sold exclusively by men, and the closest we come to a woman in the metal trade is Artemis the gilder, mentioned above. Even those trades in which women were found were practiced by men as well, and probably dominated by them.[7] The perfume trade had, according to Athenaeus, been forbidden to men by Solon, and Pherecrates, quoted above, speaks of it as if it were a feminine monopoly; but a fragment of Lysias, preserved in the same passage of Athenaeus, shows clearly enough that by the beginning of the fourth century men were involved in this business, too.[8] Whether they actually sold perfumes in the market, or had women or slaves to sell their wares for them, is not stated, but apparently the field was not devoid of men.

Virtually all of the trades mentioned were unlikely to involve more than the value of a medimnus of barley. The price of a medimnus fluctuated from three[9] to six[10] drachmas, going as high as eighteen in times of scarcity,[11] and few retail transactions involved as much as that. Surely

Aristophanes' innkeeper never charged such a bill: it took a demigod to eat ten obols' worth of meat.[12] When Philocleon knocked over ten obols' worth of bread 'and four thrown in' (whether obols or loaves is not clear), he was probably damaging more than the bread-seller would have sold to a single customer.[13] Thettale's felt hats cost an obol and three quarters apiece.[14] Nor would the stock-in-trade require purchases of more than a medimnus at a time, if supplies were either homemade or purchased fresh daily, as is likely. There were trades which dealt in larger sums, but women rarely plied them.[15]

Tradeswomen were poor women who had to earn their living, and much of the unpleasant commentary on them clearly reflects the disdain of the genteel for the uncouth. Thus Aeschylus is reproved in the *Frogs*, 'It's not decent for poets to revile each other like bakery-women',[16] and Chremylus identifies Poverty by her screams:

> POVERTY. Who do you think I am? CHREM. An innkeeper or a porridge-seller. Otherwise you wouldn't scream like that at us when nobody's done you any harm.[17]

We also hear complaints of dishonesty and greed, the common objection of the farmer to the trader.[18] While women did not sell in the market if they could avoid it — Euxitheus and his mother admit 'that we sell ribbons, and don't live in the manner we would like to'[19] — it was clearly much more respectable than working as a hired labourer. The latter was characterized even by Euxitheus as 'menial jobs worthy of a slave';[20] no such thing could have been said of petty trade, which was dominated by free men. There was a law of Solon's that 'anyone who reproaches a male or female citizen with the fact that they work in the market is to be liable to an action for slander',[21] and the laws granted preferential treatment in the market place to citizens as opposed to resident aliens.[22] The fact that men predominated in the *agora* is an indication that among the small tradesmen, as among the labourers, there were many men — presumably those who could afford it — who worked for a living while their wives did not. The ideal of the woman who occupied herself with her family was not dead in the lower classes.

In large-scale commerce women were extremely rare. Of the various merchants' marks found on amphorae of the export trade, only one appears to belong to a woman.[23] The public building accounts of Epidaurus, listing both construction workers and suppliers of building materials, include 269 different men and two women.[24] No woman, as far as we know, ever leased a mine at Laureim.[25] The accounts of the *hieropoioi* at Delos mention one tradeswoman, Comoedia: her sales to the temple consist of five drachmas for rose-perfume and eight drachmas, one obol for a jewel-case.[26] A woman named Phocis received ten drachmas to adorn an idol,[27] and another wove and embroidered garments — but a man (presumably her husband) received her pay, for the entry reads, 'to Sodamus for Aristo (*Sōdamōi hōste Aristoi*) for weaving and embroidering the garments'.[28] The accounting-inscriptions of Delphi tell a similar story,[29] as do those of the Erechtheum at Athens,[30] and the accounts of the Eleusinian treasurers mention only two women.[31]

One of these last two women, Artemis from Peiraeus, engages in a rather large transaction, selling seventy drachmas' worth of reeds to be used as building material. A sepulchral inscription, also from Athens, mentions one Elephantis who sold cloaks (*himatia*), a trade that would also have required transactions for more than the value of a medimnus of barley.[32] Both of these women appear to have been resident aliens,[33] but they were presumably subject to the same legal restrictions as citizens, and they serve to remind us that it was not the Athenian law that restricted women to petty marketing. That we find virtually no large-scale businesswomen, either in Athens or anywhere else, shows us that the Greek woman was kept out of commerce by more than the law: the ideals of her society and her own ideals, as well as the need to perform her own tasks at home, all prevented her from seeking the opportunities on which some women could capitalize.

Lending and borrowing. Loans are of two basic types, commercial and charitable. In the first type the lender always expects to receive more money than he lends, whether by repayment with interest, a share in the borrower's returns, or some other form of profit. Charitable loans are usually, but not necessarily, interest-free. The categories are not perfectly distinct; there are cases — as when a man invests money to help a friend start a business — that partake of both. Women in Greece did lend money, and they did not restrict themselves entirely to pure charity; nevertheless, we cannot find any clear indication that any women were ever professional money-lenders.

The largest transaction attested for any woman is the loan by Nicareta of Thespiae to the town of Orchomenus in Boeotia, documented in a long inscription set up by the town after the repayment of the loan.[34] Nicareta, with the consent of her *kyrios*,[35] had lent the town 10,085 drachmas and two obols; in another year she lent 2,500 drachmas, then 4,000, then 1,000.[36] The date when these loans fell due is not recorded in the inscription, but the first loan at least was overdue when Nicareta came to Orchomenus to collect it.[37] The town was unable to repay the loan, and apparently did not expect to be able to pay it with the penalties that had now accrued; Nicareta was 'persuaded' (*epithōse autan ha polis*, lines 116-17) to accept an alternative arrangement. A new agreement was made with the town, and in addition a contract was signed with the polemarchs and the treasurer: each promised to pay 18,833 drachmas within a short time (the polemarchs and treasurer at the Pamboeotian festival the next month, the city by the end of the year).

Apparently the two contracts dealt with the same money, so that the payment of one cancelled both. The contract of the polemarchs and the treasurer was secured by their own property ('the money may be exacted from the borrowers themselves and from their guarantors, from one or from many or from all, and from the property in their possession, and she may exact it in whatever way she wishes', lines 29-35). The financial embarrassment of the city is obvious; whatever Nicareta's rights were under the original contract, they were surely much better than what the city had persuaded her to accept with the heaviest personal securities it could offer. They were so much better that the city was afraid she would go back on her agreement, and refuse to accept the smaller sum offered; a clause was written into the agreement declaring that such a refusal would render the promissory notes void and make Nicareta liable to a payment of fifty thousand drachmas, almost thrice the value of the loan. Under the new contract, Nicareta was to receive only 1247 drachmas and four obols more than she had lent out – a return of slightly more than seven per cent, extremely small for two years' time even had the loan not been overdue.[38]

Eventually she got the money, though not before the polemarchs had defaulted, the year had had an extra month added to it,[39] and the city had passed a resolution that the loan was to be paid 'from all the city's revenues' (line 161). The entire transaction tells us quite a bit: that there was a woman in Boeotia at the end of the third century[40] who could lend more money than a sizable town could repay is in itself noteworthy, and that she was able to enforce payment of the principal, if not of all the penalties, will also caution us against underestimating the legal capabilities of a woman even in places where she required the consent of her *kyrios*. Nor was Nicareta the only woman to enter such a transaction: an inscription of Copae, a smaller town of Boeotia, from the same period records the town's thanks for (and 'gift' of pasturage rights for four hundred head of cattle in appreciation of) a remission of its debts to two women, Cleuedra and Olympicha.[41] But these women, and Nicareta as well, were acting in an exceptional situation. Many of the towns of Boeotia were in desperate financial trouble at the end of the third century: besides the two already mentioned, we have inscriptions from Lebadea,[42] Chorsia,[43] Acraephia,[44] and two more from Orchomenus[45] expressing gratitude for remission of debts owed either to private individuals or, in one case from Chorsia,[46] to another town. In a situation like this, a loan takes on a large element of charity, as anybody will know who has ever been asked to buy war bonds. The town of Oropus, attempting to rebuild its walls, voted automatic *proxenia* – an honorary title granting foreigners important preferential rights within the city – to anyone who would lend it a talent at 10 per cent interest.[47] The list of people who responded to the offer begins optimistically, 'the following (*hoide*) were inscribed as *proxenoi* and benefactors according to the decree'; but only one name is listed. Nicareta received little, if any, interest, and seems to have been lucky to recover her principal; Cleuedra and Olympicha had to accept payment in kind. Such loans were from the start, as the Oropus inscription shows, more patriotic service than sound finance. Nevertheless, these women are the closest thing to female bankers known to us in Greece.

The closest, that is, unless we count Hyperbolus' mother; for Aristophanes, proposing that mothers of brave men should be given *prohedria* (preferential seating at public functions) over mothers of cowards, asks,

> For how can it be seemly, citizens, for Hyperbolus' mother to sit draped in white, tresses flowing, next to Lamachus' mother, and to lend money — when really, if she were to lend someone money and exact interest, no man ought to give her interest; no, he should grab the money away violently and say, '*You're* one to have your loans bear, after bearing such a bare-faced scoundrel!'
>
> (*axia goun ei tokou tekousa toiouton tokon*).[48]

As most scholars have recognized, nothing can be made of this; Aristophanes was eager enough for the pun to spend three lines preparing for it, and he surely would not have let reality stand in his way. What transactions, if any, Hyperbolus' mother may have carried on are in no way indicated.

The other loans we hear about are on a much smaller scale. Polyeuctus' wife lent eighteen minae to Spudias — a respectable sum, but still within the bounds of the family.[49] The speaker of Demosthenes 41 implies that she had also lent him money. Whether or not these were loans at interest is not certain; the speaker mentions interest in connection with the loans of Polyeuctus and his wife, but he does not actually claim it. Eighteen minae was not a trifling sum, and the loan was witnessed by the woman's brothers, and by a sealed document that was opened and confirmed at the woman's death. The transaction involved was not truly commercial, but it was not insignificant.

The mortgage-stones of Athens, as noted in chapter 1, never mention a woman as a creditor; but we do have two non-Athenian stones that seem to do so. Neither is anything like a commercial loan. One includes the provision *hōste echein kai kratein* ('on condition of possession and control') — that is, the woman is to occupy the land for the duration of the loan,[50] perhaps in lieu of interest: this was not the normal practice, and we do not know why it was adopted here. The 'hypothecation' may mask a form of lease, or a caretaking arrangement, but it is unlikely that we are dealing with a simple loan.[51] The other stone involves only ninety drachmas, very much the smallest sum preserved in any of the *horoi*.[52] It is possible that these women made money on their loans, but they hardly seem like professionals.

A last type of loan, one that falls clearly into the category of charitable loans, is the *eranos,* a loan raised by contributions collected from a group of friends of the debtor and lent to him to meet some extraordinary expense.[53] A very problematical stone published by Fine[54] seems to include the word *plērōtria,* the feminine of *plērōtēs,* the term for a contributor to or collector of such a loan. This is the first direct evidence for women contributing to *eranos*-loans, though we should not be surprised to find it. As for women receiving *eranoi*, our only example is that of Neaera, who collected an *eranos* from her former lovers in order to buy her freedom.[55]

Aside from the *eranos* collected by Neaera, our only evidence for women as borrowers of money comes from the records of the *hieropoioi* at Delos, who lent money at interest and recorded their transactions at the end of their tenure.[56] Most of the loans are granted to men; in a number of them we find recorded the consent of a woman (usually the borrower's wife). There are also a number of loans to women, invariably with the assistance of their *kyrioi*. The chronological distribution is shown in the table below.

Decade	New Loans to Men	New Loans to Women	New Loans to Men with Women's Consent	Others[57]
ca. 250	6	0	0	1
249-240	4	0	1	0
239-230	0	0	0	0
229-220	7	0	0	0
219-210	0	0	0	0
209-200	21	1	1	1
199-190	15	6	12	2
189-180	0	0	0	0
179-170	5	1	2	1
Totals	58	8	16	5

Most of the inscriptions have come down to us in fragments, if at all, and the loans tabulated here are only a fraction of the number of loans granted by the *hieropoioi* in this period; but the lists of interest payments (also fragmentary) tend to confirm the impression that more women were borrowing money in Delos in the beginning of the second century than at the end of the third. Thus in the earlier inscriptions we find few women, and they are not paying debts that they have contracted them-

selves: Alexicrateia, appearing in the year 282,[58] is paying for one Arig-
notus, while Gorgo, who appears at the same time,[59] is paying for Chares.
Gorgo reappears in 274,[60] paying the same sum as previously, presumably
still for Chares, who is still an outstanding debtor,[61] and some time between 260 and 250 in a fragmentary line where the details have been lost.
A man pays for her in 250,[62] but there is no reason to presume that
these later debts were self-incurred any more than the first. Amphicrite
and her *kyrios* Demonous pay interest for the lands that belonged to
Pherecleides in 250;[63] I assume that these had been security for a loan
to Pherecleides, and had now come into Amphicrite's possession either
by inheritance or by sale. Nicaea pays interest in 218 for debts of her
father[64] and her brother.[65] Thus in the third century we have had
women occasionally taking over the responsibility of men's loans; but
it is only in 209 that a woman, Lyso, appears as a contractor of a new
loan.[66] Thereafter women become much more common, both in the lists
of interest payments — and in those of insolvent debtors.

We do not know what sums were involved in these loans, but if we may
judge from the sums generally lent out to men, they were not very great,
mostly less than five hundred drachmas. The women who borrow the
money are all married,[67] so they did not borrow on their own because
they lacked men to borrow for them. One woman, in fact, who borrows
with the assistance of her husband around 190 is listed eleven years later
as consenting to a loan taken out by her husband.[68] What was the difference between the two loans? Was one in fact intended for the wife's
use, and one for the husband's? Or was the difference entirely procedural?
There is no evidence that will help us answer this question now; all we
can say is that women were appearing more often at the temple, either
to contract loans or to approve their husbands' loans, than they had done
in the third century — or probably at any time before.[69]

Before leaving the subject of loans, we may add a word about guarantors. It was customary for third parties, known as *engyētai*, to offer
personal guarantees for the debtor: if the creditor could not collect from
the debtor, he could collect from the guarantor. I have not made a sys-
tematic study of the matter, but among the inscriptions I have seen, I
found no examples of a woman guaranteeing someone else's loan. Even
a creditor willing to lend to a woman preferred, it would seem, to have a
man offer his guarantee.

Wills. The power to will, which asserts the individual's rights over his
property in preference to the family's, was new to Greece in the classical period, and it was not, at first, extended to women. At Gortyn, as
we have seen, women had a good deal of legal control over their property
at the time of the Code; but even here they could not determine their
heirs. The law permitted no changes in the order of succession except by

adoption; and the rule was that 'a woman is not to adopt, nor a minor'.[70]
At Athens the rules for adoption were apparently the same: 'nobody is
adopted away from his mother', says Thrasyllus, trying to prove that
being adopted by a new father does not change one's right to inherit
through one's natural mother; but his way of putting it seems to imply
strongly that adoptive mothers did not exist — that is, that women could
not adopt.[71] Adoption involved the admission of the adopted son into a
new *oikos*, and it could not be performed except by the *kyrios* of the
family.

It is the claim of the speaker of Isaeus 10 that children were prevented
from making wills by the law 'that a child is not to be capable of performing a transaction, nor a woman beyond (the value of) a medimnus of
barley'.[72] If his claim is correct,[73] it would seem to apply for a woman
as well; and in fact, we do not find any cases of Athenian women bequea-
thing their property. A number of passages have been thought to show
bequests, but all of them may be more easily seen as gifts *inter vivos*;[74]
the only true example we have of a woman arranging for the disposal of
her property after death is Philo's mother. 'For she didn't trust this man
enough to commit herself to him when she was dying, but instead she
put her trust in Antiphanes, to whom she was no relative at all, and gave
him three minae of silver for her own burial, passing up this man (i.e.,
Philo), her own son.'[75] Whether we see this as a will or as a gift *inter
vivos* is not of great moment — if the law of Isaeus 10 prohibited one, it
prohibited the other — but the point to be noted is that it did not alienate any money from her son (who was presumably her heir). She merely
asked a friend to care for her funeral rites, and gave him money to do so;
had she not made the gift Philo would not have been richer, unless he
had been intending to skimp on the ceremonies. It was presumably for
this reason that Philo did not challenge her action as, if he was her
kyrios, he could have.

In fact, most Athenian women seem to have had little enough that they
could call their own (except their dowry, which certainly was not theirs
to bequeath). In places where women had more personal property, they
seem to have acquired more power over its final disposition. I know of
no case of a Spartan woman's will, but I find it unlikely that they were
prevented from exercising the same rights that men had.[76] The three
testamentary donations that we have — one from Calauria,[77] one from
Thera,[78] and one from Amorgos[79] — are all made in favour of cult institutions, but I doubt whether this can be taken to imply a restriction on
the women's powers; the fact is simply that private individuals did not
set up inscribed stones indicating who gave them their possessions. Two
of the wills mention the women's *kyrioi*, while the inscription of Calauria
does not — either because it is only an excerpt from the complete document,[80] or because a woman's transactions did not require the presence

of a *kyrios* at Calauria.[81] The two which do, however — one dealing with an establishment of three thousand drachmas, another dealing with unidentifiable real estate that was mortgaged for the woman's dowry — indicate once again that the formal requirement of approval by the *kyrios* did not in itself keep a woman from disposing of her property more or less as she pleased.

If women did not make wills at Athens and at Gortyn, who inherited from them? Who inherited from intestate women elsewhere? We know very little. The law in Gortyn was simple enough: 'The maternal property, too, is to be divided when she dies according to what is prescribed for the paternal property'[82] — that is, generally, to her children. The division, however, appears to have taken place only after the father's death; during his lifetime he controlled the property (*ton patera karteron emen ton matroion*), unless he married another wife. Nevertheless, he could not sell or mortgage the property unless the children were of age and consented.[83] These provisions occur immediately after the provisions cited above abolishing the economic authority of the *kyrios*,[84] and although the clause barring retroactive litigation is not repeated here, I suspect that this law, too, is an innovation. When the *kyrios* had had authority over the property of the members of his household — and this authority, in Gortyn, must have included the right to sell and mortgage property that belonged to them, for that is what had to be legislated against — it is difficult to see how the death of one would have reduced his rights. He could have sold the mother's property; he could have sold her sons' property; it is not likely that he had been prevented from selling property of the mother that had passed to the sons. When this right was abolished, the new law still left the husband his right to manage the property as long as he lived — but not to dispose of it or encumber it.

I do not know whether Athenian law specified who was heir of a woman's property. As long as her personal property was in the power of her *kyrios* during her lifetime, it would presumably remain in his power at her death, unless it formed part of her dowry; no law would be needed to establish this. But the children of a woman of some financial independence might reasonably expect to inherit from her as they inherited from their father. It was surely the daughters of Polyeuctus' wife (or rather, their husbands) who inherited her property, but I think it probable that their husbands were her *kyrioi* during her lifetime as well.[85] More promising, but in the end no more decisive, is the evidence of Apollodorus, who was certainly not his mother's *kyrios* at her death — her second husband was still alive — but who had received a quarter share of the 'maternal property'.[86] This money, apparently the money he had collected from suing Phormio,[87] was not his mother's dowry, for he could not inherit that once his mother had remarried; in fact, a quarter share of the dowry would have entitled him to 5500 drachmas, more than he

received.[88] I rather believe that he was claiming a share in the gifts given
to Archippe by Pasio in his will, out of which she had given 2000 drachmas apiece to her children by Phormio. We do not know what Apollodorus' claim was, but I suspect that he acknowledged the validity of the
gifts, and demanded an equal share for himself. If this was his plea, then
he must have claimed some right to inherit from Archippe in place of
her *kyrios,* Phormio. Unfortunately, however, we are dealing with conjecture, and other information does not help us, for we do not know
why or how the arbitrators 'persuaded' Phormio to pay off Apollodorus.
The situation is further confounded by the fact that Apollodorus asserted that his mother was an *epikleros,*[89] and may have based his claim to
inherit on this. Whether or not a less litigious son than Apollodorus
could have inherited his mother's property at Athens – whether, indeed,
Apollodorus' claim would have been allowed by a full court – cannot be
said.

Gifts. Of gifts by women to other individuals we have only the sparsest
references, all from Athens. They suffice, however, to indicate to us
that such gifts were unlikely to have amounted to much in that place.
Gifts to members of one's own family were respectable enough, but it
is doubtful whether they could have stood up in the face of opposition.
Thus Archippe, when she was dying, was (according to Apollodorus) 'no
longer *kyria* of her property . . . so as to give me as much as she wished';[90]
that is, she could not give her money to Apollodorus, since her husband,
Phormio, would oppose the gift. But it is not certain that even the husband's approval, tacit or explicit, would always suffice, for this same
Archippe did, as was just mentioned, give two thousand drachmas to her
children by Phormio, only to have Apollodorus sue Phormio for an equal
amount of money after her death, and win. The case, for the reasons
mentioned in the last paragraph, does not tell us whether or not other
women could successfully have made such preferential gifts; I doubt
whether cases involving women this rich came up very often.

  Gifts by women to other women are not recorded anywhere – not
surprisingly, in view of the overwhelmingly male sources of our information. We have, however, two examples of women giving gifts to men:
the old woman of the *Plutus,*[91] who bought the attentions of a 'dear
young man' with gifts, and a metic named Zobia who sheltered Aristogeiton, according to the speaker of Demosthenes 25, when he was fleeing
from prison, and then sent him on his way with eight drachmas and a
change of clothing.[92] The speaker is trying to arouse sympathy for the
woman, who was later (according to him) mistreated by Aristogeiton;
but he introduces her as 'a certain woman . . . by the name of Zobia,
with whom, probably, he had had sexual relations at one time'. We may
suspect that similar assumptions attached to any woman who was too

helpful, whether by gifts or by services, to a man who was not a relative.

One sort of gift to which no such stigma attached was the gift to the state, given for patriotic reasons at time of need. We have mentioned above loans of this type granted by women in Boeotia toward the end of the third century; Thompson lists in a similar vein a number of gifts given by women from the same period and somewhat later, and known from the honorific inscriptions set up by grateful citizens. One Timessa, a citizen of Amorgos, was honoured for having ransomed many fellow-citizens when they were prisoners of war;[93] Negopolis and Curasio, women of Pamphylia, contributed twenty minae apiece to the rebuilding of their city walls.[94] These gifts were exceptional; there is no shortage of inscriptions honouring public benefactors, and our three women are insignificant by comparison. But their benefactions were anything but shameful; and at the end of our period, as we have mentioned earlier, Diaeus was willing to make them compulsory for women as well as men.[95]

Dedications. Our records of dedications — objects, land, or money set aside for a god and either used for cult purposes or not used at all — present a very different picture from the one we have seen in other areas. From every place in Greece, and from every age, we have items dedicated by women to various divinities, or inscriptions commemorating such dedications. It is abundantly clear that the factors that kept women from engaging in other economic activities on a large scale never prevented them from dedicating.

This is not to say that women's dedications are as common as men's; they are much less so, the proportion for the most easily tabulated sort — altars and statue-bases[96] — giving approximately three to four men for every woman. To an extent, this may reflect a difference in property control; but I think that a greater factor is the circumstance that men had more occasions to dedicate. The successful completion of a magistracy, or an athletic victory, was an occasion for dedicating something, usually a statue or the victor's trophy; these dedications were obviously made only by men.[97] Dedications on behalf of an entire family were likely to be set up by the head of the household, though they were often set up by a husband and wife jointly,[98] or by a woman.[99] Battle-spoils were obviously the particular province of men. We might also suspect that men were more anxious to see their name or statue displayed in a public place; but the number of women's dedications hardly displays any great reticence, at least in this area.

Except for those articles which were particularly masculine (no women dedicated greaves, as one Arcadian did),[100] there was nothing which might not be dedicated by a woman as well as a man. Women dedicated land[101] and improvements to temple buildings;[102] money for sacrifices in their names;[103] statues of their relatives;[104] herms,[105] sometimes with female heads;[106] vessels for the service;[107] golden crowns;[108] every-day items.[109] There is no evidence that women's gifts were generally smaller or cheaper than those of men, and such gifts as a silver censer weighing 1300 drachmas, dedicated by an Athenian woman at the begin-ning of the fourth century,[110] should make us aware that articles were dedicated by women that were worth much more than anything that was traded by them. In Athens, one priestess was even crowned by the *demos* for dedicating some items and spending a hundred drachmas 'of her own money' on sacrifices.[111]

One second-century inscription from Paros[112] records a collection (apparently for the goddess of childbirth) whose contributors were all women. The sums vary from two obols to six drachmas, with only one possibly higher amount. We might have concluded that these women were truly donating their own pocket-money, but this does not seem to have been a project that required much. The women may have had more that they could have given, had it been asked of them.

These generalizations, it should be noted, are true for all of Greece. The remains from Athens, from Boeotia, from the Peloponnese, from the islands, all tell much the same story. Women are not more frequent as dedicators in the first half of the second century than they were in the fifth century. The only significant differences occur between various dedication-records of temples: thus the old dedications that were repaired or replaced in Oropus around 240 had been given by almost as many women as men,[113] while those included in an inventory of the second century were almost all the gifts of men.[114] In view of the uniformity of the record in other sources, I think we must attribute this and similar phenomena simply to a difference in the kind of dedications represented. An inventory including, for example, annual priestly dedications, will naturally show a heavy male bias.

It has been suggested that the dedication of an object to a divinity did not require the approval of a *kyrios* in places where other acts did.[115] Most of our inscriptions do not help us in this question, for they record the source of the object ('so-and-so dedicated') rather than the transac-tion by which it left the owner's hands. The manumission-inscriptions, most of which are written in the form of a dedication of the slave to a divinity, are no help: it is not clear, for one thing, whether their legal status is the same as that of a true dedication, and they show a suffi-ciently marked geographical variation for us to have to explain both sides of the issue – once we know why a *kyrios* is not required for a Delphic manumission, we must establish why he is required for a Boeotian one. The few inscriptions that do describe transactions do not, however, sup-port the theory that they took place without *kyrioi*. The women who contribute to the fund for renewing the clothes and vessels of an image in Lindus do so with the agreement of their *kyrioi*.[116] Nicesarete, a

woman of Amorgos, dedicates land with the agreement of her *kyrios*[117]—
not surprisingly, since the land is in fact his, mortgaged for her dowry;
the will of Epicteta, whose purpose is the establishment of a religious
foundation, is agreed to by her *kyrios*.[118] There are two exceptions, one
from the Megarid[119] and one from Calauria in the Peloponnese;[120] but
these are not sufficient to be used as examples for a general rule, and they
may either be due to the omission of the *kyrios* by the stonecutter or to
a difference in the laws of these localities, for in neither is the presence
(or absence) of a *kyrios* attested for any other transaction.

How are we to explain the great frequency of women's dedications?
Even were we to accept the theory outlined in the last paragraph, it
would not help us, for the requirement of consent of the *kyrios*, as we
have seen, was not what prevented women from entering other transactions. But it is clear that the major factor which did keep women from
large-scale economic activity, namely, the division of functions between
male and female, was not a factor here. Religion in Greece was never a
male monopoly — it was, on the contrary, just about the only institution
of Greek society that was suffused with women from the top to the bot-
tom, from the priestesses and prophetesses to Sostratus' mother, who
'goes in circles around the whole deme, sacrificing'.[121] For a woman to
appear too often in the market might be demeaning; for her to appear at
religious functions was not. Buying, selling, and lending she might do
within limits, for those were essentially her husband's job; dedicating and
sacrificing were the business of both husband and wife. For this reason
we do not find an increase in the frequency of women's dedications in
the Hellenistic period. Already before that time, dedication was, like
other religious acts, an essential part of the woman's role.

One word of caution is in order: there is no reason to presume that the
property dedicated by women had originally been theirs. The very community of property between husband and wife which, legalized in the
concept of family property, generally resulted in the husband's control-
ling the wife's resources, might here work in the opposite direction. The
person who is mentioned as the dedicator of an object is not necessarily
the person who provided the money, but the person who incurred the
obligation to the divinity: when a woman in labour vows a statue, she
may have to get the money for it from her husband, but the statue will
bear the woman's name.[122] So the dedications, while they do indicate
that women could incur obligations concerning large sums of money, do
not necessarily mean that the money was theirs for other purposes. A
man who might think twice about refusing money vowed to a divinity
could still be firm in refusing new clothes to his wife.

6
The Dowry

Marriage in Athens was a contract between the bride's father and the groom. The form of the marriage was a conditional gift:

> PATAECUS. I give you this woman for the procreation of legitimate children. POLEMON. I accept. PATAECUS. And three talents' dowry. POLEMON. And all is well.[1]

Traces of a similar concept survive in the Christian wedding ceremony: the father brings the bride to the altar and gives her to the groom. At Athens, however, the gift of the bride was no empty formality, but a reflection of the actual state of affairs. The bride herself could not legally enter into the contract; only if she was given away by the appropriate man was the marriage valid and the issue legitimate.[2] Scattered throughout the literature we find mention of the considerations that go into — or that should go into — the choice of a bride,[3] or the choice of a son-in-law.[4] No one discusses the choice of a husband, since that was not the woman's prerogative.

Arranging this marriage was the primary responsibility of the family into which a woman was born. This responsibility fell in the first instance upon the head of the family — the father, if he was living; otherwise a paternal brother or, failing those, the paternal grandfather[5] — and we have already seen the seriousness with which it was taken. Along with the wedding, indeed, almost essential to it, went the responsibility of providing a dowry; and this was a matter that determined more than any other what the woman's economic status would be in her new family.

The dowry at Athens.[6] Just as marriage, ideally, dominated the social life of an Athenian woman, so the dowry, ideally, dominated her economic affairs. Both ideals were truest among the upper classes. The dowries mentioned in the orators vary from ten to fifty minae, while property actually belonging to the women mentioned was, as we have already seen, very slight.[7] Among women of this class, the dowry represented more money than they were likely to control in their entire life, and it was able to serve them in ways that their personal possessions could not.

The first purpose served by the dowry was the attraction of a suitable husband. It is doubtful whether Athenian girls really grew up without ever seeing the light of day, but it is certain that girls of good family did not mix freely with men, and were unlikely to attract a husband by their personal merits. A girl's family might be an asset: the speaker of

Lysias 19 claims that he and his father chose their wives because they were daughters of worthy men,[8] and an orator with a case at hand might even claim that no man would turn down a true friend's daughter.[9] But in the absence of a friend both true and generous, the dowry was an important matter. A woman without a dowry was in danger of being unmarried all her life, as litigants with daughters did not fail to remind the court: 'For who would ever take a dowerless wife from a penniless man in debt to the state?'[10] A large dowry, on the other hand, might attract an otherwise unattainable husband. It was a sign of Callias' wealth, not merely his consideration, that he was able to offer his daughters any bridegroom they wanted,[11] and the younger Alcibiades claimed that his maternal grandfather's wealth had made all the best youth of Greece suitors for his mother's hand.[12] Isaeus in two places implies that it would be extraordinary for a wealthy groom to accept a dowerless wife, or one with a small dowry;[13] this is, of course, Isaeus speaking, but there can be little doubt that there was a tendency for wealthy men to receive large dowries.

The only legal obligation that the groom acquired toward the wife upon receipt of the dowry was her maintenance, for which he was responsible as long as he held it. During the marriage this 'obligation' cannot have meant very much, since it was the normal duty of a man to feed his wife and all the other members of his household; in practice it meant that in case of divorce, or in case the marriage failed to take place (as that of Aphobus and Demosthenes' mother),[14] the wife's *kyrios* could sue the husband to pay for her upkeep out of the interest on the dowry, computed at the rate of 18 per cent.[15] In effect, then, this obligation was essentially a matter between the husband and the woman's *kyrios*: a matter that might work to the wife's disadvantage, if she was caught in the middle of a struggle about who should be feeding her.

Ownership and control. The dowry itself belonged in no legal sense to the woman. She could not dispose of it, since it was worth more than a medimnus of barley. Its management belonged, as did the management of the property she brought with her, to her husband.[16] Her husband, on the other hand, could dispose of it freely, even too freely: Menander's *Epitrepontes* shows us an old man hurrying to obtain his daughter's divorce before her dowry is spent.[17] It could be confiscated for the husband's debt.[18] The only legal restrictions on the husband's rights were the claims of the woman's *kyrios* in case of divorce, childless death, or state confiscation of the husband's property.[19]

This being the case, it is strange to see the dowry being referred to regularly as if it were the woman's. The wife of one debtor begged the creditors not to touch the furniture, which was part of her dowry: 'leave

the furniture', she cried, 'and don't take anything of mine'.[20] Mantitheus
tried to demonstrate that his mother had a dowry, for her brothers were
rich and unlikely 'to rob their own sister';[21] Demosthenes, speaking in
his own person, called the dowry 'hers' (*ta ekeinēs*).[22] This surely does
not reflect a division of use; there is no evidence I know of to indicate
that women were ever likely to manage their own dowries as they managed household expenses.[23] It reflects a much broader power, through
which a well-dowered wife could dominate the economic life of the
family. Menander warns against marrying a woman whose dowry is out
of proportion to one's own wealth: 'When a man who is poor chooses
to marry and accepts the property that comes along with the wife, he
is giving himself, not taking her',[24] and Plutarch says the same: 'Those
who marry women far above themselves become without realizing it
their dowries' slaves, not their wives' husbands'.[25] Similar sentiments
may lie behind a fragment of Euripides, 'Even though free, he is a slave
of his marriage bed, having sold his body for his dowry'.[26]

These are not isolated statements,[27] nor are they bits of romantic
advice against marrying for money. They are warnings against a phenomenon that was very real to the Athenians, even if it had no legal basis.

How did a man become a slave to his dowry? The wife had one clear
source of practical power: if she chose to divorce her husband, he had
to return the dowry to her *kyrios* — a procedure which might be impossible if he had spent it, and would in any event be disagreeable if his
personal estate was not worth much more than the dowry.[28] There must
have been men at Athens who, after some profligate or unsuccessful years,
possessed less money than they had received as a dowry; such men could
avoid bankruptcy only by keeping the favour of their wives, and there is
little doubt that they would be considered 'their dowries' slaves'.

But not all slaves are slaves to power or to threats, nor did all wives
have to be ready to divorce their husbands to get their way. The Athenians considered the dowry to be the wife's contribution to the family
treasury, and the wife who contributed more than her husband had a
good claim to be considered the senior partner. This appears most
clearly when Xenophon's hero Ischomachus finds it necessary to persuade his wife otherwise: 'For I am laying out everything I own into our
common treasury, and you have deposited everything you brought into
our common treasury. And we shouldn't calculate which of us has contributed more; instead, we should recognize clearly that whichever of us
should be the better partner — that one is contributing the item of greatest value.'[29] The moral obligation under which a man was put when he
accepted a large dowry made Gorgias in the *Dyscolus* hesitate about his
marriage:

(GORGIAS.) My sister I give to you for a wife, and as for taking
yours — I'm all right. (SOSTRATUS.) What do you mean, 'all right'?

(GO.) It doesn't seem pleasant to me to live high off other people's efforts. I'd rather save up my own money. (SO.) You're talking nonsense, Gorgias; don't you think you're worthy of the match? (GO.) I think I'm worthy of her, but I don't think it's worthy for a man with a little to take a lot.[30]

Once married, he might find himself the object of considerable scorn if he failed to support his wife as her dowry deserved. Theophrastus' badmouth, the *kakologos*, chooses this fault for one of his tidbits: 'and stinginess — there's nothing like it. To give you an idea: his wife brought him a talent's dowry, and bore him a son, and he gives her three coppers for treats, and forces her to wash in cold water on New Year's day.'[31]

Not everybody was daunted by moral obligation or public scorn. Menander presents a character who seems able to overcome his better feelings: 'He got a dowry of four talents of silver, but he doesn't consider himself his wife's servant; he sleeps away from home, and pays a pimp twelve drachmas a day'.[32] Against behaviour like this there is, should tears and protests fail, no defence except divorce. The girl's father attempts to effect a divorce,[33] but the girl herself objects.[34] What is to be learned from this? Only that Athenian women were liable, like the rest of us, to love their spouses, and that for a couple to break up was a difficult emotional matter then as now. Obvious as such a statement is, it is nevertheless worth keeping in mind when speaking of divorce as a remedy to a woman's problems: the sickness might have become quite serious before a wife would take the remedy.

One woman who tried it was Alcibiades' wife Hipparete, whose troubles were documented in gory detail by Pseudo-Andocides: 'After getting a dowry bigger than any Greek ever got,[35] he had the nerve to bring prostitutes, both slave and free, into the same house, until he forced his wife, a perfectly modest woman, to go to the archon, to divorce him according to the law. And that was where he really showed his power: he called together his cronies, snatched the woman out of the *agora*, took her away forcibly, and showed everybody what contempt he had for the archons and the laws and the other citizens'.[36] The story is a very sad one; Plutarch adds that the woman did not live long thereafter.[37] But there cannot have been many such stories. Few Athenians could have got away with what Alcibiades could; and even Alcibiades had to collect a gang for the purpose. Normally a wife, once she had decided to leave her husband, must have been able to count on the support and protection of her family.

The dowry and economic class. Among the lower economic strata, dowries were of course lower. Most of the preserved *horoi* deal with dowries of twenty minae or less, and these are still the dowries of people with real property.[38] It is conceivable that the dowry disappeared entirely in the lowest citizen classes; there are certainly dowerless women in the orators,[39] and even the smallest dowries on the *horoi* were well beyond the reach of the poorest citizens of Athens.[40]

We should nevertheless be wary of presuming that there was a proportional relationship between a father's wealth and the dowry he gave to his daughter. The evidence we have on the subject is meagre, but it does not support such an assumption. Ciron, a man whose fortune amounted to somewhat more than a talent and a half,[41] gave his daughter a dowry of twenty-five minae; when he failed to recover the full amount at his son-in-law's death, he gave her away a second time with ten minae.[42] Endius, who possessed three talents, was alleged to have given the daughter of his adoptive father ten minae; the speaker of Isaeus 3 claims that no adopted son would dare give a legitimate daughter less than a tenth of the estate. [43] Onetor, on the other hand, possessing more than thirty talents, gave a dowry of either a talent or eighty minae, but Demosthenes gives no indication that this was a parsimonious sum.[44] At the other end of the scale, Demosthenes' father gave his daughter two talents out of fourteen, his wife eighty minae; but these were testamentary bequests, and the sum for the daughter must have included the wherewithal to maintain her for ten years, until she was of marriageable age.[45] Diodotus' will provided a talent apiece for his daughter and his wife, out of an estate that appears to have amounted to somewhat more than thirteen talents.[46] Pasio left his wife five talents, some three talents and forty minae of which were, probably, all that was technically her dowry;[47] out of a total worth of some sixty talents,[48] this was still somewhat less than a tenth.

These dowries are all from wealthy people; but they show a wide variation in percentage of the giver's estate, from almost twenty per cent in the case of Ciron[49] (estimating his total fortune to have been slightly more than two talents) to less than five per cent for Onetor. In actual monetary value, on the other hand, we saw a rather smaller range of sums.[50] This should not surprise us; surely there were other factors that affected the size of the dowry besides the fortune of the man who gave it. A man with many daughters must have given each a smaller sum than a man of similar fortune with only one daughter;[51] and since the major purpose of the dowry was to attract a husband, the sums will have depended in part upon the competition. Even if Onetor had had three hundred talents, there would have been little need for him to settle more than a single talent on his daughter; an amount on that order put her among the most attractive matches an Athenian could make. The family of Callias, who seem to have been more generous, were clearly using dowries as a form of ostentation.[52]

Dowries of the poor. At the other end of the economic scale, we may suspect that dowries represented a much greater proportion of the family's wealth. The poor of Athens were not in direct competition with the Onetors and the Hipponici; but they, too, must have found it difficult to get a bridegroom if they had no money to offer, and it was a matter of pride to offer as much as they could, or more. That citizens of Myconos offered dowries above their ability to pay is epigraphically attested,[53] and it is reasonable to believe that the same was true at Athens. Menander's Gorgias, a pauper who has just been given half a farm, has to be talked out of giving his sister a talent's dowry,[54] and the entire plot of Plautus' *Trinummus* revolves around a man who feels honour-bound to dower a girl for whom he is responsible, even though her suitor is willing to accept her dowerless. The dowry, in Athens, was a necessity, and like necessities at all places and at all times, it must have taken up a greater part of the budgets of the poor than those of the rich. The strain placed on the poor by the competition for bridegrooms may have been behind the Solonian legislation against dowries.[55]

Wealthy people, as we see from the orators, usually did not include the wife's trousseau in the evaluation of the dowry. She brought her clothing with her without legally binding her husband to return it in case of divorce; he, for his part, was likely to return it anyway. This was not a matter of law, but of politeness; legally anything could be valued in the dowry, as long as it was actually delivered to the groom's household.[56] Among the lower classes, this conventional generosity is less likely to have obtained. A man who was hard-pressed to provide a dowry might well have preferred to inflate the figure by including his daughter's trousseau; he may also have been more careful to make sure that everything he gave would be returned in case of divorce. Our only direct evidence for this practice among the poor comes not from Athens, but from the dowry-inscription of Myconos, where three dowries specifically mention that clothing (*esthēs*) was included in the sum: it is precisely these three whose cash balances are not paid in full.[57] In Athens such a practice was certainly legal; but in the absence of evidence about poor women's dowries, we cannot be certain that it was common, or indeed that it was found at all in ordinary cases.

To what extent the poor of Athens were able to dower their daughters, however, depended not only upon their own fortunes, but upon the fortunes and the generosity of their friends and relatives. It was considered a deed of piety to provide dowries for poor relatives, and we have numerous testimonies of such benefactions. Thus the speaker of Lysias 19, after describing his father's liturgies, adds, 'and furthermore, he also helped some of the impoverished citizens give away their daughters and sisters, at his own expense',[58] an act which he classes with the ransoming of prisoners and providing money for funeral expenses. Aristomenes appears to have performed a similar favour for the mother of the speaker

of Isaeus 10, although the speaker, in his eagerness to gain his grandfather's property, from which the encumbrances have now been removed,
maintains this to have been part of a plot against him.[59] Chaerestratus in
the *Aspis*, 'since he is a good man',[60] is ready to dower his niece when her
brother fails to return from battle. A letter attributed to Plato discusses
his responsibility for dowering his grandnieces: 'My friends and I have
to give in marriage any of these women who marry in my lifetime; it will
be too bad about those who marry later. I don't have to give away any
whose fathers are richer than I; but now I am the wealthiest of them, and
I even gave away their mothers, along with Dion and others';[61] here we
see the members of a family taking collective responsibility for raising
their daughters' dowries. Particularly noble, according to Demosthenes,
was the example of Satyrus the comic actor, who came to Philip after
the fall of Olynthus and requested him to free the captive daughters of
one of Satyrus' *xenoi*, so that Satyrus could give them away with dowries.[62] We see here the extent to which one might go to see to it that a
friend's daughters suffered 'nothing unworthy either of ourselves or of
their father';[63] even a man of ordinary decency might be expected to
take a similar interest in a brother's family. Attacks on men who failed
to do so are preserved for us by the orators.[64]

The most famous beneficiaries of dowry-assistance were the daughters
of Aristeides, who were said to have been dowered by the state; it is
worth noting, perhaps, that their dowry was less than a third of the cash
grant to their brother, who also got one hundred plethra of land and four
times his sisters' living allowance.[65] Probably the oddest such case was
Neaera's alleged daughter Phano. Epaenetus, caught with Phano in what
Stephanus claimed was adultery (the term, in Greece, included offences
with the plaintiff's daughter as well as his wife), paid a ransom for his
freedom, then charged Stephanus with having framed him. The dispute
was settled on the following terms: 'What happened concerning the
imprisonment (i.e., Stephanus' holding of Epaenetus for ransom) is to
be completely forgotten, and Epaenetus is to give Phano a thousand
drachmas towards her wedding, since he has slept with her often. Stephanus is to make Phano available to Epaenetus whenever he is in town
and wishes to have relations with her.'[66] Here the lover not only contributed to the girl's hope-chest, but did so on condition of her continued
favours! In reality, of course, no true marriage was contemplated by such
provisions. Phano remained – or became – a *hetaera*, like her alleged
mother; the ransom was said to be 'towards her wedding' (*eis ekdosin*)
in order to make Stephanus' acceptance of it on behalf of a girl he
claimed as his daughter more respectable; and the last clause, ensuring
Epaenetus of her 'availability', was added to protect him against a
second charge of adultery.[67]

The examples quoted are not from lower-class people, except for

Phano, who had connections; they are dealing for the most part with well-to-do Athenians, who, having fallen on hard times, were helped out by their families. Whether or not a chronically poor man was likely to have rich relatives to whom he could turn for help is a much harder question to solve, and one that goes beyond the limits of the present study. All we can say is that if a man could get financial assistance, it is likely to have been most available, and most welcome, for the dowering of his daughters.

The dowry after marriage. The protection afforded a woman by her dowry did not cease when she was divorced or when her husband died. As long as the money was in the hands of her former husband or his heirs, she was entitled to maintenance from the interest. In the case of a woman who returned to her former household, this may have been a a matter that affected her only indirectly; her brother (or, indeed, any member of her family) was not likely to let her starve while waiting for the dowry to be returned,[68] and the suit would affect her only in so far as it would enable (and at least morally, obligate) him to maintain her on a higher level.

A woman who had children at her husband's death, or who claimed to be pregnant, was entitled to remain in her husband's household.[69] If the children were adults, they became her *kyrioi* and were responsible for her maintenance; if they were minors, she was apparently maintained out of their estate. This seems, at least, to have been the situation with the mother of Demosthenes, since it was Demosthenes who, as heir of the estate, demanded from Aphobus the reimbursement for maintenance which Aphobus owed.[70] The pregnant mother remained under the protection of the archon[71] until the birth of the child; thereupon a guardian was presumably appointed, who would also be the woman's *kyrios.*

Once the dowry either returned to the *kyrios* or passed to the sons, its legal existence seems to have been at an end. The responsibility of the sons for their mother's maintenance was independent of her dowry, and the responsibility of her *kyrios* does not seem to have differed from his responsibility before the marriage — that is to say, it was a matter of family ties rather than legal responsibilities.

If the woman was still marriageable, it was the duty of the *kyrios* to marry her off again. This responsibility was not perhaps as pressing as the marriage of a virgin, at least if the woman had children; thus Demosthenes, as often as he upbraids Aphobus for not marrying Demosthenes' mother, does it from a financial point of view ('He neither returned (the dowry) itself nor paid her maintenance-allowance').[72] He uses very different language when speaking of his sister: 'Nor did they feel shame — if not pity — that my sister, who had been deemed worthy of two talents by my father, was to get none of the things that were proper;

but as if they had been some sort of enemies, rather than friends and bereaved relatives, they paid no attention at all to their family ties.'[73]

But if the matter was not an emergency, it seems to have been taken seriously enough by Athenian men, and there are numerous attested cases of women married for a second time;[74] some, in fact, never returned to their fathers' houses, but were betrothed by their dying husbands, along with dowries at least as large as those they had brought with them.[75] Once a woman had returned to her family, she still required a dowry for a second wedding, and while it was legal, and not unexampled, to give the second husband a smaller amount than the first, it was clearly the feeling of Athenian men that such behaviour required a good excuse. The speaker of Isaeus 8 feels compelled to offer such an excuse: 'My grandfather received her back, and since he did not recover as large a dowry as he had given — because of the impoverished state of Nausimenes' affairs — he gave her away again to my father, and gave a dowry of a thousand drachmas along with her',[76] as opposed to the twenty-five minae which her first husband had received. And Mantitheus professes disbelief at the suggestion that well-to-do Athenians would have done such a thing: 'Nor is it likely that Menexenus and Bathyllus, who had a lot of money themselves, and who had recovered the dowry at Cleomedon's death, would rob their own sister'.[77] Phaenippus went so far as to list his mother's dowry among his debts.[78] It is not easy to see what he had in mind — whether he considered the money a debt to her, in that he was obliged to find another husband for her, or whether his father was still alive but retired, and he considered the dowry a debt to her former *kyrios*, to whom he could be obliged to repay it if his mother should return to her family's house after his father's death or a divorce[79] — but neither possibility, in the case of a woman whose son was grown and in charge of the *oikos*, would offer much justification for him. An inscription of the *poletai*, on the other hand, distinguishes the land of the widow — apparently land that had been mortgaged against her dowry — from the land of her husband's heirs;[80] so the claim might have been credible in another situation.

Whether or not there were circumstances in which the dowry did not have to be returned to the wife's *kyrios* is a question over which scholars have been able to exercise their wits, since there is no direct evidence. Only two cases suggest themselves: (a) that of a foreign woman betrothed to an Athenian citizen by another citizen 'who claimed that she belonged to him' (*hōs heautōi prosēkousan*)[81] and (b) adultery. In the first case, the law itself should satisfy us that the dowry was not returnable, for the *kyrios* who had married the girl off with such a claim lost his civic rights and had his property expropriated;[82] it hardly seems likely that he could then go to the husband whom he had tricked and demand his money back. He surely had no recourse at law, being deprived of civic

rights.[83] It is equally dubious whether his sons could inherit his claim to
the dowry, should he have died between the marriage and the divorce;
rather than come to court with the information that their father should
have lost his citizenship and his property, they were probably well ad-
vised to leave the matter alone.

In the case of adultery, we are not helped much even by indirect evidence. At Ephesus, adultery on the part of the wife forfeited the dowry;[84]
but Ephesus was not Athens. An attempt was at one time made to show
that Plango, the wife of Mantias, had never received her dowry back because she had been divorced on the grounds of adultery; but the argument, which was *ex silentio* in the first place, has been well disposed of
by Wolff.[85] Beauchet argued that 'since the return of the dowry ordin-
arily operates to the profit of the person who had given it, it is impossible for the giver to suffer from a fault which is foreign to him';[86] but
this is an argument which can be turned around with equal force: why
should the husband (who is required to divorce his wife, and may have
some difficulty returning the dowry) suffer for a crime that is not only
not his, but has in fact been committed against him? If indeed the cuckold was required to return the dowry with the wife, then the Athenian
courts were offering good reason for him to remain silent and go along,
in spite of the laws, with his wife's adultery. There is no proof that they
did not do so, but it is hard to imagine.[87] In the Athenian courts, where
precedent had no legal standing, anything that was not explicitly and
unambiguously stated in a written law was open to argument.[88] The
jurors were sworn to uphold the law, and they apparently took their
oath seriously; but in the absence of precedent, consistently applied
interpretations — what we like to call 'the letter of the law', as if every
law had only one possible correct interpretation — counted for much
less than emotional appeal and ostensible moral rectitude. The Attic
orator, retained by a cuckold who wished to keep his dowry, would be
likely to write him a speech emphasizing the grievous injury to the husband, the unspeakable avarice of the *kyrios* who wished to profit from
his daughter's (sister's, niece's) crime, the danger to the state and to
public morals when well-dowered wives would be able to practise adultery with impunity. If Demosthenes' estimation of his audience was
anywhere near correct, any one of these arguments would carry more
weight with them than finely-drawn legalisms. And the law, in Athens,
was what the jurors thought it was.[89]

Old age. If a woman had borne sons, she was entitled to be supported
by them in her old age, as was their father. Her children had to provide
her with lodging and food,[90] and could be prosecuted by any citizen for
abusing her.[91] She was under the particular protection of the archon or,
if she was a metic, of the polemarch.[92] According to a law quoted by

Aeschines, it was forbidden for anyone to speak in the assembly 'who strikes his father or his mother, or fails to provide them with food or lodging',[93] and he accuses Timarchus of violating the law by wasting the property from which he could feed (and on which he could bury) his mother.[94]

Legally, then, a woman was never as thoroughly protected as she was in her old age. In fact, the care with which parents are treated by the laws testifies to their actual powerlessness once they had retired from their property and left it in the hands of their children. The protection of the archon was extended also to orphans, *epikleroi,* and pregnant widows remaining in their husbands' houses; to all those, in short, who were easily abused by the members of their *oikoi.* Aeschines' description of Timarchus' mother, 'begging and pleading' (*hiketeuousēs kai antibolousēs*) for him not to sell the land, shows the situation in its pathetic aspect; the aged Philocleon's tipsy complaint to the flute-girl, 'Now I don't have control of my own property, because I'm young, and very closely guarded. My son watches me carefully, and he's grouchy, and besides, he's a cumin-splitting-cardamum-scraping skinflint. He worries about me, afraid that I'll waste all the property, since he doesn't have any father except me',[95] shows behind its comedy the same child-like dependence of the parent on the child. Abuse of one's parents was considered to be a particularly heinous offence, and we must presume that the normal Athenian treated his mother and father, as have most peoples, with a good deal more reverence than is customary today; the laws were intended to chastise the exceptions. How common the exceptions were, and to what extent they were indeed restrained by the law, goes beyond the limits of our study; for us it will suffice to point out that a woman's rights to maintenance continued throughout her life, if she had sons, and included the right to burial and maintenance of cult at her grave after death.[96]

As for the childless woman, she presumably remained in the house of her *kyrios.* She had no legal claim to maintenance from her relatives,[97] and was dependent upon their willingness, and ability, to keep her. Much can be surmised about the life of such women, but nothing is known.

The dowry outside of Athens. We have concerned ourselves thus far only with Athens. Most of our evidence has come from literary sources, chiefly from the orators; for the rest of Greece, where literary evidence is scanty, much less can be said. We have no grounds to infer that the laws, customs, or social functions of the dowry were identical throughout Greece, or even that they were anywhere quite what they were at Athens; and only in isolated cases have we any grounds to deny it. There is only one general principle that we can state, and it is based on inference rather than evidence: namely, that where women were more directly

involved in economic affairs — as they were, on the evidence of the preceding chapters, in many places in Greece — the dowry is unlikely to
have dominated their economic life as thoroughly as it did at Athens.

In Delos, where the women seem not to have dealt much directly with
property until the second century, there is reason to suspect that as they
became more actively involved, they acquired more control over their
dowries. This, at any rate, is what seems to be implied by the sudden
increase in the number of loans that are 'agreed to' by the wives of the
borrowers. We find in the inscriptions dated 200 or earlier forty-two
new loans contracted by men: one records the agreement of a man,[98]
two the agreement of the borrower's wife,[99] and one that of two people
of whom the first is illegible and the second is a wife — whether of the
borrower or of the other consentor is not clear.[100] Of thirty-five new
loans to men in the second century, twelve are agreed to by the borrower's wife,[101] one by his mother,[102] and one by a woman whose
relationship cannot be determined.[103] The change is noteworthy, but
its explanation is only conjectural. I suspect that at this period Delian
women were coming to be considered the owners of their dowries, so
that their agreement was required (or desired) before real estate that
was mortgaged for a dowry (or that formed part of a dowry, if that was
customary at Delos) could be used as security for a loan. The simultan-
eous increase in female debtors may point in the same direction, for
control of her dowry will have given a woman real security on which to
borrow.

The Amorgian *horoi* seem to indicate the same development. One of
them records that the owner of the lands has hypothecated them with
his wife's agreement (*synepichōrousēs tēs gynaikos*),[104] and another
records a *prasis epi lysei* by a husband and wife of lands that were all
originally acquired by the husband;[105] in both cases, we must presume
that the woman's agreement was necessary because the land, although
belonging (at least in the second case) to the husband, was mortgaged
for her dowry. Our presumption is strengthened by the fact that in both
stones the woman agrees with a *kyrios* other than her husband. He was
presumably her original *kyrios*, to whom the land was legally obligated,
and whose consent was thus desired before more encumbrances could be
placed on it. Most striking is the *horos* that records Nicesarete's dedication of real estate assessed in her dowry (*apotetimēmenon . . . eis tēn
proika*),[106] a dedication which is performed, indeed, with her husband's
consent (though not with that of her former *kyrios*), but which certainly
shows a much more direct use of the dowry than was possible for an
Athenian woman.

At Gortyn, according to Wolff,[107] there was no *proix*, and indeed
there was not, in the sense in which Wolff uses the word, that is, the
dowry as it existed at Athens. But there was a dowry at Gortyn. Much

of the legalism surrounding the Athenian dowry was absent, for a woman
of Gortyn could own property, and was entitled at the end of the marriage to 'her own property . . . which she had had at the time of the
marriage', as well as part of the produce of her married life;[108] at her
death, her children inherited her property.[109] This being so, the purposes
of the dowry required no more than a gift to the woman at her marriage;
but such gifts were certainly given, and probably no less regularly than
at Athens. The Code refers to them with the provision, 'If the father
should wish during his lifetime to give to his daughter upon her marriage,
he is to give as prescribed, but no more. Anyone to whom he has already
given or pledged is to have that, but she is not to inherit anything more
(of the paternal property)'.[110] This legislation, restricting the size of the
dowry to the girl's share of the inheritance (i.e., to half a son's share),
seems to imply in its last phrase the existence of even larger dowries
before the introduction of the law. A further requirement was the wit-
nessing of the dowry: 'When the property is divided, three or more
adult free witnesses are to be present. If he should give to a daughter,
the same applies'.[111] The presence of witnesses was common, but not
required, at Athens.[112]

The connection of estate division with gifts to the daughter is not for-
tuitous, for a woman's dowry in Gortyn was her share of the estate. Upon
receipt of a dowry from her father, she lost her claim on the estate;[113]
after the estate had been divided, she had her marriage-portion and could
expect no dowry from her brothers.[114] It is unlikely, however, that most
women had to wait for their father's death before receiving their share.
The possibility of a gift 'to his daughter upon her marriage' during his
lifetime was, as we have seen, considered by the Code (gifts to sons were
not), and a girl who received nothing from her father would have been
at a disadvantage in competition with fatherless girls who had already
received their inheritances. Ephorus, apparently describing the situation
that we find in Gortyn, considered the daughter's share to be her dowry:
'The dowry, if there are brothers, is half of a brother's portion'.[115] He
was not misunderstanding the situation; the dowry and the inheritance
were in fact identical. If the money was given at the wedding by the
father, we should call it a dowry; if it was received at the father's death,
an inheritance; but its function in the woman's life was the same in
either case. Both the origin of the woman's special inheritance rights —
an anomaly in Greek law, where women did not generally inherit anything at all in the presence of equally close males — and the restriction
of those rights to daughters (sisters of the deceased would not inherit
anything if there were brothers) are to be explained as a procedure to
guarantee (and, at least by the time of the Code, to limit) a woman's
dowry, not as a survival of a hypothetical proto-Cretan matriarchy.

The fact that a daughter's inheritance was simply her dowry under another guise will also explain to us the peculiar restriction of the inheritance law, whereby certain forms of property, including the town-house, were divided among the sons only, even if there were daughters in the house.[116] These items were the essentials of the inheritance: a man did not give his daughter his family home as a dowry, and the law did not legislate such a gift at his death. After the sons, who were the true heirs, had divided the items that were the essentials of the estate, the law set aside one-half of a brother's portion out of the remainder to take the place of the dowry the daughter would have received from her father had he survived.

Since the dowry (or inheritance) of a Gortynian woman was her personal property, it naturally followed her in case of divorce, or of her husband's death; upon her death it passed to her children. As regards her membership in a family, the rules were apparently the same as those at Athens: if her husband died childless, the woman left his household; if there were children, she was permitted to do so, whence we may gather that she could also remain.[117] If she does leave, she may go with a gift from her husband: 'she is to marry, taking her own property and whatever her husband may give according to the law before three adult free witnesses'.[118] This gift is given, like the dowry, in the presence of three witnesses and is not considered by the Code in the case of divorce:[119] it is precisely the phenomenon we have observed at Athens of a husband dowering his wife on his deathbed. At Athens, testamentary dowries seem generally to have been larger than those arranged by living fathers for their daughters,[120] and the only case in which we can compare a woman's first dowry to that granted by her dying husband shows the latter to have been substantially larger.[121] In Gortyn, where the woman possessed her original dowry automatically, provision was made for her husband on his deathbed to increase the sum. Both at Athens and at Gortyn, the purpose of the gift must have been to make the widow more attractive to a prospective husband, and to ensure that the marriage actually took place once the husband was not there to arrange it. In a later provision, these gifts were restricted to a hundred staters; so were gifts by a son to his mother, which presumably would also be given for her remarriage.[122]

The law of Gortyn expresses itself in different terms from that of Athens, and has certain very considerable differences in substance. But the differences of expression should not blind us to similarities where they exist. The Code describes gifts given to daughters at their marriage, duly witnessed, which follow the wife when she leaves the household, which pass to her children at her death, which are in need of sumptuary legislation to restrict their size, and which may be increased by a husband on his deathbed. Ephorus called them *phernae*. Would another Greek have called them *proikes*?[123] We don't know; but it is clear that we are dealing with an institution very closely related to the Athenian dowry.

The chief differences between the Athenian dowry and the Gortynian were three. Most notable is that the Gortynian dowry was considered to belong to the woman, not to her *kyrios,* and could not be alienated by anyone but her.[124] The second important difference is that the dowry of the Gortynian woman belonged to her of right, as part of the law of inheritance, whereas an Athenian man was under no legal compulsion whatsoever to dower his daughters.[125] Even in Gortyn, the father was not obliged to furnish a dowry at the time of the marriage; but the bride was nevertheless assured of her eventual share. The third difference is not — at least in origin, for the Code is clearly interested in curbing dowries, not raising them[126] — a legal difference but a social one: in no case that we know of at Athens did the daughter receive as much as half a brother's portion of the estate. Here, however, we should not express ourselves with too much certainty, for our Athenian information comes from the upper classes where the dowry was likely to form a smaller part of the estate than elsewhere.

Even less is known about Sparta, and what we do know is obscured by various idealized tales about the 'Lycurgan constitution'. But it is clear from Aristotle that dowries were given in his day, and he considered the practice one of the causes of Sparta's weakness: 'and almost two-fifths of all the land belongs to women, both because there are many *epikleroi,* and because they give large dowries'.[127] The statement is an interesting one, since in Athens a woman did not own her dowry, nor was an *epikleros* full mistress of her patrimony; no matter how large the dowries, or the number of *epikleroi,* Athens would not have belonged to the women. We might suspect that Aristotle was merely using his terminology loosely, as the Athenians did when speaking of dowries; but our other evidence seems to support the conclusion that Spartan women were indeed possessors of wealth in their own right. The example of Cynisca has been mentioned, of whom Xenophon says that she showed with her victory 'that this creature (the horse) is an indication not of manly virtue (*andragathia*), but of wealth';[128] we may add the mother and grandmother of Agis IV, who was, according to Plutarch, the wealthiest of all the Lacedaemonians — indeed, it is the wealth of the Spartan women that he cites as having been one of the great obstacles to Agis' reforms.[129] If Aristotle could attribute such wealth to the size of Spartan dowries, we must conclude that women at Sparta, as women at Gortyn,[130] owned their dowries; and while we have no information as to the actual power of Gortynian wives, it is clear that the women of Lacedaemon were the mistresses of their property.

7

Patterns in Women's Economics

• •
•

What does it all mean? We have a series of still photographs from different places and different times, and the patterns that seem to arise are, as I said in the introduction, subject to differing interpretations. I have tried throughout to give facts precedence over theory, for the more of ourselves we project into history, the less we can understand the ancients, whether good or bad, and the less we can learn from them; but nothing has been learned at all unless we examine the patterns that do emerge from the evidence. These patterns do not, in the case at hand, completely fit what was to be expected (what, indeed, I myself had expected) on the basis of received opinion. I can only state the truth as it appears in the field of this study, and leave it to others to see whether or not the same patterns apply to other areas of Greek society.

Greek society and Greek law. A person who has read the Athenian orators and comes to deal with the law of Gortyn is likely to feel himself in another world. There are tribes and serfs, and government seems to rotate among families, rather than individuals; women marry 'whomever they please', inherit half a brother's portion from their father's estate, and hold their property in their own name. The reader who was expecting something like Athenian law might think he was dealing with a document of another society entirely, and indeed, some venturesome scholars have attempted to explain Gortynian society as if it were closer to the Iroquois or the Alamanni than the Athenians.

It is surprising, then, to see how closely the institutions of Athenian society are paralleled in Gortyn. In Gortyn, as in Athens, there is an *oikos,* and a man is its head, despite the law's abolition of his economic powers. Women marry when they are of age, and are given a dowry when they do; if their fathers are dead, their brothers once provided the dowry as in Athens, but now the women can claim it of right. When they are divorced, or when their husbands die without children, they return to their former *oikos,* and take their dowries with them. During their marriage they occupy themselves with 'weaving within the household'. Their inheritance rights, except for the special provision guaranteeing a daughter's dowry, are parallel to those of the Athenian woman: this indicates strongly that family structure, too, was similar, that is, that the Gortynians had the same ideas as the Athenians as to who was a near relative and who was a distant one. It is perhaps most striking to find the institution of the *epikleros*, under a different name, indeed, and with differences of detail, but quite recognizably the same institution that in Athens appeared to serve purposes that had no place at Gortyn. I found all this surprising, and others have simply refused to believe it. Should the law not have made more difference?

In fact, the problem recurs throughout our subject, and it is not a matter that applies to Gortyn alone. A similar shock of recognition is felt when we realize that Athenian women, without any law authorizing such a thing, are performing transactions that get their validity from the agreement of their *kyrios*; Delian women, too, are availing themselves of the Athenian woman's freedom in small transactions, though the 'law of the medimnus' was peculiarly an Attic one. In the manumissions there are places where women require a *kyrios* to manumit, and there are places where they do not; but the matter does not seem to affect the frequency of their manumissions.

The matter, in fact, is not as surprising as all that; for there was behind Greek society a historical unity that did not exist for Greek law. The Greeks had entered Greece, Ionia, and the islands, in successive waves of invasion over a period of several hundred years; although each group had distinguishing characteristics, both in language and in culture, their speech and behaviour were mutually intelligible and had a common basis. This common basis was even more apparent within each dialectical group. Law, however, was formulated in Greek states only after they separated into independent *poleis*; and then each city formulated its own law. The law was based heavily on the preexisting culture: monogamy, inheritance by proximity of relationship with males preceding females, and the structure of tribes, clans, and households, were just a few items that reappear throughout Greece, in practically every system of law we know.

But law is not simply a reflection of the society that produces it; it is a systematization and rationalization. Now, the same institution may be rationalized in many different ways: inheritance, for example, can be seen merely as a way of recycling the goods of a dead man; or of regulating the leadership of a household when its leader dies; or of carrying out the wishes (or presumed wishes) of the dead; or of guaranteeing the survivors a livelihood. In some cases, there will be no practical difference whatever rationalization we adopt; in others, our understanding of the institution's function will demand that we fit the law to our understanding, and in fact, much of a society's legal change comes about because of new rationalizations of old institutions. If marriage is designed to build up a household, a childless marriage is not really a marriage at all; if it is designed to secure companionship for husband and wife, the presence or absence of children should not affect it.

The lawmakers of the various Greek cities did not all adopt the same rationalization of their institutions. Although the institutions themselves were similar throughout Greece, the understanding of them differed from place to place; the more so as they must already have diverged in many particulars by the time of the great legislators. The result of this was that the various legal codes that were built differed not only in details, but in fundamental principles, while the societies that followed them retained a great similarity. The understanding of the epiclerate in Gortyn was totally different from that in Athens, but the institution itself was remarkably similar. Tribes, on the other hand, existed in both places, but in Athens they served purely as political subdivisions, while in Gortyn they still determined a man's choice of a bride.

It is natural, in the course of time, for two developments to take place. First of all, there tends to be an internal rationalization, that is, an increasing reform of the practical law to fit the dominant principle, once that has been adopted: one may think here of the great changes that eventually had to be made in American law to fit the principles of 'freedom of religion' or 'due process of law'. Secondly, there is a competition among varying forms of law, resulting eventually in the lapse of some and the spread of others, often by conquest. As the first principle operated, it will have tended to make the laws – and the societies, for society does indeed change in reaction to law – of the various Greek cities more distinctive; as the second operated, both by persuasion and conquest, it will have tended to lead to the disappearance of local laws and their replacement with others, often on the Athenian or Spartan model. In law, as in language, the period of dialects gave way to a period of *koine,* a common speech. But in the classical period that we have been discussing neither of these two developments was far advanced. The essential unity of Greek society, based on an ancestral unity in a period in which the society's customs had grown up, remained strong. The laws of its various localities were clearly distinct, but since in those cases we can observe they had not yet restructed the social institutions in a way as fundamental as can happen over a period of centuries, the basic unity remains visible behind the legal diversity.

The law and the individual. Among the various possible understandings of an institution, the law may choose one, compromise among many ('freedom with responsibility') or define an order of precedence among them ('your rights end where his nose begins', i.e., freedom from assault takes precedence over freedom of action). Citizens in their everyday dealings, however, are not necessarily so consistent, nor do they necessarily accept the law's choice of principles. This is, of course, one of the major sources of employment for judges and juries; but much of the citizen's behaviour will never get to court, whether or not it is legal. It is not true, then, that 'women in Athens could not own property'. The case is rather that women in Athenian *law* could not own property; that is, when the matter reached court, the property would be treated as belonging to their *kyrios*. But in everyday transactions many women did in fact behave as if their property was theirs; and if the matter did not reach court, then it really does not much matter what the court might have decided about its legality. This is not to say that the law was a dead letter, for it was not; the whole body of Attic oratory shows us as much. What it does show us is the limits of any body of non-religious personal law as a determinant of personal behaviour. And it makes clear how a law can fall into disuse, when people stop thinking its violations a matter worth bringing into court. Similar statements can be made about the position of the *kyrios* throughout Greece, or throughout those parts of Greece where the *kyrios* exercised an economic function, and they suggest themselves for other matters as well, but others will have to determine how true they are in areas outside the field of this book.

Paternalism in Athens. A particular matter worth noting is the structure of the law in Athens. We have discussed it at length in every chapter of this book, but it is worth mentioning in summary if only because it is so easy to get a false picture by looking at parts of the whole.

Since a woman's sphere in life was her family, her active life did not really begin until her marriage. The marriage itself, as we saw, was arranged by her father and her prospective husband; she was simply passed from the house of one *kyrios* to the house of another, with some money or property going along with her as a dowry.

But concomitant with the patriarchal marriage-rules was a pervasive paternalism, a solicitude for the bride's interest that was seen in terms of family responsibility. This paternalism was based, of course, on a presumption that men were more intelligent than women – a presumption so basic to Athenian male society that they rarely bothered to state it directly, though it is possible to adduce sources.[1] Perhaps most interesting is the Didot papyrus, where a woman is portrayed as taking it for granted: 'But you'll say I don't understand. Maybe it's possible that I am foolish, I won't deny it; but, Father, if a woman hasn't got intelligence to judge other matters, she may still have some sense about her own affairs'.[2]

It has been presumed[3] that such a belief would mean that women were held in contempt; since that is demonstrably not the case, as anyone knows who has read Greek tragedy or seen Greek art, the existence of the belief has been denied. But there was no need for contempt to be involved; each sex was considered to have a proper role for which it was fitted, and intelligence, beyond such understanding as was necessary to manage the day-to-day affairs of a household, was not thought necessary or desirable for the Greek woman.[4] It followed from this, as well as from the inherited patriarchal family structure, that the most important decisions of a woman's life were made for her, not by her.

This being the case, many scholars, particularly legal scholars, have written of Athenian women as if they were treated as slaves or as objects. Thus, for example, Erdmann: 'She was in her entire legal position actually more a part of the family property, whose worth was originally even realizable in cash by bride-purchase, than a real legal subject who could be an independent possessor of rights and responsibilities.'[5] This is a very superficial view even of the epiclerate; as a general view of Athenian women's legal position it is nonsense. Murder of a woman was punishable as murder, not as damage to her husband.[6] I know of no one who has ever claimed that a female citizen could legally be enslaved, or assaulted, or slandered, or that the prohibition on these would have fallen under property law. *Hybris* (a general charge covering serious injury or offence) was culpable against a woman as against a man; but then, so was *hybris* against a slave.[7] It is always easy to believe of other people, particularly people very long ago or very far away, that they establish systems on principles of utter foolishness; but neither the epiclerate nor a hypothetical purchase-marriage (which was not the form in Athens, at any rate) should convince us that the Greek lawgivers were unaware that women were people.

Athenian men did recognize that women were people, and they were interested in their well-being; but they would not entrust to a woman the power to guarantee that welfare. Protection of women was thus expressed not through direct rights, but by a system of rights and obligations of men. I know of no better definition of paternalism.

The men normally responsible for looking after the woman's welfare were, of course, the men of her family; but the law recognized that there were cases in which a woman needed protection against the men of her own family. In these cases — abuse of an *epikleros*, abuse of parents, divorce — or in cases where the family rights and responsibilities were themselves to be determined, as the adjudication of an *epikleros*, the eponymous archon took charge of the matter.[8]

It was thus the head of her family who chose her husband for her, and though we do know of cases where the women were allowed free selection,[9] these were exceptional. Normally the father, or whatever male relative had inherited his position as *kyrios*, would make his own choice. But, as far as we know there were only two considerations that were likely to determine his action: his daughter's welfare, and that of his family.

These two rarely conflicted in the economic sphere, for an Athenian woman's prosperity had, as we have seen, little to do with personally-held assets; it was rather the wife of a rich family who could be considered wealthy. This was the consideration of the father in the Didot papyrus: 'But you (says his daughter), as you tell me, are going to give me now to a rich man, so that I shouldn't live out my life in grief',[10] though she, a true heroine of the New Comedy, is more interested in preserving her original marriage with the man she loves. Demosthenes attacks Meidias by describing his ostentation: 'He built a house in Eleusis so big that it overshadows everything in the place, and he takes his wife to the mysteries, or anywhere else she wants, with his white Sicyonian team, and he himself swaggers around the *agora* with three or four attendants, naming funnels and demi-tasse and saucers so that passersby can hear.'[11] If Meidias' wife lived in luxury in the house at Eleusis, if she was driven around with the Sicyonian team, it was not by virtue of her personal wealth, but by her having married a rich man. It was also on the basis of her husband's wealth that liturgies were performed in her name, as was noted above.

Marriage into a rich house could, of course, have its disadvantages. Demosthenes accused Apollodorus of high living in terms very different from those employed against Meidias: 'Now you wear a wool coat, and you free one *hetaera,* and give a dowry to another — and this when you have a wife — and you go around with three boys for your attendants, and live wildly for all to see',[12] and Alcibiades' wife, who had to put up with even worse abuse, does not seem to have been made happy by her husband's wealth. But even against her husband, a woman was always dependent upon her family: mistreated by Alcibiades, she went to her brother for protection.[13] Demosthenes tells a similar story about Aristogeiton: 'and in addition to not keeping his hands off his mother, as you just heard from the witnesses, he also put his own sister — not by the same father; she was his mother's daughter, whom she had given birth to somehow (I'll pass over that), but his sister nevertheless — he put her out for prostitution, according to the charge of the suit, which that excellent brother, the one who is now pleading for him, brought against him on their behalf.'[14] Here we are dealing with a half-sister, not a wife, and with a story rather less likely than that of Alcibiades' wife; but it is still notable that the girl's protection against her brother was another brother.

It is possible to argue that the paternalism of Athenian law and society was no more than a cloak surrounding the patriarchy, and that the society itself was truly designed for the exclusive benefit of its male members. Such an argument, I think, would be more valid in a contemporary situation than it would be for ancient Athens. For Athens had no need of a cloak; the patriarchy of the law and the society was completely unchallenged. Efforts have been made to invent a Greek 'feminist movement' out of such works as the *Lysistrata* and the *Medea,* but there is nothing to indicate that the Athenians saw them that way: the *Lysistrata* no more makes a 'comic proposal' that the city be turned over to the women than the *Birds* makes a 'comic proposal' that a city be founded by Birds, or the *Peace* a 'comic proposal' that peace-loving Athenians should fly to heaven on dung-beetles. Athenian patriarchy was extremely stable, and indeed survived for centuries in spite of great political upheavals. Nobody tried to hide it. The paternalistic interest which we find throughout was rather the result of the patriarchy, or perhaps we should say that the two went hand in hand: once the women had no power of their own, it was only the men of their family who could guard their interests. And since their relationship with their husbands and fathers was not, in general, an adversary relationship, the men usually did so.

This arrangement was not without benefit for the woman: her modesty was not infringed by the necessity of transacting her business in person. her position within the family was guaranteed and respected, and her larger economic affairs were, or were supposed to be, managed, or mismanaged, for her. Few women today would consider this adequate recompense for the loss of their independence; but it is unlikely that the women of Athens put the same value on independence, which was considered by the men, at least, a trait more proper to a *hetaera* than to a respectable woman.

Perhaps more to the point, it has become clear from the previous chapters that for all the legal and social paternalism, those women who were in a position to be independent — women with large dowries and rich *epikleroi* — did indeed dominate their families' economic lives just as they would have if their money had been their own. In their case we glimpse what it was that made the patriarchy so stable: the patriarchy existed, for these women, only when they chose to call upon it. If they did not wish to be bothered with the day-to-day management of the farm, well, that was their husbands' business; but if he wanted to sell it, or did not want to sell it when she did, he had a powerful opponent. On the other side of the economic scale, where the women who worked for a living as the men did, there was a similar practical equality in spite of legal distinctions; and while we may surmise that in Athens, as at other places and times, it was in the middle classes that the pressure to conform to the society's ideal was strongest, there is no reason to believe that the law that was so flexible for other women was ironclad for the moderately comfortable.

Now, in a society whose laws are written, but whose women are largely illiterate, the women will tend to be more interested in the actual situation than the legal one, while the men will often show a reversed priority. We are all familiar from popular literature with the man whose wife agrees calmly to all his pronouncements of principle — he is the head of the family, he will have the final decision, he will make up his own mind — and then watches him accede to her practical advice. When both man and wife have undergone the same education, this situation can only be viewed as one with a winner and a loser, but which is which will depend upon whether we are more interested in abstract principle or in concrete decision. When the man has been educated to think in abstracts and the woman has not, each leaves this discussion perfectly satisfied: the man has won his abstract points, the woman her concrete one.

In Athenian society, the situation was similar. The society was an extremely patriarchal one in theory, not only legal theory but the generally accepted social understanding of the people. However, in day-to-day actions, as we saw, the patriarchal structure may have counted less than the particular resources of the individuals involved: here the women could hold their own with the men, if their economic and social standing permitted it. The men were satisfied with the situation; although they recognized that a rich woman was not dominated by her husband, they did not thereby think that the patriarchy was endangered. The women have not left us their opinion; but it is possible (though it need not be the case) that the stability of the system indicates that they were satisfied with their practical abilities, and willing to accept the theoretical disabilities. Occasionally, of course – and particularly in the law courts – these could become painfully real; but as long as they did not, the women may have been willing to accept severe restrictions outside of the family in return for importance and idealization within it.

Patterns in Greece at large. While women's economic role was always a limited one, there was no movement to restrict it further: their rights to inherit, such as they were, were never abridged, nor was their freedom to manage small amounts of money tampered with. But was there any movement in the other direction?

The evidence of the papyri, coming from outside Greece and not dealt with in this book, has led scholars to believe that there was a material change in the economic position of women in the Hellenistic age, in which women became much more prominent in the larger dealings of economic life.[15] This certainly appears to have been the case for those Greek women who went to Egypt, whence the papyri come; but there are few traces of it in the documents of Greece proper. Much of this lack may be due to the nature of our documents, which rarely extend over a period of time long enough to show any development. It is true that most of the individual inscriptions in which we find women transacting important business date from the later Hellenistic period; but since the non-Athenian documents are much more abundant for these years than for the earlier centuries, we may have no more than an accident of preservation. The only concrete evidence of change that we have is in the Delos inscriptions, where the women clearly became more active at the close of the Hellenistic era. It is surprising to see the change come so late, particularly in as cosmopolitan a place as Delos; and we may perhaps have an indication that the changes in the condition of women took place first outside of Greece – possibly because of contact with foreign cultures, or the conditions of settlement – and spread only later to the mainland and the islands.

Within Greece, our geographical information is very patchy. We know much about Athens and about Gortyn, and we know something about Lacedaemon, Delphi, and Delos. Documentation for the rest of Greece varies from poor to nonexistent. Perhaps the only generalization worth making is that as the limitations placed on the woman's external activity both by the law and by the culture were intimately connected with her role in the family, these limitations tended to disappear in other contexts. The greater independence of Spartan and Gortynian women is certainly connected with the dominance of communal institutions in these places; the dependence of the Athenian woman, on the other hand, is surely connected with the strength of the Athenian family. The members of the Athenian family were much more interdependent than the members of a family in Sparta or Gortyn, where the communal institutions, segregated by sex, had prospered at the expense of the family; we may suspect, on the other side of the coin, that the Athenian woman who occupied herself with her household had a larger and more respected function than a Spartan woman who did likewise. Where the family was a less important unit, it ceased to dominate the lives of men or women as thoroughly as it did in Athens; and the law of Gortyn came to reflect the difference.[16]

When trying to gauge the direction in which Greek society was moving, it is important to remember that we know very little about the proto-Greek state of affairs. To what extent the principles of Athenian family organization were either innovation or archaism is, in the present state of our knowledge, impossible to determine. The scholar who would deal with 'origins' must remember that the proto-Greeks were not simple; if there are universal characteristics of a primitive society, the Greeks were separated from them not by decades, but by millennia. He must also remember that an institution is not necessarily old because it is obsolete, or new because it is vigorous.

In my introduction, I asked what a woman did in ancient Greece, and indicated that I would deal only with part of the question. Many matters remain to be investigated. For example, the early upbringing of children, the management of domestic slaves, and the production of food and clothing were matters of great importance to Greek women; each deserves more than a few paragraphs in a general 'story of the Greek woman', which is what they have hitherto been given. For other questions, I am not even sure that the material exists to answer them: What was a Greek woman's cultural universe? Was it the same as the men's? Was it based on literature or on stories or on gossip? What in the world was an Athenian girl doing during the years 'indoors' before she was married?

Scholars thus far have not succeeded either in building an independent history of women or in integrating women into the general fabric of Greek history. The latter goal, I believe, is hopeless; what we know about Greek women indicates that they had precious little traceable effect on the wars and reigns that we call 'history'; nor can those women who did be said to represent the true history of women. But the former, too, is not going to be an easy task. Because of the nature of women's world, lines of causality are very different in it from those in the men's world. The traditions of individual families count for much more, and the vagaries of outside society for much less, than they do in men's history. To deal properly with women's history, we will need an open mind as to what constitutes 'history', for it surely will not be wars and reigns. We will need an open mind about periodization: is there a 'Renaissance period' of women's history after the 'mediaeval period'?

I have, throughout the book, avoided the common debate on the 'status' of Greek women, whether it was 'high' or 'low'. They had, in Greek society, the status of women: this was a status distinct from that of men, or children, or slaves, and our purpose must be to determine what that status was and to try to understand the people who lived with it, and who made of it an honourable or a dishonourable estate by their own actions and experiences. We must examine the matter in all its subtleties and complexities, and see it in a historical perspective. We must ask not, 'What was her status?' but rather, 'How did this aspect come to coincide with that one? How did they develop out of the previous state? What effect did they have on succeeding generations?' There is no shortcut to understanding.

Appendix I : Size of Dowries

· ·

The following table will indicate the range of attested dowries, as well as the discrepancies among the sources:

Amount of Dowry[1]	Attic Horoi	Other Horoi	Tenos	Myconos	Orators	Literary Sources[3]	Wills[4]	Menander
0 – 500 dr.	4	0	0	0	0	0	0	0
500 dr. – 10 min.	3	0	0	1	3	0	0	0
10 min. – 20 min.	10	1	3	4	4	0	0	0
20 min. – 30 min.	2	1	0	0	4	2	0	0
30 min. – 40 min.	1	0	0	1	5	0	0	0
40 min. – 50 min.	1	0	0	0	2	0	0	0
50 min. – 1 tal.	1	0	0	0	2	0	2	1
1 tal. – 2 tal.	1	0	0	1	3	0	2	2
2 tal. – 3 tal.	0	0	0	1	0	0	0	3
above 3 talents	0	0	0	0	0	2	1	1

Header note: Source[2]

The chief things to note from this table are that the dowries in the orators are almost all between ten and fifty minae (the three sums in line two are all ten minae); that those on the *horoi* are mostly twenty minae or less; that the dowries granted in wills tend to be very much larger than those granted by a living husband; and that Menander's dowries are hopelessly exaggerated. As a last word of caution, it should be noted that we do not know whether or not the sums on the *horoi* always represent the total dowry.

See further the discussion in Finley, 79-80, ibid., 175, Table D, and Thompson, 99-113.

Appendix II : Προίξ and Φερνή

Two words for 'dowry', προίξ and φερνή, are attested in classical Attic, and they often appear to be interchangeable. The Suda's entry is laconic enough to be reproduced in full:

φερνή: προίξ

But a good deal of literature has grown up around these two words, centering on the problem that while items are spoken of as φερναί that would not be προῖκες,[1] there is no evidence in any of the classical material of a method of dowering a bride other than the προίξ. Many solutions have been proposed,[2] but the chief difference between them in the classical period is certainly that φερνή is poetic and προίξ is not. Thus in the whole of oratory, with its many battles over dowries, the word φερνή occurs only once – and then in description of a mythical event; even there the scholiast substitutes the word προίξ in his explanation.[3] In tragedy, on the other hand, the word φερνή occurs ten times, the word προίξ only once – and then in a fragment whose tragic origin is extremely doubtful, and which is more likely from New Comedy.[4] In the less pedestrian language of the historians, we have two examples of φερνή,[5] both of them describing foreign customs analogous to, but not identical with, the Athenian dowry. It would appear that the term προίξ was, in the classical period, particularly Attic; outside of Athens the term is regularly φερνή, with the obvious result that those gifts spoken of as φερναί tend to reflect non-Attic law. Homeric usage knows neither word in its classical sense. The word ἕδνα is used both for bride-price and for dowry,[6] though προίξ occurs twice with the meaning 'gift',[7] a meaning which survives in the classical προῖκα, 'for free'.

The poetic term φερνή is, as we should expect, used more broadly than προίξ, and in places where the latter would be inappropriate. Eustathius noticed two uses for the word, one identical with προίξ and one not.[8] We need not therefore postulate the existence of a separate institution called the φερνή in the classical period. For the Hellenistic era, when φερνή begins to be used commonly in everyday prose, the evidence is chiefly Egyptian, and must be evaluated separately, in the context of the development of *koine*[9].

Appendix III : Dowry and Trousseau

.· ·.

Along with the dowry we occasionally find mention of *himatia kai chrysia*, the personal effects of the wife.[1] It has been presumed by most scholars[2] that these could be included in the valuation of the dowry or not, the only restriction being the same as that on anything else sent along with the bride, viz., that if it was not included in the valuation, it was not recoverable in case of divorce or childless death.[3] This view is denied by Wolff, who believes that the wife's trousseau was never included in the evaluation of the dowry.[4]

It is certainly true that the orators present a number of cases where the trousseau is mentioned as a sum over and above the dowry,[5] but there seem to be as many where they do not. These Wolff disposes of in various ways; we shall take them one at a time.

The easiest is the Myconos dowry-inscription: [6]

> Sostratus betrothed his daughter Ar. to Eparchides, and gave a dowry of one thousand and three hundred drachmas; of this, one thousand drachmas (are) those included in the five-hundred-drachma *eranos*[7] which Alexicles collected, in which Callistagoras took part, and he added a hundred drachmas of silver, and clothing assessed at two hundred drachmas . . . . Callixenos (betrothed) his daughter Time-crate to Rhodocles, and gave a dowry of seven hundred drachmas: of this, clothing worth three hundred . . . . Ctesonides, son of Thar., betrothed his sister Dicaie to Pappias, son of Pa., to be his wife, and a dowry of a thousand (drachmas) of silver and clothing worth five hundred . . .

It seems reasonable to assume — though Wolff is willing to make another suggestion[8] — that the *esthēs* (clothing) of these dowries was the same as that of all marriages with which clothing is mentioned, that is, the wife's trousseau; and it is in the first two instances explicitly included in the sum of the dowry. But this is at any rate not an Athenian inscription, and cannot prove anything about Athenian practice.

From Athens, however, is Isaeus 8.8, a harder nut to crack: ἐπεὶ συνοι-κεῖν εἶχεν ἡλικίαν, ἐκδίδωσιν αὐτὴν Ναυσιμένει Χολαργεῖ, σὺν ἱματίοις καὶ χρυσίοις πέντε καὶ εἴκοσι μνᾶς ἐπιδούς. ('When she was of an age to be married, he gave her away to Nausimenes of Cholargus, giving along with her twenty-five minae, including clothing and jewelry'). Here Wolff does away with the problem by punctuating differently: ἐπεὶ συνοικεῖν εἶχεν ἡλικίαν, ἐκδίδωσιν αὐτὴν Ναυσιμένει Χολαργεῖ σὺν ἱματίοις καὶ χρυσίοις, πέντε καὶ εἴκοσι μνᾶς ἐπιδούς.⁹ He offers no translation, but presumably takes it to mean, 'When she was of an age to be married, he gave her away with clothing and jewelry to Nausimenes of Cholargus, giving along with her twenty-five minae'. This reading, however, is impossible. For one thing, it presumes σύν to mean 'with', which in classical oratory is always expressed either by μετά or by ἅμα. Σύν, on the relatively rare occasions when it occurs in the orators, nearly always means 'including', which it cannot mean here if taken with ἐκδίδωσιν. The most notable sign of the change from the archaic and poetic usage to the usage of classical prose is Isaeus 3.68: ὁ γὰρ νόμος διαρρήδην λέγει ἐξεῖναι διαθέσθαι ὅπως ἂν ἐθέλῃ τις τὰ αὑτοῦ, ἐὰν μὴ παῖδας γνησίους καταλίπῃ ἄρρενας· ἂν δὲ θηλείας καταλίπῃ, <u>σὺν ταύταις</u>. οὐκοῦν <u>μετὰ τῶν θυγα-</u><u>τέρων</u> ἔστι δοῦναι καὶ διαθέσθαι τὰ αὑτοῦ· ἄνευ δὲ τῶν γνησίων θυγα-τέρων οὐχ οἷόν τε οὔτε ποιήσασθαι οὔτε δοῦναι οὐδενὶ οὐδὲ τῶν ἑαυτοῦ, where the speaker substitutes the more normal μετά for the archaic σύν of the law.¹¹

But even if we were to allow σύν the meaning of 'with', in defiance of the universal practice of the Athenian orators, the sentence would still make poor reading according to Wolff's punctuation. What in the world would the speaker mean by 'he gave her away with clothing and jewelry, giving along with her a dowry of twenty-five minae'? Had the jurors suspected Ciron of giving his daughter away naked? Why are the clothing and jewelry mentioned, if they had nothing to do with the dowry?

The reason that they are mentioned is to inflate the dowry. The speaker is attempting to prove his own legitimacy, and to do this he must show that his mother was legally married. A dowry was a sign of legitimate marriage (though there could be legitimate marriage without it), and he is careful to mention his mother's; he has included the value of her trousseau in order to be able to quote a better figure. This explains why he must say, 'including clothing and jewelry, he gave a dowry of twenty-five minae': were we to consider the dowry alone, the sum would have been less. But the use the speaker is making of the figure also points up the unreliability of his statement: it does not at all indicate that the clothing *at the time* was reckoned in with the dowry, but simply that he is including it when he says 'twenty-five minae'. If anything, the fact that he felt it necessary to preface a mention of the trousseau to his estimate of the dowry would seem to suggest that the two had been counted separately at the time of the wedding.

Most of Wolff's discussion centres on Demosthenes 41.27, a passage so bizarre that it must be quoted at length. The speaker is suing for, among other things, ten minae which he claims are still outstanding on his dowry of forty minae. This is a larger dowry, apparently, than his opponent Spudias has received, and the speaker realizes that he must justify his claim. First he argues that Polyeuctus, their father-in-law, had the right to give one daughter a larger dowry than the other; continuing, in paragraph 26, he says ἀλλ' οὐδὲν ἔλαττον εἶχες, ὡς ἐγὼ διδάξω. πρῶτον δ' ἐφ' οἶς ἐξέδοτο τούτῳ, λαβὲ τὴν μαρτυρίαν.

ΜΑΡΤΥΡΙΑ

(27) Πῶς οὖν οὐδὲν ἔλαττον ἔχει, φήσει τις, εἰ τούτῳ μὲν ἐν ταῖς τετταράκοντα μναῖς ἐνετιμᾶτο τὰ χρυσία καὶ τὰ ἱμάτια τῶν χιλίων, ἐμοὶ δ' αἱ δέκα μναῖ χωρὶς προσαπεδίδοντο; τοῦτο δὴ καὶ μέλλω λέγειν. ὁ μὲν γὰρ Σπουδίας, ὦ ἄνδρες δικασταί, παρὰ τοῦ Λεωκράτους ἔχουσαν τὰ χρυσία καὶ τὰ ἱμάτια τὴν γυναῖκ' ἔλαβεν, ὧν ὁ Πολύευκτος προσαπέτεισε τῷ Λεωκράτει πλεῖν ἢ χιλίας· ἐγὼ δ', ἄπερ ἔπεμψέ μοι χωρὶς τῆς προικός, ὅσ' ἔχω μόνον, πρὸς τὰ τούτῳ δοθέντ' ἐὰν ἀντιθῇ τις, εὑρήσει παραπλήσια, χωρὶς τῶν εἰς τὰς χιλίας ἀποτιμηθέντων. (28) ὥστ' εἰκότως ἐν ταῖς τετταράκοντα μναῖς ἐνετιμᾶτο ταῦθ', ἄπερ ἀπετετείκει τῷ Λεωκράτει καὶ πλείω τῶν ἐμοὶ δοθέντων ἦν. καί μοι λαβὲ πρῶτον μὲν τὴν ἀπογραφὴν ταυτηνὶ καὶ λέγ' αὐτοῖς, ἄπερ ἑκάτερος ἡμῶν ἔχει, μετὰ δὲ ταῦτα τὴν τῶν διαιτητῶν μαρτυρίαν, ἵν' ἴδωσιν ὅτι καὶ πολλῷ πλείω χρήματ' ἔχει, καὶ περὶ τούτων ὁ Λεωκράτης ἐνεκάλει, καὶ ταῦτ' ἔγνωσαν οἱ διαιτηταί. λέγε.[12]

'This computation can be shown to be a piece of oratorical jugglery devised to deceive the judges', says Wolff,[13] and that it is; but it is a singularly inept juggling act. To this day scholars are not quite certain what the speaker wanted the audience to believe; they are, however, quite satisfied that it was a lie, and that in fact Spudias had received thirty minae with his wife, and another ten minae's worth of trousseau, while the speaker is claiming forty minae free and clear, exclusive of his wife's trousseau. It is doubtful whether an account so opaque even on fifth and sixth reading was very lucid to the judges; in fact its purpose was more to confuse than to deceive.

'The passage', writes Wolff, 'bears witness to a desperate effort on the part of the speaker to create the impression that Spudias has received as much as, or even more than, himself. As this necessitates taking into account the jewelry and clothing of Spudias' wife, the speaker is forced to bring into the reckoning his own wife's trousseau. In order that he still obtain a seemingly balanced account, he mentions these objects as received "apart from the προίξ", while at the same time dismissing as not received the amount by which his προίξ actually surpassed that of his opponent, and thus cunningly changing the sentence, which begins as though it were aimed at a comparison of the trousseaux, into a comparison of the total amounts received by both parties. Actually the jewelry and apparel of Spudias' wife were also not valued and kept apart from the dowry proper. This follows from the speaker's tacit admission, in the opening sentence of sect. 28, that it was he, not Polyeuctus, who included their value in the total valuation set for Spudias at 40 minas, and it is also proved by the evident circumstance that his estimate of their monetary value was based on the price paid by Polyeuctus to his former son-in-law, Leocrates.'[14]

Wolff's estimate of the speaker's purposes is sound; his description of the actual state of affairs is not at all certain. There is no 'tacit admission in the opening sentence of sect. 28' that the speaker is responsible for the valuation of forty minae; the word εἰκότως, from which Wolff derives this admission, implies quite the opposite. One does not say, 'I am probably including that', but one may say, 'he probably included that'. The speaker's meaning is, that Spudias' wife's trousseau, which according to the testimony at the end of section 26 was worth a thousand drachmae, was probably identical with the clothing for which Polyeuctus had paid Leocrates more than that sum, that is, that the total value received by Spudias, thirty minae plus a trousseau was more than the forty minae at which it was estimated. The speaker has in fact made no mention of the total value of Spudias' dowry before the witnesses testified; when he anticipates the question as to how come Spudias' wife's trousseau was 'reckoned in with the forty minae', the forty minae in question can only be those just mentioned by the witnesses. The question is nonsensical if the witnesses had testified to thirty minae's dowry, and ten minae's trousseau reckoned separately. Thus we must presume — as most scholars always had — that the witnesses testified that Spudias had received a dowry of forty minae, which included ten minae's worth of *himatia kai chrysia.* To presume that the figure of forty minae had never been mentioned before the beginning of section 27 would only remove the passage yet further away from sense.

We have found, then, some difficulty with Wolff's hypothesis; both the speaker of Isaeus 8 and the speaker of Demosthenes 41 clearly include the trousseau of the wife in their computations of the dowry, and their so doing indicates that such a process was at least conceivable. We have no concrete proof, however, that it was conceivable because it was done in the assessment of the dowry; it might be argued that it was conceivable because it was done by gossips and by lawyers trying to inflate the total value. In the first case our information comes from an unreliable speaker, and in the second from inference.

On the other hand, there is no evidence at all to argue that the exclusion of the trousseau was universal; neither explicitly nor implicitly do any of our sources testify to that. On the contrary, there is one clear instance which, to my knowledge, has never been mentioned in this context: Aphobus, Demosthenes' guardian, who was appointed to marry Demosthenes' widowed mother, took her jewelry as part of her dowry,[15] and the fact that he never married the woman does not require us to believe what Demosthenes never asserts, that there was anything irregular about the items he took. This method of making up a dowry was not, indeed, the rule in the upper classes; but it was certainly in use at Myconos, and as it was certainly legal at Athens, we must assume that it was not unknown there either.

Appendix IV : Inheritance of the Dowry

· ·

The Athenians conceived of the family as being eternal. The death of a member brought about no changes in the positions in the family, but simply the sucession of that member's legitimate adult sons (where these existed) to his rights. This was the case with the head of the household: an estate whose *kyrios* left legitimate sons passed to them automatically, without being subject to legal adjudication.[1] Succession to the wife's privileges by her sons was similarly direct.

The dowry was given by the *kyrios* of the bride — by the head of her household, ideally her father — to ensure the maintenance of her and her descendants as members of the groom's *oikos*. As long as the bride remained in the husband's household, her dowry remained with her; her husband, being *kyrios* of the household, was also *kyrios* of the dowry, and had a responsibility to maintain his wife. With the wife's death, if there were children, nothing changed except the cast of characters. The husband remained *kyrios* of the household and of the dowry,[2] and he may have been responsible for maintaining her children, at least to the extent that he had been responsible for maintaining her.[3] At the husband's death, *kyrieia* of the dowry, as of the household, passed to his children; if they chose to divide the estate (that is, to set up a number of new households), only those children in whose households there were descendants of the wife's family (that is, only the wife's children) became *kyrioi* of the dowry. If the husband died during the wife's lifetime and she remained in the household, her children became *kyrioi* of her dowry immediately; they also inherited from their father the responsibility for her maintenance.

Legitimate sons, then, succeeded to the rights of their mother's family upon her death, and to the rights of their father's family upon his death. None of this changed the relationship of the dowry to the household; it simply replaced a member of the family with his descendants. In the event that there were no legitimate children, this was impossible; as the bride's family now had no descendants in the groom's *oikos*, the dowry returned to the family that had given it.[4]

The only case where conflict arises in this scheme is that in which a woman was divorced or widowed and returned to her father's house, leaving behind children in her husband's house. In this case the dowry followed the woman, not her children; and as it was thereby removed from the *kyrieia* of their father, they did not become *kyrioi* of it upon their father's death.[5]

We find, then, that the various cases with regard to inheritance of the dowry may be reduced to two principles: (a) the dowry is given by the head of the bride's household to the groom as head of his household, and remains with the latter as long as the bride or her descendants do; (b) as long as the bride is alive, the dowry is attached to her household in preference to that of her children. Whether or not there were any limitations to the operation of these two rules — whether, for example, a husband would have to return the dowry if, after his wife's death, her sons were to die — I do not know.

Abbreviations

• •

I have tried to make all abbreviations readily recognizable; for
any which are not, the reader is referred to the *American Jour-
nal of Archaeology* 74 (1970) 3-8, ibid. 69 (1965) 199-201,
the *Oxford Classical Dictionary* (second edition), and LSJ
(see below). The reader should also note the convention of
writing (And.), (Dem.), etc. for 'Pseudo-Andocides', 'Pseudo-
Demosthenes', etc., i.e., a work found in the manuscripts of
Andocides or Demosthenes and published among his works
but probably written by somebody else. For the speeches of
Demosthenes, some of whose authenticity is still *sub iudice,*
I have followed the judgment of Blass in his edition. Since
all the speeches come from the courts of fourth-century Athens, the spurious 'Demosthenic' orations are not of less value
than the authentic ones for historical purposes.

The following abbreviations should be noted:

AJA	*American Journal of Archaeology*
And.	Andocides
Ar.	Aristophanes
Arist.	Aristotle
BCH	*Bulletin de Correspondance Hellénique*
Beauchet	L. Beauchet, *Histoire du droit privé de la république athénienne* (Chevalier-Marescq, Paris 1897; reissued Rodopi, Amsterdam 1969)
CP	*Classical Philology*
CQ	*Classical Quarterly*
CR	*Classical Review*
Dar.-Sag.	Ch. Daremberg and Edm Saglio, *Dictionnaire des antiquités grecques et romaines* (Hachette, Paris 1877-1919; reissued Akademische Druck- und Verlagsanstalt, Graz 1972-3)
Dareste et al.	see RIJG
Davies	J. K. Davies, *Athenian Propertied Families, 600-300 B.C.* (Oxford University Press 1971)
Dem.	Demosthenes
Erdmann	W. Erdmann, *Die Ehe im alten Griechenland* (Volume 20 of *Münchener Beiträge zur Papyrusforschung und antiken Rechtsgeschichte;* Beck, Munich 1934)

Fine	J. V. A. Fine, *Horoi: Studies in Mortgage, Real Security, and Land Tenure in Ancient Athens (Hesperia,* Supplement 9, 1951)
Finley	M. I. Finley, *Studies in Land and Credit in Ancient Athens, 500-200 B.C.* (Rutgers University Press, New Brunswick 1952)
Guarducci	see IC; Lex Gort.
Hafter	E. Hafter, *Die Erbtochter nach attischem Recht* (G. Fock, Leipzig 1887)
Harrison	A. R. W. Harrison, *The Law of Athens* (Oxford University Press 1968-71)
Herfst	P. Herfst, *Le travail de la femme dans la Grèce ancienne* (A. Oosthoek, Utrecht 1922)
Hruza	E. Hruza, *Beiträge zur Geschichte des griechischen und römischen Familienrechtes* (G. Böhme, Erlangen & Leipzig 1892-4)
IC	*Inscriptiones Creticae,* ed. M. Guarducci (Libreria dello Stato, Rome 1935-50)
IG	*Inscriptiones Graecae,* ed. Deutsche Akademie der Wissenschaften, Berlin (de Gruyter and G. Reimer, Berlin, 1873-date; the name of the editing academy has varied with political changes). Roman numerals refer to volume numbers, superscripts to editions (e.g., IG II^1 = second volume, first edition)
Ins. Dél.	*Inscriptions de Délos,* ed. F. Durrbach et al. (Champion, Paris 1926-50)
Isae.	Isaeus
Isoc.	Isocrates
Lacey	W. K. Lacey, *The Family in Classical Greece* (Thames and Hudson, London 1968)
Lex Gort.	The large law-inscription of Gortyn, most easily accessible in the edition of R. F. Willetts, *The Law Code of Gortyn (Kadmos,* Supplement 1, 1967) or of Guarducci, IC, vol. IV, no. 72; cited by column and line
Lipsius	J. H. Lipsius, *Das attische Recht und Rechtsverfahren* (Reisland, Leipzig 1905-15; reissued G. Olms, Hildesheim 1966)
LSJ	H. G. Liddell and R. Scott, *A Greek-English Lexicon,* revised and augmented by Sir H. Stuart Jones, with a supplement (Oxford University Press 1968)
Lys.	Lysias

Men.   Menander. Line numbers are given according
to *Menandri Reliquiae Selectae*, ed. F. H.
Sandbach (Oxford University Press 1972).
The reader is warned that, thanks to the large
and numerous new discoveries of Menander
fragments, the numbering of other editions
will not necessarily correspond to this

RE   A. Pauly, G. Wissowa, and W. Kroll, *Real-
encyclopädie der klassischen Altertumswis-
senschaft* (Druckenmüller, Stuttgart 1893)

REG   *Revue des Etudes Grecques*

RIJG   R. Dareste, with B. Haussoulier and T. Rein-
ach, *Recueil des inscriptions juridiques
grecques* (Leroux, Paris 1891-8; reissued
Rome 1965)

SEG   *Supplementum Epigraphicum Graecum*

SGDI   H. Collitz, F. Bechtel, O. Hoffman, *Sammlung
der griechischen Dialekt-Inschriften* (Vanden-
hoeck & Ruprecht, Göttingen 1884-1915)

SIG³   W. Dittenberger, *Sylloge Inscriptionum Graecarum,* third edition (Hirzel, Leipzig 1915-24)

Thompson   M. Thompson (Bohn), *The Property Rights
of Women in Ancient Greece,* unpublished
doctoral thesis, Yale University, New Haven
(1906)

Willetts   see Lex Gort.

Wolff, RE   H. J. Wolff, προίξ RE 23 A (1957) 133-70

Wolff, *Traditio*   id., 'Marriage Law and Family Organization
in Ancient Athens', *Traditio* 2 (1944) 43-95,
reprinted in id., *Beiträge zur Rechtsgeschichte*
(H. Böhlau, Weimar; in German translation)

Wyse   W. Wyse, *The Speeches of Isaeus* (Cambridge
University Press 1904; reissued G. Olms, Hildesheim 1967)

Notes

..

PREFACE

1. 'Some Observations on the Property Rights of Athenian Women', CR 20 (N.S.) (1970) 273-8.

2. M. Thompson (Bohn), *The Property Rights of Women in Ancient Greece*, doctoral thesis, Yale University, New Haven (1906). I saw this worthwhile work only after finishing an early draft of this book, and while I did not need to make significant changes, I did have to revise some of my claims to originality. My thanks are due to Professor Louis Feldman of Yeshiva University for bringing it to my attention.

3. For this and other books referred to by the author's surname see Abbreviations, pp.108-10

4. For the *epikleros*, and other technical terms of Greek law, see the Glossary, pp.153-4.

5. In addition to Hafter's monograph and the sections by Beauchet, Lipsius, and Harrison on the subject, see L. Gernet, 'Sur l'Epiclérat', REG 34 (1921) 337-79.

6. Beauchet's discussion is insufficient, but others have generally contented themselves with mentioning the outlines of the institution, usually as an incidental part of another topic. The rights of the *kyrios* and the interrelationship of the members of the family are properly a topic for a work on the family; Lacey, while he has a good deal that is worthwhile, does not explore adequately the economic and legal matters involved.

INTRODUCTION

1. The reader interested in the material from outside Greece, mostly gathered from papyri and concerned with Egypt, is referred to C. Vatin, *Recherches sur le mariage et la condition de la femme mariée à l'époque hellénistique* (de Boccard, Paris 1970) and C. Préaux, 'Le statut de la femme à l'époque hellénistique, principalement en Egypte', *Recueils de la société Jean Bodin* 11, part 1 (Brussels 1959) 127-75, and the bibliographies contained in each. The topic is also dealt with by Thompson in her last chapter.

2. See G. H. Macurdy, *Hellenistic Queens* (Johns Hopkins Press, Baltimore 1932) and Vatin, op. cit., 57-114. Easily the best study of the economic and social aspects of prostitution is H. Herter, 'Die Soziologie der antiken Prostitution im Lichte des heidnischen und christlichen Schrifttums', *Jahrbuch für Antike und Christentum* 3 (1960) 70-111. For the problems of slavery in general

see the bibliography in M. I. Finley (ed.), *Slavery in Classical Antiquity* (Heffer, Cambridge 1960) 229-35; I know of no work dealing with the differences in function and status between male and female slaves.

CHAPTER 1 : TYPES OF PROPERTY

1. (Dem.) 46.14.
2. *Ta heautou diathesthai*, ibid; cf. Dem. 20.102.
3. A collateral relative, where there were no sons, was not a true heir in the same sense that a son would have been – unlike the son, for example, he could take possession of the estate only after a court had awarded it to him – and the law did not assert his 'family' right against the deceased's 'personal' right to dispose of it as he pleased. This was not the case before Solon: Plut. *Sol.* 21.
4. Aeschines 1.170-2: see Harrison I, 114n.1.
5. Isae. 11.41.
6. ibid. 42.
7. (Dem.) 43.31.
8. He argued her case in court (ibid. 32), and so must have been her *kyrios* at the time of the earlier trial. She was *epikleros* of her father Eubulides (ibid. 13, 20, 55, 74), but probably not of her cousin Hagnias.
9. IG II^2 1594-1603; SEG XXI 578, 579. Cf. Plato's will (Diog. Laert. 3.41-2), which adds seven more male property owners.
10. IG II^2 1579-89; SEG XII 100, XIX 132-5, XXI 564; M. Crosby, 'The Leases of the Laureion Mines', *Hesperia* 19 (1950) 189-312, and id., 'More Fragments of Mining Leases from the Athenian Agora', ibid. 26 (1957) 1-23. I do not include the inscriptions which list the property confiscated and sold in 415 or 414 in connection with the profanation of the mysteries and mutilation of the herms. For these see Pritchett, 'The Attic Stelai', ibid. 22 (1953) 225-99. The condemned were, of course, all men.
11. SEG XII 100, lines 67-71.
12. cf. ibid. lines 44-5, 79-80, and Crosby, *Hesperia* 19, no.5, line 4.
13. If she remained in the household, and if the children were hers, they would have been entitled to keep the money; but if she was planning a second marriage – Charmylus could even have betrothed her to another on his deathbed, as Demosthenes' father and Pasio did to their wives (Dem. 27.5, 45.28) – her dowry would have to be delivered to her new husband, and if she was not the children's mother, or if she chose to leave the household, it would be returned to whatever relative now became her *kyrios* (see Wolff, RE, 151-4). In either of the latter two cases, the only simple way to mention the land as long as it was still in the hands of the guardians and mortgaged for an unpaid debt would be as Charmylus' wife's land. Less likely, I think, is the suggestion that she had inherited this land independently, in which case the failure to mention her name will be a simple matter of delicacy: see Schaps, 'The Woman Least Mentioned: Etiquette and Women's Names', CQ 27 (N.S.) (1977) 323-30. But although some orators tend to avoid mention-

ing women by name, inscriptions in general show no such reticence, as the numerous dedications by and in honour of women testify.

14. He is mentioned on the same stone, SEG XII 100, line 48.
15. Crosby, *Hesperia* 19, no.3, line 13.
16. On the *epikleros,* see chapter 3.
17. Landowners are generally mentioned in the nominative or genitive in these inscriptions, but this woman appears in the accusative. The accusative, in fact, has no place in the formula, and it is difficult to see what she is doing here.
18. IG II^2 2684-757; SEG XIX 184, XXI 655-60; Fine, chapter 1 no.19, chapter 2 no.21; Finley nos.14, 17, 18, 22, 24, 53, 54. We may add also the few mortgage-stones describing hypothecation, IG II^2 2758-62; Finley nos.6, 3A.
19. IG II^2 2492, 2493, 2495, 2497; SEG XXI 644, XXIV 203. The sex of the lessee of 2497 is guaranteed by αὐτῷ in line 7. In the same group are four sales of land for a water conduit (SEG XIX 181, 182; IG II^2 2491, 2502), whose three identifiable sellers are likewise men.
20. IG II^2 2659-83; Fine, chapter 1 nos.6-8, 12, 25, chapter 2 nos.7-10, 25; SEG XVII 59, XXI 653-4, XXIV 206-7. The same meaning is presumably to be attributed to IG II^2 2765 and 2766, although the word προλξ does not appear on either stone; see Kirchner's note in IG II^2. Harrison I, 236n.3 is apparently in some confusion when he assumes otherwise, for he recognizes that 'in Athens not a single *horos* names a woman in any context other than a dowry', but includes these two stones as 'some other inscriptions'. The stones, however, are certainly *horoi,* and as such cannot be taken as indications that the women actually owned the land. *Horoi* were not set up on unencumbered land.
21. IG XI 135-289; Ins. Dél. 290-498. The little evidence from before this period (315-155 B.C.E.) comes from IG I^2 377, II^2 1633-53: we find no women, but the stones are few and fragmentary.
22. IG XI 2 287 A, lines 14-15, 182.
23. Ins. Dél. 316, line 17; cf. 338, line 10.
24. Arist. *Pol.* 1270 a 23-5.
25. Lex Gort. IV 31-43. As we shall see when we come to discuss the dowry, this was not really a restriction on women's right to own property.
26. ibid. IV 46-8.
27. ibid. II 48-50; it is differentiated from *oti k'enupanei,* 'what she weaves within', which is the produce of her industry. The provision mentioned is absent from the divorce rights of the female serf, ibid. III 40-4, who had no land.
28. BCH 56 (1932) 3-5. All the owners whose property was confiscated were foreigners. As for the earlier period, nothing conclusive can be shown from the rentals of confiscated real estate: these were political confiscations, and the absence of women may be due as well to political as to economic inactivity (*Fouilles de Delphes* III, fasc. 5, (Ecole française, Athens 1932) nos.15-18, with Bourget's commentary ad loc.). The absence of women among the lessees of the confiscated land (twenty-four men and one city leased the land) is also inconclusive, for the buying of confiscated goods was itself a political act; cf. Herodotus 6.121.2.
29. P. Salviat and C. Vatin, 'Le Cadastre de Larissa', BCH 98 (1974) 247-62.

30. IG XII 5 544 B, 1075 B, 1076, 1078.
31. ibid. 872, 875.
32. IG VII 43. She is not a priestess who has bought this land for the temple; if so, it would be unnecessary for her to instruct the citizens concerning the use of the land's income, as she does in lines 7-15.
33. τοῖς ὑπάρχουσί μοι αὐτοκτήτοις χωρίοις, IG XII 3 330, line 32.
34. ibid. 327, lines 9-12.
35. IG IX 2 458.
36. Diog. Laert. 5.12. Also noteworthy are mortgage-stones from Amorgos (IG XII 7 412) and Lemnos (Segre, 'Iscrizione greche di Lemno', *Annuario della Regia scuola archeogolica italiana di Atene* 15-16 (1932-3) 298-9, no.6; text reprinted in Finley, no.10) in which land is probably hypothecated to women (the Lemnian stone may have a minor as creditor, but this is less likely). The hypothecations may be connected with the delivery or return of the women's dowries. A stone from Cos (Paton and Hicks, *Inscriptions of Cos* (Oxford 1891) no.152) mentions a woman in connection with a plot of land, but it is impossible to determine what the connection is.
37. SGDI 1684-2342; *Fouilles de Delphes* III, fasc.1, no.565; fasc.2, no.229; fasc.3, nos.1-4, 6-9, 11-14, 26, 205; SEG XIV 427.
38. IG V 2 345, 429; VII 3198-9, 3301-412; IX^1 1 34-42, 120-6; IX^2 1 passim; IX 2 passim; XII 3 336-7; 3 Supp. 1302-3; SGDI 1346-65; SEG XV 293, 370; XXIII 478; XXIV 606. Much older are IG V 1 1228-33, from Taenarum in Laconia, and SGDI 1161, from Olympia.
39. Such was the case at Delphi, where eighty-six of the women appear with nobody 'approving', and at Naupactus. In Boeotia, on the other hand, women who manumit alone are very rare. See below, pp.49-50.
40. See IG IV^2 1 353-79, IV^1 529.
41. L. Mitteis, *Grundzüge der Papyruskunde,* juristischer Teil (Teubner, Leipzig 1912) 226-7.
42. IG VII 3083, 3364. Cf. 3363 (a man frees his mother's slave), 3348 (a man frees a slave who serves him and his parents), 3322 (a woman frees her grandmother's slave).
43. IG VII 3323-5, IX^1 1 42; cf. VII 3333 and IX^2 1 671, where a woman frees a servant serving herself and her husband, and VII 3085, which may show a similar case. Particularly interesting is VII 3378, where of two slaves both of whom (apparently) serve both husband and wife, one is freed by both and one by the husband alone. See below, p.49.
44. Plautus, *Casina* 284-91 implies that there were cases in which a father could, and his son could not, free a slave who served the son; but whether we are seeing the power of a Greek *kyrios* or of a Roman *paterfamilias* is impossible to tell. What is clear (the plot of the play depends on it) is that slaves belonging to the same household might have various allegiances within the family.
45. IG VII 3201; SGDI 1761. There are many more in which sons, daughters, wives, and mothers add their consent.
46. At least one case of disputed ownership seems to be preserved in IG VII 3372: see Schaps, 'A Disputed Slave in Boeotia', *Zeitschrift für Papyrologie und Epigraphik,* 20 (1976) 63-4.
47. Purchase: (Dem.) 59.18 (for the date, note that the 'little child' of the pas-

sage was a grown *hetaera* in 373/2, ibid. 35). Sale: ibid. 29, 'they bought (Neaera) free and clear from (Nicarete) according to the city's law to be their slave', where the expression νόμῳ πόλεως, 'according to the city's law', may imply that such a sale would be illegal at Athens, perhaps because it involved a woman selling a slave, that is, an item worth more than a medimnus of barley.

48. ibid. 46. She may have purchased them outside Athens. It is not clear whether Phrynio claimed the maids, who had been hers, or merely his own movables, which were awarded to him by the arbiters.

49. Xen. *Mem.* 3.11.4-5. Here we know nothing of the legal title to the slaves, but simply that they, or the money to buy them, came from a lover.

50. Dem. 45.28; cf. Demeas' gift to Chrysis, Men. *Sam.*, 381-3.

51. IG II² 1553-78; SEG XVIII 36, XXV 178, 180.

52. The δίκη ἀποστασίου, cf. IG II² 1578. It is not known whether or not all slaves were manumitted by this process; it is possible that these inscriptions record only cases of contested liberty. See most recently D. M. Lewis, 'Attic Manumissions', *Hesperia* 28 (1959) 237-8.

53. Lys. 23.9-11.

54. Theophr. *Char.* 22.10.

55. Neaera (see below, p.12) behaved on this assumption, and even in his anger Demeas gives Chrysis her slaves (ibid.) Phaedra's nurse is with her in her husband's house (Eur. *Hipp.*), and the old man of the *Iphigenia in Aulis* was part of Clytemnestra's trousseau (Eur. *Iph. Aul.* 43-8). Cf. also Aesch. *Supp.* 975-9. The greater laxity of property restrictions with regard to slaves is apparent as early as Homer, where, as Thompson, 14, points out, the dowry was already given with the woman, not to her (see *Il.* 9.148, 22.51, *Od.* 1. 278), but Penelope had two slaves whom her father had given to *her* at her marriage (*Od.* 4.735-7, 23.227-9).

56. (Dem.) 25.56.

57. ibid. 59.35, 46.

58. Lys. 12.19.

59. Dem. 41.11.

60. Xen. *Mem.* 3.11.4.

61. (Dem.) 47.57.

62. See Wolff, RE, 147-50.

63. Lys. 12.19.

64. Isae. 2.9.

65. Dem. 45.28. The repetition of the terms in the body of the speech indicates the authenticity of the inserted will. For the general question of the trustworthiness of the documents inserted in the text of Demosthenes, see Drerup, *Über die bei den attischen Rednern eingelegten Urkunden* (Teubner, Leipzig 1897). None of the documents pertaining to the study at hand appears to be spurious.

66. This distinction was made by Wolff, *Traditio*, 57. Cf. also Lys. 32.5-6.

67. Isae. 3.35. For the meaning of 'assessing it as part of the dowry' (ἐν προικὶ τιμήσας) see Wolff, RE, 137. The pleonasm of the passage may indicate that the last clause is a quote from the law.

68. Not γάμου, as Reiske proposed; cf. Wyse, 313-4 (ad loc.), with whom I agree although Lipsius, 491 n.74, did not.

69. Dem. 41.27. The speaker's argument rests on an unspoken, and probably untrue, assumption that Spudias' wife had a new trousseau that was not reckoned in the dowry, in addition to the old trousseau that 'probably' (εἰκότως, ibid. 28) was. See further Appendix III, pp.102-4.

70. A man who remarried immediately could of course have given them to his new wife (if she was the same size) or, like Plautus' Menaechmus, to his mistress; but this was hardly a gentlemanly way to behave, and in general the husband probably had little use for his wife's dresses.

71. τὰ ἐκ τῆς οἰκίας καὶ ὅσα ἦν αὐτῇ ὑπ' ἐκείνου περὶ τὸ σῶμα κατεσκευασμένα ἱμάτια καὶ χρυσία, καὶ θεραπαίνας δύο, Θρᾶτταν καὶ Κοκκαλίνην, (Dem.) 59.35. That τὰ ἐκ τῆς οἰκίας is to be understood with ἱμάτια καὶ χρυσία is indicated by the compromise effected; for if it referred to other items acquired in Stephanus' house, there would have been nothing of her own for her to keep.

72. ibid. 46.

73. Men. *Sam.* 381-3.

74. Similar are the transactions for a woman's *uestem, aurum* when buying her as a *hetaera* (Plaut. *Curc.* 344, *Persa* 669). Since the women involved are slaves, their clothing presumably belongs to their masters, who furnished it; but it still follows them, not its owners, when they are sold.

75. See IG V 1 1564a, Paus. 6.1.6 and Frazer's commentary ad loc.

76. IG VII 303, lines 55ff.

77. See, chiefly, Lex Gort. IV 23-7. The fines imposed in certain cases of divorce and pilferage (ibid. II 52, IV 12-14, and elsewhere) indicate that unmarried women had money, but they are not direct evidence for the status of that money during marriage.

78. IG VII 3172.

79. IG IX[1] 1 278. The husband is mentioned alone at first because of the phrase διὰ προγόνων εὔνους ὑπάρχων, 'a benefactor by ancestral tradition'; it is the husband's family that has a link with the *technitae*. But the gift, as the inscription goes on to explain, came from both husband and wife.

80. ibid. 694. I follow H. L. Ahrens' view (*De Graecae linguae dialectis* (Göttingen 1839-43) II, 225) that we are dealing with a man and wife, Aristomenes and Psylla. Note that they give separate (and equal) gifts: in Athens we should have expected all the money to be given in the husband's name, or at most to be given jointly.

81. IG IV[2] 1 46, if the lady was really granted immunity from public burdens (ἀτέλεια), would show us a married woman of the fifth century rich enough to have liturgies, from which the inscription exempted her; but ἀτέλεια is, unfortunately, merely a conjecture based upon parallel grants to men.

82. Ins. Dél. 362 B, line 11 (209 B.C.E.); 406 B, lines 16, 25, 38, 46, 49, (c. 190 B.C.E.); 442 A, line 215 (179 B.C.E.).

83. IG IV[1] 840. It is quite possible that the total estate was larger, and that we have only a portion of the will: see Dareste et al. II, 114.

84. IG XII 3 330.

85. ibid. 329.

86. IG V 2 461, lines 5-8.
87. Cynisca: see above, n.75. For the date of her victory, see C. Robert in Hermes 35 (1900) 195. Euryleonis: Paus. 3.17.6. Cf. Paus. 3.8.1, 'After Cynisca other women, particularly from Lacedaemon, had Olympic victories, but the most glorious as a victory was hers'. The victory of Belistiche, the *hetaera* of Ptolemy Philadelphus (ibid. 5.8.11) may also be mentioned, though one must be extremely careful in using Hellenistic court personnages as evidence for other Greeks. (The 'victor' in the chariot-race was the owner of the team, not the man who drove them).
88. IG IX 2 526.
89. IG II² 2313, 2314. It is not surprising that the only women we know to have won victories at the Panathenaea were not Athenians.
90. Polyb. 38.15.6 (ed. Buettner-Wobst).
91. See, e.g., IG II² 2332-5, V 2 438-42.
92. Dem. 27.53-5.
93. id. 41.11.
94. id. 36.14-16.
95. Ar. *Lys*. 492-7. A similar passage occurs in id. *Eccl.* 210-13. Wilamowitz commented on πολεμητέον ἔστ' ἀπὸ τούτου, 'Nicht unlogisch, sondern kurz. Geld, das der Krieg braucht, kann eine Frau nicht verwalten.' Wilamowitz, like the Probulus, shared the prejudices of his time and place; I share those of mine in disagreeing. But the contrast between τἄνδον and 'Geld, das der Krieg braucht' is significant: it was only household expenses that women managed, not land-purchases or business expenses (and, of course, not the war treasury).
96. Plato, *Leg.* VII 805 e. Cf. (Dem.) 59.122 (where the wife should be 'a faithful guardian of the household goods (τῶν ἔνδον)'), Arist. *Eth. Nic.* 1160 b 34 (where the husband 'gives over to her whatever is proper for a woman'), and Lys. 1.7 (where the plaintiff's wife was 'a clever and thrifty housekeeper, one who kept a close eye on everything').
97. Ar. *Thesm*. 418-23.
98. Men. *Sam*. 301-3.
99. Xen. *Oec*. 3.12. That Xenophon has financial matters in mind is evident from what follows: '. . . For wealth comes into the family, in general, through the husband's business, but most of it is spent through the wife's management' (ibid. 15).
100. ibid. VII 3.
101. Dem. 41.8-11, 17, 21.
102. IG IV¹ 801.
103. (Dem.) 50.60-61.
104. Aeschin. 1.170: rightly rejected by Harrison I, 114n.1, as being of no legal significance, the passage is nevertheless talking about a situation that was known to the Athenians.
105. The only one of which we know is the banquet given at the Thesmophoria, which Isae. 3.80 mentions with the addition of 'such other liturgies in the deme as ought to be borne in one's wife's name from an estate of that size' (cf. ibid. 6.64). What the 'other liturgies' were (if they were anything more than a rhetorical flourish of Isaeus') was unknown to Wyse, and is no more apparent to me.

106. Aeschin. 1.183.
107. (Dem.) 59.16. It may be suggested that she is not fined because she was not the one who contracted the marriage; but this consideration does not seem to have kept the foreign women from being sold. It is possible, however, that the two clauses of the law are not parallel, but deal with somewhat different types of union, as Wolff, *Traditio*, 65-6 suggests.
108. A similar explanation may apply to an Arcadian sacred law of the sixth or fifth century (SEG XI 1112, XXII 320; the translation here given is that of Carl Darling Buck, *The Greek Dialects*, University of Chicago Press 1955, p.197): 'If a woman wears a brightly coloured robe, it shall be dedicated to .... If she does not dedicate it, being ill disposed in respect to the rite (?), let her perish, and whoever is demiurgus at that time shall pay thirty drachmas. If he does not pay, he shall be charged with the impiety. Let this have validity for ten years . . . . ' The text is uncertain, and its circumstances unknown; but all its editors agree that the magistrate has to pay for the woman's impiety. The woman is cursed (Robinson's first assumption, that she was killed ('A New Arcadian Inscription', CP 38 (1943) 191-9), seems extreme), but not fined.

CHAPTER 2 : ACQUISITION

1. Dem. 57.45.
2. Ar. *Thesm*. 446-9.
3. Crates ap. Plut. *Mor.* 830 C (=XXXXVII fr. 5 Diels, with an alternate reading that need not concern us here).
4. Xen. *Oec.* 10.10-11, in response to his wife's request for advice on how to improve her appearance.
5. This was true of men as well, though the Crates passage, and the relative frequency of male workers as opposed to female, suggests that a man would normally work before he would ask his wife to do so. See in particular Claude Mossé, *The Ancient World at Work*, tr. Janet Lloyd (Norton, New York 1969) 25-30. Farming was a respectable occupation; but it was not one in which women took much of an independent part, as Herfst, 13-17, notes.
6. Xen. *Mem.* 2.7.
7. ibid. 2.7.5.
8. id. *Oec.* 7.41.
9. Ar. *Thesm.* 400-1. The widow produced in quantity and took orders in advance, ibid., 457-8.
10. id. *Ran.* 1349-51.
11. Xen. *Mem.* 2.7.6.
12. Lex Gort. II 51, III 26, 34.
13. *Od.* 5.61-2, 10.220-3, 7.108-10.
14. IG II^2 1553-78; SEG XVIII 36, XXV 178, 180. There are also a number of women designated as παιδίον, either 'servant' or simply (as in 1576, line 60) 'child'.
15. IG II^2 1556, line 18; *Fouilles de Delphes* III fasc.3, no.26, line 6.
16. IG II^2 1559, lines 60, 63; ibid. 2934.
17. ibid. 5592.

18. IG I² 473.
19. IG II² 1578, line 5. She may have been a leather-seller (σκυτόπωλις) as easily as a true cobbler (σκυτότομος, *σκευτεύτρια), according to M. N. Tod, 'Epigraphical Notes on Freedmen's Professions', *Epigraphica* 12 (1950) 11. Herfst, 33, saw another in IG II 5, 772 b, col. I, line 24 (=II² 1558, line 14); but this is apparently a man (cf. Kirchner's note ad loc. in IG II²; his reading is approved by D. M. Lewis, 'Attic Manumissions', *Hesperia* 28 (1959) 218, line 456, and by Tod, loc. cit., 8). Lewis (loc. cit., 222, line 91) adds a female horse-currier, if one can believe his reading; but as he admits (ibid., 231), 'An *hapax legomenon* ψηχιστρία with extraordinary spelling (he reads ποηκιστρί(α)) is not encouraging'. πο, he adds, is unknown in Attica or indeed, by the time of the inscription, anywhere in Greece.
20. Herfst, 24-32.
21. Reproduced in Dar.-Sag. II², 1127, fig. 3041. A Homeric simile (*Il.* 4.141 ff.) mentions a woman painting ivory, but it is not speaking of a Greek. We also possess the tombstone of a κυκλιστρία, probably a professional acrobat.
22. SIG³ 1177.
23. Herfst, 52-3, cf. 78-9.
24. See below, pp.61-3.
25. This responsibility was imposed by law for his parents, and for his divorced wife until he returned the dowry, but it was certainly a matter of propriety for his wife during marriage, his minor sons and his unmarried daughters and sisters as well.
26. The resignation of one's property in favour of a natural or adopted son – as, for example, in Men. *Dysc.* 731-40 – need not concern us here, as it was unlikely to take place in favour of an heiress, who would not manage the estate herself.
27. Lex Gort. X 33 - XI 23; cf. Dareste et al. I, 482; Guarducci IV, 168 (ad loc.); Willetts, 30.
28. Dem. 20.102, Arist. *Ath. Pol.* 35.2, Plut. *Solon* 21.3-4.
29. Arist. *Pol.* 1270 a 21.
30. Isoc. 19.51.
31. See, e.g., C. Préaux, 'Le statut de la femme à l'époque hellénistique', *Recueils de la société Jean Bodin* 11, part 1 (Brussels 1959) 167-9.
32. (Dem.) 46.14.
33. Arist. *Pol.* 1270 a 21:ὅπως μὴ ἦ τοῖς συκοφάνταις ἔφοδος.
34. Ar. *Vesp.* 583-9; Isae. 1.41; (Arist.) *Pr.* 950 b 5-8.
35. Isae. 7.9.
36. id. 11.8.
37. ibid. 41-2. Theopompus claims that the girl's natural father made a tidy profit out of his guardianship, but his assertions are not to be trusted. Cf. Davies, 88.
38. cf. IG XII 1 115, 379, 818, 854, 894; SGDI 3706 VI, line 61; P. Le Bas, *Voyage archéologique* (Paris 1870; reissued Hildesheim and New York 1972), Partie V (Asie Mineure), nos.115, 507. These inscriptions, mostly of uncertain date, attest little more than the word θυγατροποία.
39. (Dem.) 46.24-5; the will is in Dem. 45.28.
40. Dem. 27.5, 29.43.

41. Lys. 32.5-6.
42. ibid. 4.
43. Lex Gort. III 18-22, 29-30, X 15-20, XII 1-5.
44. Wyse, 515 (ad Isae. 6.28).
45. Beauchet III, 677-8; Wyse, loc. cit.; Lipsius, 564-5; Harrison I, 152. The Gortynian parallel suggests that the ability to make a limited will to protect the members of one's family may be a common Greek feature, rather than a post-Solonian innovation as these scholars maintain.
46. Thus in IG VII 3083 (from Lebadeia in Boeotia), a man leaves his son instructions to free a slave after the slave has served the boy's mother for ten years — instructions that would more likely have been given to the mother along with the slave, if that had been legal; but since the son would now be her *kyrios*, the slave was part of his patrimony and he was the one to free her.
47. cf. also the will of Conon, Lys. 19.39-40, which left less than half his estate to his son; much of his fortune may have been in Cyprus (ibid., cf. 36), out of the reach of the Athenian courts. As Harrison (loc. cit.) says, 'testators would have to make nice calculations' in deciding how large a portion they could leave to others without having the will overturned in court.
48. SIG^3 1014, lines 150-64 (*c.* 250 B.C.E.). Epicteta of Thera received deathbed instructions from her husband and, two years later, from her son (IG XII 3 330, lines 8-9, 16-19); from which, if either, she inherited cannot be stated.
49. Her new husband presumably became *kyrios* of them; in the meantime, it is more likely that she controlled them herself, despite the fact that she could not be their *kyria*.
50. *Pace* Willetts, pp. 18-20, who postulates for Gortyn a system of cross-cousin marriage on the basis of 'parallels' from the Iroquois and from India [sic] but without any evidence at all from any part of Greece.
51. On great-uncles and great-aunts see below, p.125n.65. On the entire subject of this section see D. Schaps, 'Women in Greek Inheritance Law', CQ 25 (N.S.) (1975) 53-7.
52. (Dem.) 43.51, Isae. 11.1-2; cf. Wyse, 680-1, and Harrison I, 130-49.
53. The term in Gortyn was πατροιῶκος, but the rules were analogous.
54. Lex Gort. IV 31-43 and V 9-28.
55. IG IX^2 1 609. An inscription from Aetolia (ibid., no.2) is too fragmentary to give us any clear information, but the order appears to be: sons, daughters, brothers or sisters, and at least one other category. It is impossible to tell certainly whether or not males exclude females here.
56. Isoc. 19.6-9. The half-sister claimed *ab intestato*, while the speaker of the oration disputed her claim on the basis of a will.
57. IG V 2 159.
58. Plato, *Leg.* 925 c - d.
59. Wolff, *Traditio*, 63.

CHAPTER 3 : THE *EPIKLEROS*

1. IG IX^2 1 609, describing the terms of a land division in Naupactus, mentions daughters as heirs and says nothing about their becoming *epikleroi*; but the language is not such as to exclude the possibility entirely.

2. Thus Isae. 10.4, explaining how his mother allegedly became an *epikleros*, mentions the death of her father, brother, and sister, but not her mother; similarly the general case in Isae. 3.64. Cf. Hafter, 12-13. The only apparent exception is Polyeuctus' wife, who obviously controlled some money after her husband's death (Dem. 41.9); but we do not know where this money came from, or what her legal title to it might have been; and both her daughters were already married, in marriages that were not challenged either at her husband's death or her own.

3. cf. Andoc. 1.118 (the estate was not in fact as badly off as that; see below, pp.30-1, Isae. 10.16.

4. id. 3.64, 10.19; Andoc. 1.117 ff.; (Dem.) 53.54; the Suda's requirement of 'the entire property' must thus be taken to refer to all the *epikleroi* of a given estate, as opposed to beneficiaries of limited testamentary bequests.

5. cf. Pollux 3.33, περιόντος τε τοῦ πατρὸς καὶ ἀποθανόντος.

6. Such at least is the point of the uses in Dem. 53.29 and in the fragment of Agathias cited in the Suda s.v. ἐπίκληρος, where the girl's place in the succession is not at all what the authors have in mind.

7. Ar. *Vesp.* 583-9.

8. (Dem.) 46.18-19. The law does not, in fact, define the term *epikleros*, and explicitly recognizes that a woman fitting the 'definition' might not be one (ἐὰν μὲν ἐπίκληρός τις ᾖ . . . ἐὰν δὲ μὴ ᾖ) – as indeed she might not: her brother, for example, might have died and left a son.

9. Isae. 10.2. If the archon in fact compelled the speaker to identify his mother as the sister of Aristarchus, he obviously did not recognize the speaker's mother as an *epikleros*: see Wyse, 649-51.

10. (Dem.) 46.20.

11. That it applied to the *anchisteus* is stated by Isae. 10.12 and id. fr. 25 Thalheim; the only claims, real or hypothetical, against an outsider ((Dem.) 46.19-20, Isae. 3.50, Men. *Aspis* 270-3) are against men who, according to the claimants, were never entitled to the property. It has been argued (by Hruza I, 91n.7, followed by Beauchet I, 466) that the claimant of Isaeus 10, by not claiming in his own name, shows that he did not have this right; but it is not clear that he is, in fact, claiming for his mother (cf. Wyse, 650). Isae. 3.55, also mentioned by Hruza and Beauchet, is irrelevant, for the children of Xenocles and Phile cannot have reached majority by the time of the speech; cf. ibid. 31. If anything is suggested by this speech, it is quite the opposite of Hruza's thesis: see ibid. 50. According to the purpose of the law as explained in the text, Hruza's understanding is reasonable, for the *epikleros* could indeed leave a husband who was not the *anchisteus* and return to her family; so she will not have needed extra protection against him. But it is not clear that she could do so without having to marry her next-of-kin, and she may not have been able to recover her fortune, and in any event, the theory is not necessarily true simply because it fits my own hypotheses. The tendency of the Attic courts was to extend the laws protecting the *epikleros* as far as they could, a fact which argues against Hruza's understanding.

12. Isae. 10.12.

13. ibid. 8.31.

14. id. fr. 25 Thalheim.
15. Hypereides fr. 192 Blass: 'When I was registered, and the law, which ordains that the children, when they are two years past puberty, are to be *kyrioi* of the *epikleros* and of all the estate, granted me the recovery of what had been left to my mother'.
16. Unlike the dowry, which the wife ἐπιφέρει ('brings along') and the husband λαμβάνει ('takes'). For the property of the *epikleros* cf. also ἡ τῆς ἐπικλήρου οὐσία, Aeschin. 1.95; τῶν ἑαυτῆς, Isae. 3.46; τὰ ἑαυτῆς, ibid. 62.
17. Dem. 14.16. For 'liturgies' see the glossary.
18. That only one son could succeed, and he only by adoption, 'is the most likely view *a priori*', says Harrison I, 135, and so accepts it; but the first part of the hypothesis is explicitly denied by the sources cited in notes 12-15, and the second implicitly by (Dem.) 43.11-13 and Isae. 3.73.
19. The adoption of Eubulides, son of the speaker of (Dem.) 43, was designed to make him Hagnias' cousin's son, and thus eligible for Hagnias' estate; so whatever its consequences for his grandfather's estate it was not entirely restricted to religious duties. The posthumous adoption of Aristarchus II in Isae. 10 also left him with the property of his adoptive father.
20. Isae. 2.13, 3.68, 10.13.
21. Hruza I, 91n.7.
22. The case is that of Sosias in (Dem.) 43; cf. Hruza, loc. cit.
23. See Harrison, loc. cit.; Gernet, 'Sur l'Epiclérat', REG 34 (1921) 356 (cited incorrectly in Harrison, loc. cit., n.1); Wyse, 360-2; Beauchet I, 470-3; Hruza, loc. cit. A Coan inscription (Paton and Hicks, *Inscriptions of Cos* (Oxford 1891) nos.367, 368; see their commentary, pp.258-9) may indicate that variation was possible: in one family, rights to participation in certain *sacra* are inherited only by that son who bears the name of his maternal grandfather, while in another both sons appear to inherit, although neither bears his grandfather's name. This suggests that one son could be designated as the grandfather's heir to the exclusion of the others, but that if he was not, all brothers shared equally. The son's 'preferment' here did not eliminate his claim from his father; in neither case was any son adopted into the maternal *oikos*. Much caution, however, is in order. This is Cos, not Athens; the 'excluded' son shared in the rites anyway through his father, and may simply have neglected to mention his maternal claim; and we are dealing with religious rights, not property rights.
24. Isae. 3.64.
25. id. 10.19.
26. For a good review of the literature, see Harrison I, 309-11.
27. Ter. *Adel.* 650-9.
28. This passage was first adduced by U. E. Paoli, 'La legittima aféresi dell' ἐπίκληρος nel diritto attico', *Miscellanea G. Mercati*, vol. V (=*Studi e Testi*, 125; Biblioteca Apostolica, Vatican 1946) 524-38.
29. Wyse is puzzled by the absence of references to the relative claims of a son born to an outsider and one born later to the *anchisteus*: 'the point is vital (to Isae. 8.30-4), but it is passed over in silence' (p.609). It is passed over because the hypothetical case put there by the speaker assumes that his mother had no children at his grandfather's death; otherwise she would not

have been liable to adjudication – that is, once there were children born to
an outsider, there could not be legitimate children born later to the *anchisteus*. (This is not to say, of course, that the speaker there is pretending he
does not exist; what he is pretending, for the sake of argument, is that he is
his opponent's son.) Wyse's treatment, here as elsewhere, suffers from his
unsubstantiated (though common enough) assumptions about the epiclerate
– the chief of those being that 'all the rules concerning the ἐπίκληρος are
a violation of equity' (p.609), because she 'was herself inherited as an appendage to the property' (p.608). The prevalence of arguments from equity,
and the consistent refusal of the sources – despite the terms and procedure
of the law – to treat the *epikleros* as an 'appendage to the property' bother
Wyse not a whit, since he considers Isaeus a gross liar. That Isaeus, as Greek
lawyers in general, did not shrink from the *suppresio veri*, from the *suggestio
falsi*, from the improper inference, or from the other tools of his trade, is
certainly true, and has not always been properly appreciated by scholars;
but there is no need to create new contradictions in his speeches by noting
that they contradict our own improper deductions.

30. This right apparently belonged to the father as long as no children had been
born of the marriage (see below, p.143n.33), and I suspect that this right,
passing to the next-of-kin on the father's death, is the basis for his power to
claim the girl. It must be noted, however, that the father's right is not completely certain, and we have nothing to indicate whether such a right passed
to the next-of-kin when the girl was not an *epikleros*. The residual rights of
the father to dissolve the marriage are not to be confused with the economic
control exercised by the *kyrios*, which passed to the husband at the moment
of marriage.

31. That a daughter born to the *epikleros* did not prevent *epidikasia* is suggested
by the claim of Androcles to the hand of Euctemon's daughter (Isae. 6.46),
who already had a daughter of her own (ibid. 32) – though the claim is an
odd one, as the speaker notes, since Androcles also asserted that Euctemon
had left legitimate sons.

32. Dem. 41.

33. (Dem.) 44.10.

34. The last is the promise of Chaerestratus in Menander, *Aspis* 266-9; cf. the
law in (Dem.) 43.54, discussed below, and Isae. 10.6 (if the speaker's mother
really was an *epikleros*). This may not have been possible if another relative
wanted to claim the *epikleros*: see below, p.35.

35. (Dem.) 43.51. The law begins with the case of daughters not because it 'takes
for granted and therefore does not mention sons' (Harrison I, 130n.4), but
because it is part of a code, and follows, as the first clause shows, on the
rules of testation – that is to say, it follows closely (though probably not
immediately) on the law quoted in (Dem.) 46.14, which restricts itself to
the case 'if there should be no legitimate male children'. The code thus
began by stating that sons inherit from their father – a law which hardly
had to be quoted to an Athenian court, and so has not been preserved –
continued with the provisions for testation in the absence of legitimate sons,
then went on to state the laws of succession that applied where no will had
been made. The speaker of (Dem.) 43, who was not representing Hagnias'

son, has no need to quote the first two sections; nor does Theopompus in Isae. 11.1-2.

36.   Isae. 3.68, 10.13, 3.42. The provision is not mentioned in 2.13, since Menecles had no daughters.

37.   See above, pp.26 and 121n.11.

38.   (And.) 4.15, where Alcibiades allegedly hopes to gain his father-in-law's money by killing his brother-in-law; Dem. 41; (Dem.) 44, where the son of the *epikleros* claims the estate of his maternal grandfather's brother, which implies that he has succeeded to his grandfather; Isae. 3.46, 50, 55, 62, all affirming the rights of a legitimate *epikleros* against an adoptive brother (also next-of-kin) who did not marry her; id. 8.31, spoken by a grandson whose mother predeceased her father, and so never became an *epikleros*.

39.   Isae. 10.19. This alleged fear is doubted by Wyse (ad loc.), since the speaker's father had received his wife from the very men who were now supposedly threatening to take her away; for a plausible defence of the speaker's contention, see Paoli, 'La legittima afèresi', *Miscellanea G. Mercati*, vol. V (=*Studi e Testi*, 125; Vatican 1946), 535-8.

40.   Men. *Aspis* 264-73.

41.   Isae. 3.55.

42.   Andoc. 1.117-21.

43.   On this see Davies, 261-5.

44.   Lys. 14.28; cf. Davies, 268-9.

45.   Isae. 3.42, 68, 10.13. We do not know if adoption changed incest-taboos; his adoptive sister, being now ὁμοπατρία but still not − according to Isaeus 7.25 − ὁμομητρία, would be permitted in any case.

46.   It is worth noting that while the father could not exclude a son from inheritance − since a man with sons could not adopt − a man with many daughters (and no sons) could exclude all but one of them by adopting a son who would marry one of the daughters. The same rule was established by Plato in the *Laws* (XI 923 e), as Thompson, 62, points out.

47.   Dem. 41. 3-4.

48.   ibid. 5.

49.   See Thompson, 65; Lipsius, 543; Harrison I, 136n.2; Lacey, 141.

50.   See Lacey, chapters 1, 3, 4. On the importance of having a descendant, rather than a collateral, succeed to the *oikos*, see D. Asheri, 'L'οἶκος ἔρημος nel diritto successorio attico', *Archivio giuridico Filippo Serafini*, ser. VI, vol. 28 (1960) 8-24.

51.   A nephew, Isae. 6.6, 7.5-7, 13-14; a brother-in-law, Dem. 41.3; a first cousin's son, Isae. 9.2-4. The speaker of Isaeus 2, a sometime brother-in-law whose sister had been divorced and remarried before the adoption, finds it necessary to explain away the fact that the deceased could find no nearer relative to adopt (Isae. 2.20-2).

52.   Isae. 11.49, (Dem.) 43.11, 44.41. See further Thalheim, RE 1 A (1893) 397-8, s.v. Adoption.

53.   (Dem.) 43.15.

54.   See ibid., and Isae. 3.73.

55.   As, for example, in Isae. 11.49. For other objections to this theory, see L. Gernet, 'Sur l'Epiclérat', REG 34 (1921) 358-67.

56. Dem. 57.41.
57. id. 30 Hyp.
58. Isae. 6.46.
59. And. 1.121.
60. Arist. *Pol.* 1303 b 18.
61. ibid. 1304 a 4-13.
62. id. *Ath. Pol.* 56.6, 58.3; (Dem.) 46.22.
63. This is stated by Apollodorus, (Dem.) 46.22 (ἀνεπίδικον μὴ ἐξεῖναι ἔχειν μήτε κλῆρον μήτε ἐπίκληρον), but not by the law there, which says only that no one is to inherit an estate without *epidikasia* (ἀνεπίδικον δὲ κλῆρον μὴ ἔχειν). Apollodorus is probably correct in his interpretation of the law's intent, at least as far as pertains to the next-of-kin; but since the *epidikasia* was the only legitimate marriage possible in this case, it was unnecessary to mention the *epikleros* here. He is not correct in inferring that an *epikleros* may never be married to an outsider.
64. Arist. *Ath. Pol.* 43.4; cf. (Dem.) 43.5. For the λήξεις cf. (Dem.) 46.23, Isae. 3.30, 4.2.
65. On this interpretation, the son of the deceased's cousin was within the preferred circle, but if he was dead, his own son was not. Another possibility is that one's descendants always inherited one's own claims, and the limitation μέχρι ἀνεψιῶν παίδων was a 'horizontal' one, limiting the inner circle to second cousins (the deceased and his second cousin were the children of first cousins, after all). Other interpretations have been proposed. Cf. A. R. W. Harrison, 'A Problem in the Rules of Intestate Succession at Athens', CR 61 (1947) 41-3; J. C. Miles, 'Attic Law of Intestate Succession', *Hermathena* 75 (1950) 77; L. Lepri, *Sui rapporti di parentela in diritto attico* (A. Giuffrè, Milan 1959) 8-13. It is not certain that the Athenians were themselves agreed on this point, for there was no lack of confusion as to the precise intent of the various provisions of this law, nor any body of precedent to resolve the confusion.
66. (Dem.) 43.51, Isae. 11.1-2. See Beauchet I, 426-35, III, 441 ff.; Wyse, 348-9, 680-1 (ad Isae. 11.2); Lipsius 540-61; Harrison I, 143-9. Wyse attempts to restrict the succession to paternal relatives, but his reasoning is faulty and contradicts the explicit testimony of the orators. Beauchet's view, that the rights to the *epikleros* extended indefinitely, is followed here with some reservations. The law is not perfectly clear, and the text he cites (Isae. 3.74) does not prove his point. The fact that we do commonly meet *epikleroi* married to outsiders suggests that the right to claim her did not extend indefinitely; so does the term *anchisteus* (cf. Harrison I, 143). But this possibility cannot be proven, either.
67. Thus Endius' brother, whose mother was Pyrrhus' sister, says that he and Endius would have been able to obtain Pyrrhus' daughter (if he had one, which the speaker denies) by *epidikasia* (Isae. 3.74); cf. ibid. 63, where maternal uncles are said to have a claim; also And. 1.124, Dem. 45.75. Wyse's objections (see previous note) have no Athenian evidence whatsoever to support them. Plato's rules (*Leg.* XI 924 e - 925 c) are quite different, being based on the principle that no one is to have two estates, and on a willingness to allow the girl a choice in certain instances.

68. i.e., the estate is divided among all the members of a given generation who have living descendants, whether they themselves be alive or dead at the time of the division, and then the share of each dead member is divided among his descendants, always applying the principle that females are excluded in the presence of males. That division actually was *per stirpes* is a presumption of scholars, though nowhere attested; see Harrison I, 144n.2 and the literature cited there.

69. See Men. *Aspis* 254-6. Seniority, too may have applied *per stirpes*, so that (for example) the son of the elder uncle would come before the younger uncle; I do not know of any evidence on this aspect of the law's application.

70. Arist. *Ath. Pol.* 42.5.

71. (Dem.) 43.16.

72. ibid. 5.

73. The term 'betrothal' is used as a convenience, though *engye* is not parallel with our 'engagement'. Athenian marriage took place in two steps, of which *engye* – the father's 'handing over' the bride to the bridegroom – was the essential first step. Without it, the marriage (except of an *epikleros*) was not legitimate.

74. (Dem.) 46.18.

75. Wyse, 501 (ad Isae. 6.14), and Wolff, *Traditio*, 75. Harrison I, 12 misunderstands the law when he claims that 'nothing is said of (the legitimacy of) children born of a woman married by ἐπιδικασία'. For the law to order the marriage was all that had to be said.

76. Arist. *Pol.* 1270 a 28-9.

77. Andoc. 1. 117-21.

78. Isae. 6.51.

79. Ar. *Vesp.* 583-7.

80. Plut. *Solon* 20.2-5. For the correct interpretation of this law, which Plutarch misunderstood, see Dareste, 'Une prétendue loi de Solone', REG 8 (1895) 1-6 (=Dareste, *Nouvelles études d'histoire du droit* (Larose, Paris 1902) 31-7. Lacey, 89, 104, and 276n.31, still follows Plutarch's misinterpretation, as had Thompson, 65n.1; LSJ s.v. ὀπυίω understands it properly.

81. Isae. 6.13.

82. Men. *Aspis* 266-7.

83. Pl. *Leg.* XI 925 a.

84. Lex Gort. VII 52 - VIII 8.

85. The worst that could happen to the husband of a dowered woman was that he would be left, in case of divorce, without the money to repay the dowry; for *epiklērou kakōsis*, on the other hand, see below, p.38.

86. Aeschin. 1.95; for a royal Spartan case, see Plut. *Cleom.* 1.1-3.

87. Men. fr. 582 Koerte (=585 Kock).

88. id. fr. 334 (=403); cf. 333, 335 (=402, 404).

89. Arist. *Eth. Nic.* 1161 a 1-3.

90. Or 'for the family' (τῷ γένει, the MS reading, rather than C. F. Hermann's conjecture τῷ γ'ἑνὶ, which I have translated in the text) – that is, the entire family need give away only one *epikleros*, and the others must fend for themselves. This would seem to be against the whole purport of the law, but

Thompson, 64-5, is uncertain.
91. (Dem.) 43.54. Harpocration s.v. ἐπίδικος and Diod. Sic. 12.8.3, quoting the figure of five minae without qualification, are probably being brief rather than accurate. The provision of a fine for the archon's ignoring the case suggests that even he could not be counted on to pay attention.
92. Isae. 1.39.
93. And. 1.118-19.
94. Eustathius 1246, (12). We do not know the date of this innovation.
95. Diod. Sic. 12.8.4.
96. Arist. *Ath. Pol.* 56.6, 58.3; cf. (Dem.) 35.48, Dem. 37.33, Lys. 15.3.
97. Arist. *Ath. Pol.* 56.6; Pollux 8.38 (where Meyer's προσηκόντως is right. It was not the duty of the girl's husband to notify the archon (as Paoli, 'La legittima afèresi . . . ', *Miscellanea G. Mercati*, vol. V (=*Studi e Testi*, 125; Vatican 1946) 529n.23, suggests), for there was nothing for the archon to do unless a claimant appeared; the advertisement for counter-claims took place only after the original λῆξις); Isae. 1.39 (note ταῖς μεγίσταις ζημίαις), 3.46. Cf. Lipsius, 349-50.
98. (Dem.) 43.75. On the severity of the penalties see Isae. 1.39, 3.47, 62, Dem. 37.46.
99. Isae. 3.46-7, Harpocration s.v. κακώσεως.
100. Because it was not before the archon: Dem. 37.45-6.
101. Lipsius, 531-2.
102. (Dem.) 40.4, 59.8.
103. ibid. 59.112-3, Hypereides 1.13.
104. Dem. 45.74-5.
105. Lys. 12.21.
106. Dem. 30.33. For cases of remarriage arranged at death, see ibid. 27.5, 36.8; at divorce, ibid. 30.11, 57.41. The last case in Dem. 36.28-30 is certainly divorce (from Aegina); the first two may be either divorce or death.
107. Diog. Laert. 5.12.
108. Isae. 7.11-12, (Dem.) 44.10.
109. Diod. Sic. 12.8.4.
110. Plato, *Leg.* XI 924 d-e.
111. SEG I 211; the text is available in C. D. Buck, *The Greek Dialects* (Chicago University Press, Chicago 1955) 207, no.22.
112. IG IX^2 1 609, c. 500 B.C.E.
113. ibid. 2, c. 223 B.C.E. (the inscription itself is much later).
114. IG XII 3 330, lines 81-2.
115. Herodotus 6.57.4. The word πατροῦχος may be a corruption (with Ionicized spelling) of πατρωιόκος, the term used at Gortyn. It is identical in meaning with *epikleros*, which is not attested in Doric.
116. ibid. 7.205.1; cf. W. W. How and J. Wells, *A Commentary on Herodotus* (Oxford University Press 1912) ad loc. (How and Wells are wrong in seeing an *epikleros* in Lampito (Hdt. 6.71), since her father Leotychidas had a legitimate son in Zeuxidamus).
117. Arist. *Pol.* 1270 a 26-9.
118. Plut. *Cleom.* 1.2.

119. Lex Gort. VIII 40-2. Whether or not the Athenian definition included the paternal grandfather as well is still *sub iudice*: see Harrison I, 136-7, Gernet, loc. cit. (above, p.122n.23) 339-45, Beauchet I, 415-16.
120. Lex Gort. VIII 15-27.
121. ibid. VIII 8-12.
122. ibid. VII 35-52, VIII 8-12.
123. ibid. VII 52 - VIII 8. The town-house apparently constituted the most essential part of the inheritance, and passed to the 'true' heirs of the household even when the rest of the estate was divided − between the *patroikos* and the *epiballon* here, or between sons and daughters as in IV 31-9 (see p.86-7).
124. The presumed meaning of ὐπόδρομος...ἐβίον, ibid. VII 35-7.
125. ibid. VII 35-52.
126. ibid. VIII 20-30. I know of no satisfactory explanation for this provision. Willetts (ad loc.) says, 'the matter is presented in this way because the married woman, by becoming an heiress, has acquired a quite new status, as a result of which her existing marriage has to be reaffirmed or abandoned'. This is not an explanation but a paraphrase, substituting for the concrete terms of the text the abstract nouns and adjectives which English prefers. What was it in her new status that cast doubt on her marriage? Dareste et al., I, 473-4, say that it is her new wealth, which enables her to find a better husband, but it seems odd for a marriage to be dissolved merely because one of the partners becomes rich; besides, the *patroiokos* is hardly given a broader choice than she had when her father was alive. Guarducci, IC IV, p.164 (ad loc.) postulates that the older law, like the Athenian, permitted the *epiballon* to dissolve the marriage where there were no children. This seems to go some distance towards explaining the text, but problems remain. λείοντος ὀπυίεν, 'while the husband wishes to (remain) married', seems to imply that the situation might be different if the husband also wanted a divorce, but why? and how? Cf. following note.
127. Dareste et al., loc. cit. proposed the *epiballon*, which seems strange, since he had no further rights to her property if she maintained her marriage, or to her person if she dissolved it. Guarducci, loc. cit. suggests her children; but why should it be necessary to divide with her own heirs? The only party who suffers financial loss by the divorce is her husband; but why should he get nothing if the marriage has not produced children? The answer may lie in the fact − if it is a fact − that marriage among the Greeks was not considered complete until the birth of children (see Wolff, *Traditio*, 46-50); but I can hardly offer this solution with certainty.
128. Lex Gort. VIII 30-6.
129. Lex Gort. VIII 42-53, XII 6-19. The new provisions of the latter passage also include 'orphan-judges' (ὀρπανοδικασταί), whose title indicates that they were state officials, but whose possible absence (XII 6-7) would seem to imply that they were specially appointed in each case, i.e., that they were state-appointed guardians. For this possibility cf. also IG IX^2 1 654 g, where a woman is ὀρφανοφύλαξ for her own children − very likely a private function rather than a true magistracy. Cf. below, p.132n.38.
130. A. C. Merriam, 'Law Code of the Kretan Gortyna', AJA 2 (1886) 40.

131. Diod. Sic. 12.15.
132. Diog. Laert. 1.56. In the case of an *epikleros*, whose heir could get the money by marrying her, the law may not have worried about murder.
133. ἐξ ἐπιτροπευομένης δὲ τούτω γενέσθαι, Isae. 6.13, cf. Wyse ad loc.; cf. also, for paternal uncles taking care of orphans, Isae. 10 Hyp., id. 1.9, Dem. 27.4.
134. Lex Gort. VII 29-35.
135. If it was the uncles, then they were entitled to half the income (see above), leaving nothing for the *patroiokos*; if it was the *patroiokos*, then it is odd that the house should be mentioned, for she in fact kept all the property.
136. Lex Gort. IX 1-7.
137. ibid. XI 31-45.
138. ibid. VIII 8-20.
139. This would explain why the town house usually was not inherited by women, but might be in the case of the *patroiokos*, who was restricted to marrying within her tribe (it is not known whether or not other women were so restricted). But cf. below, pp.86-7.

CHAPTER 4 : ECONOMIC AUTHORITY OF THE *KYRIOS*

1. See, e.g., IG XII 1 764, lines 25-6, 31-2, etc. But cf. below, p.150.
2. See IG XII 1 764, lines 39-40, 80-1, 84-5, 87, 88-9, 103-5, 123-5; in lines 108-9 a man gives independently once, and once in partnership with his brother, indicating that an estate might be shared in part while each brother retained property outside of the shared portion. I know of no epigraphical study of the question of shared inheritance – how common the practice was, what geographical and historical development it showed – but the evidence contained in lists such as these and in manumission-inscriptions, beside that of Attic and Gortynian law, would seem sufficient to repay such an investigation.
3. Such is the contention of the speaker of Isaeus 6, who speaks of 'the large estate (which) Euctemon owned with his son Philoctemon, big enough . . . for both of them to perform the greatest liturgies for you' (6.38). Wyse, 528 (ad loc.) maintains that 'Euctemon alone was the legal owner. "The estate of Philoctemon" is a fiction of the orator'; but the 'fiction' was sufficiently real to impose on Philoctemon a trierarchy on which he was killed (ibid.27), so he must have had some legal standing in the estate. His power to bequeath it, however, was contested by the speaker's opponents (ibid. 56). Euctemon, in any event, was certainly not his *kyrios*. It would seem from Dem. 41.4 that a similar situation obtained between Polyeuctus and his adopted son Leocrates, who finally separated 'with Leocrates taking back what he had brought into the estate'. Leocrates, before the separation, was able to make contracts as to the disposition of the estate after Polyeuctus' death (ibid. 5), but I do not know what his rights were during the latter's lifetime.
4. This was doubted by Hruza I, 69-72; he was followed by Beauchet I, 216-23, who stated that 'le kyrios conserve les pouvoirs qu'il avait antérieurement sur la femme, sauf ceux dont il a fait délégation expresse ou tacite au mari' (222). Hruza's argument was based on a concept of the term *kyrios* which

appears much too rigid, according to which the husband could not have been *kyrios* if he did not possess the right to give his wife in marriage. Beauchet saw the *kyrios* as holding an 'office' which should be the same regardless of its holder; but the Greeks were able to recognize that a man's relationship to his wife differs from his relationship to his daughter, and still to see him as head of his household. There is no evidence to indicate that a husband did not exercise the economic prerogatives of the *kyrios*, and we certainly find many husbands doing so; the claim that all these husbands were *kyrioi* by virtue of special appointment or of some other kinship seems weak. Cf. Wyse, 286-7; Lipsius, 484n.46. T. W. Beasley, 'The Κύριος in Greek States Other than Athens', CR 20 (1906) 252, cited IG XII 7 55 and 58 in support of Hruza; but he has misunderstood the use of the word *kyrios* in these inscriptions.

5. See Dem. 30.7, 57.41, in which the brothers, not the divorcing husband, perform the actual betrothal.

6. Father, IG VII 3327; brother, ibid. 3379, 3385, cf. 3198; husband, ibid. 3317, 3322, 3330, 3359, 3372, 3412, cf. 3199; son, ibid. 3311?, 3326, 3353, 3371.

7. ibid. 3331, 3333, 3366, 3367, 3374, 3377. In 3315 a *hiera* of the Mother of the Gods joins in the manumission without consent of the *hierarchos*.

8. ibid. 3329, 3357, 3365?, 3387, cf. 3199. In 3199 the husband and the son (or father-in-law) of one manumittor are present as 'friends' to the other; if the two women are related, as is suggested by their joint ownership of the slave, then the 'friends' are not complete outsiders. In 3329 one of the friends is Kallon, son of Timiadas, who must be, if not a brother, at least a relative of the woman, Kallo, daughter of Timiadas. Cf. ibid. 3381, where a freedwoman's manumittors act as her *kyrioi*.

9. The one exception is ibid. 3385, where both the woman's brother and her brother's sons are apparently present: the brother may himself have been retired, so that his sons were in fact his *kyrioi*.

10. Th. Homolle, 'La loi de Cadys sur le prêt à intérêt', BCH 50 (1926) 3-106 (=*Fouilles de Delphes* III, fasc.1, no.294). To show the reader what is known and what conjecture, I append the Greek text:

Γυ[ν]-
[αἴκα μὲν γυναι]κὶ δὲ μὴ χρῆσαι [αἴ κα] μὴ ἐπαωή[σ]-
[ηι ἑκατέραι ὁ] ἀνήρ. αἰ δὲ χήρα ε[ἲ γυν]ά τις, υἱὸν β-
[εβαιώσαι ἠβέ]οντος ἤτ[ο]ι ἐπ᾽ ἐ[γγυα]τᾶ ἐνὸς ἀνδρ-
[ὸς ἐξ ἀγχίστων] χρησάτ[ω].[17]

11. Men. *Aspis*. 133-6, 254-6. In the case of the *epikleros*, of course, no such leeway could be allowed, for the economic benefits that went to the girl's *kyrios* could lead to serious fights among her relatives.

Some scholars have attempted to learn the Athenian rules as to who was *kyrios* of a woman from the law quoted in (Dem.) 46.18 (Hruza I, 54-67; Beauchet II, 335-50); but this law (quoted above, p.34) deals only indirectly with the question, being primarily concerned with the legitimacy of marriage and the legitimacy of children (Wyse, 285; Wolff, *Traditio*, 75. The two are not exclusive). It seems furthermore to presume by the expression τὸν κύριον ἔχειν, 'the kyrios is to marry her', that the *kyrios* of a woman without father, brother, or grandfather is already determined. But it does indicate who was *kyrios* in the first instance as far as concerns the power of betrothal, and it is interesting to note that an inner circle is described – father, paternal grandfather, paternal brother – outside of which more leeway is allowed: ὅτῳ ἂν ἐπιτρέψῃ, 'that person to whom he shall turn her over'. For a good summary of the debate as to the 'he' who is the subject of the verb ἐπιτρέψῃ, see Wyse, 285-6; recent views are mentioned in Harrison I, 20n.3.

12. IG VII 3172, XII 3 330.
13. IG VII 3378, cf. 3358, 3359.
14. Note Bromias the flute-player, who receives 180 drachmas or more without a *kyrios* (IG XI 2 287, line 85; Ins. Dél. 290, line 107; 316, line 116, cf. IG XI 2 159 A, line 62; Ins. Dél. 372 A, line 98; 442 A, line 197; 444 A, line 28).
15. e.g., SGDI 2054, where a man's daughter consents to the manumission; 2017, where his wife, son, and daughter consent; and others. The only participle used of the *kyrios* is παρών, 'being present': the various verbs signifying agreement (συνευδοκῶν, συνευαρεστῶν, συνεπιχωρῶν, συνεπινεύων) are used to indicate the consent of third parties who claim, or who may in the future claim, an interest in the slave. See Dareste et al, II, 253-4, and H. Lewy, *De civili condicione mulierum graecarum*, Bratislava, 1885, 56-8.
16. IG IX² 1 616, 621, 636 b, 638.9, 639.2, 11, 12. There are others, of course, in which a man and woman manumit jointly (ibid. 624 e, f, 632, 638.11, 640 b), but these indicate nothing about the woman's competence to act alone.
17. IG IX¹ 1 122, 123. Each of these seems to include the 'agreement' (not as *kyria*) of another woman.
18. ibid. 109.
19. Dittenberger (ibid. ad loc.), noting that the slave is referred to only as the father's, not as the daughter's, suggests that 'nullum superstitem habebat Meneclia necessarium, qui post patris mortem tutoris (κυρίου) officium sustineret'; and so the city had to ratify her actions. But the job of the *kyrios* was not simply to approve transactions, but to safeguard the welfare of the family, provide maintenance, legal protection, etc. It is conceivable that women with no near relation might be put under the protection of a magistrate (though the rules determining the *kyrios* seem to have been lax enough in this case for her to be able to select one), but the functions of a *kyrios* would hardly be performed by decree of the senate and the people for each transaction – indeed, who would introduce such a motion, if not the girl's *kyrios*? Paris' suggestion (BCH 11 (1887) 339) that Stephanus had performed a service to the state is possible, though Dittenberger's objections to it are worth consideration; it is also possible that Lampron's inheritance was either divided or contested between Menecleia and the public treasury.
20. IG VII 3314. Ibid. 3345 seems to have no *kyrios*; but Dittenberger's reconstruction fits neither the normal formula (in which καὶ αὐτ[ή] has no place) nor the lengths of the other lines as he has reconstructed them. I have not seen the stone, but am dubious about considering this another exception.
21. IG VII 3198, 3199, 3307, 3309, 3330, 3379; cf. 3366, 3386, where the agreement of another party, not the *kyrios*, is similarly postponed.
22. ibid. 3172.

23. The reader who would like to choose among *a priori* arguments may see Beasley, 'The Κύριος', CR 20 (1906) 251.
24. IG XII 5 872 passim, 875, line 30.
25. ibid. 7 412.
26. SIG³ 1012, line 28; ibid. 1006; Paton and Hicks, *Inscriptions of Cos* (Oxford 1891), no.152.
27. IG XII 3 330.
28. Ins. Dél. 362 B, line 11; 406 B, lines 16, 25, 38, 46, etc.
29. C. Blinkenberg, *Lindos: Fouilles de l'acropole, 1902-1914* (W. de Gruyter, Berlin 1941) vol. II, part 1, no.51 a II lines 34-5, 54-5 (=IG XII 1 764, lines 98-9, 118-19), b I lines 11-12, c I lines 47-8, c II lines 44-5.
30. P. Le Bas, *Voyage archéologique* (Paris 1870) Partie V (Asie Mineure) no.323.
31. ibid. 415 (but here the girl is apparently a minor).
32. SIG³ 1014, lines 119-25.
33. SGDI 1356 (=RIJG II, 315 no.49). Dareste et al. are probably correct in seeing this as a form of manumission.
34. IG IV¹ 840; Cf. RIJG II, 114.
35. The payments and loans are as follows:

without *kyrios*	with *kyrios*
5 drachmas (IG XI 2 161 A, l. 93)	
5 dr. (Ins. Dél. 354, l. 52)	
8 dr. 1 obol (IG XI 2 203 A, l. 65)	
	10 dr. (IG XI 2 161 A, ll. 31-2)
10 dr. ½ ob. (ibid. 199 A, l. 11)	10 dr. ½ ob. (ibid. 158 A, l. 27)
	10 dr. ½ ob. (ibid. 162 A, l. 24)
	12 dr. 1 ob. (?) (Ins. Dél. 372 A, ll. 56-8)
20 dr. (5 ob.) (ibid. 158 A, l.26)	
20 dr. 5 ob. (ibid. 161 A, l. 30)	
25 dr. (ibid. 287 A, l. 194)	
	40 dr. (ibid. 443 C, ll. 16-22)
	59 dr. 5¼ ob. (IG XI 2 287 A, l. 182)
	130 dr. (Ins. Dél. 354, l. 41)
	150 dr. (ibid. 362 B, l. 11)
	300 dr. (ibid. 399, ll. 122-3)
	833 dr. 2¼ ob. (IG XI 2 287 A, ll. 14-15)

36. Ins. Dél. 354, ll. 41, 52.
37. IG XI 2 162 A, lines 23-4; 199 A, line 11.
38. IG IX² 1 654 g. I believe that the word ὀρφανοφύλαξ must be taken here to mean no more (or at best little more) than ἐπίτροπος, 'guardian', despite its use elsewhere (Xen.? *de Vect*. 2.7) of a magistracy (probably the archon or the polemarch: cf. Arist. *Ath. Pol.* 56.6-7, (Dem.) 43.75, Lang. Scholia Augustana ad Dem., 172, references which do not seem to leave room for another magistracy dealing with orphans, and note as well the absence of any such magistracy from any of the speeches of the orators in which mistreated orphans are discussed, e.g. Dem. 27-9, Isae. 11). The scholiast on Soph. *Ajax* 512 recognizes both meanings for ὀρφανιστής: ὀρφανισταί, ἀρχὴ

Ἀθήνησι τὰ τῶν ὀρφανῶν κρινοῦσα· ἢ ὀρφανιστῶν, τῶν τῆς ὀρφανίας
ἐπιτρόπων.
39. SIG³ 1014, lines 119-25.
40. IG VII 3317.
41. Ins. Dél. 442 A, lines 213-14; cf. ibid., p.347, 'Additions et corrections' ad
    loc.
42. Isae. 10.10. The limit of a medimnus of barley apparently applies to the
    woman only; the child's incapacity was presumably absolute.
43. Scholiast on Ar. *Eccl.* 1026; the Aristophanes passage itself is an obvious
    allusion to the law.
44. Dio Chrys. 74.9.
45. L. J. Th. Kuenen-Janssens, 'Some Notes upon the Competence of the Athe-
    nian Woman to Conduct a Transaction', *Mnemosyne* (3rd Ser.) 9 (1941) 199-
    214. Those who see a glass as being half-full will agree with Kuenen-Janssens
    that 'women had considerable freedom of action corresponding to the gener-
    ally accepted importance of the part they played within the house' (ibid.
    214); those to whom the glass is half-empty will say with Wolff that 'Athe-
    nian women lived a modest life in seclusion' (Wolff, *Traditio*, 46). Both have
    in mind, as G. E. M. de Ste. Croix points out ('Some Observations on the
    Property Rights of Athenian Women', CR 20 (N.S.) (1970) 278), only that
    economic class that could often have spent larger sums had the law allowed
    it.
46. Lys. 31.21. For the value of a medimnus of barley, see below, p.136nn.9-11.
47. Dem. 41.8-9.
48. id. 36.14-15.
49. IG II² 1672, line 64.
50. See below, p.137n.32.
51. Fine, chapter 1, no.28. The reading of this stone is most uncertain (see the
    comments of Finley, 188), but the word πληρώτρια does seem to occur,
    and its only likely meaning, particularly in view of the context, is 'organizer
    of (or, less likely here, 'contributor to') an *eranos*-loan – in the feminine.
52. A. Desjardins, 'De la condition de la femme dans le droit civil des Athéniens',
    *Mémoires lus à la Sorbonne dans les séances extraordinaires du Comité Impé-
    rial des Travaux Historiques et des Sociétés des Savants. Histoire, Philologie
    et Sciences Morales,* 8 (1865) 616-18.
53. For the date of the speech see Wyse, 652.
54. Ar. *Plut.* 986.
55. Lys. 31.21; on the date of the speech see Gernet's note (Lysias, *Discours,* ed.
    L. Gernet and M. Bizos (Paris 1967) vol. II, 173).
56. Wyse, 659-60, hesitates before agreeing with the common opinion; de Ste.
    Croix, loc.cit. (above, n.45), 274-6 is the only scholar to disagree.
57. IG II² 1558, lines 63-5; cf. ibid. 1570, lines 3-5, which may be either a
    woman or a child.
58. Fine, chapter 1, no.12.
59. E.g., προικὸς ἀποτίμημα Τιμοδίκε[ι] Φιλίππου Ἀναγυρ(ασίου) θυγατρί, IG
    II² 2662.
60. This is the explanation of Finley, 183. It is also possible that the mixed form
    of the stone (*apotimema,* not *prasis epi lysei,* was the usual way to secure a

dowry) indicates that the stone was set up after divorce or the husband's death, when the repayment of the dowry was due, the *kyrios* having accepted a delay for a set time on security of the land.

61. As he could elsewhere: cf., e.g., Ins. Dél. 372 A, lines 132-4.

62. Dem. 41.8-9.

63. Van den Es, *De jure familiarum apud Athenienses* (Lugd. Bat., 1864), 160-1, followed by Beauchet II, 354-5; Lipsius, 535n.72; Erdmann, 55; Kuenen-Janssens, 'Some Notes . . .', *Mnemosyne* (3rd Ser.) 9 (1941) 202; Harrison I, 114n.1.

64. Dem. 41.9.

65. id. 36.14. If Isaeus' law was the basis of Apollodorus' claim, this would explain why he waited until Archippe's death: he could now claim that part of the money should be returned to him, as one of Archippe's heirs. But see below, pp.69-70.

66. Lys. 31.21. It would have been much more disgraceful if Philo had formally approved the instructions for someone else to bury his mother, and the speaker would probably have mentioned it if it were true.

67. (Dem.) 50.60. She was able to make the gifts to her other sons, since Phormio did not object to them; that she seems to have given each only a quarter-share (see below, p.140n.88) suggests that Apollodorus was, for once, telling the truth.

68. This is true of Archippe (otherwise Apollodorus would have been justified in his argument that Phormio could not marry her, (Dem.) 46.13), and apparently of Artemis the reed-seller and Elephantis the cloak-seller (see below, p.137n.33).

69. Isae. 7.31, cf. 44.

70. Dem. 27.55.

71. It is not certain whether a woman might be *epikleros* to her brother or grand-father, and Hruza I, 118 was probably correct in his judgement: 'hier heisst es sich bescheiden und die ars nesciendi üben'. (Later writers have expressed themselves with more certainty, as Wyse, 655-6, Harrison I, 113, and de Ste. Croix, loc. cit. (above, n.45), 276, but not because any new evidence has appeared on the question). Still, there were certainly heiresses who were not *epikleroi* by the Gortynian definition, and who were hardly likely to be adjudicable: a uterine sister, for example, might inherit while her own father and brothers were still alive.

72. Lest the reader wish to eliminate this possibility *a priori*, I am grateful to Mr de Ste Croix for informing me that much of a woman's property under English common law became the freely alienable property of her husband, reverting to her at his death only if he had not disposed of it. The law was first reformed in 1870: see the Encyclopaedia Britannica, Eleventh Edition (1910) vol. 14, s.v. 'Husband and Wife', pp.2-3.

73. Lex Gort. IV 48-51, V 1-3. Cf. below, p.148n.114.

74. Lex Gort. XI 14-17, XII 1-5; cf. below, p.87.

75. Lex Gort. VIII 20-21.

76. ibid. III 44 - IV 17. The law deals only with children born after divorce, and does not attempt to enforce the husband's authority during marriage; but cf. below, p.59.

77. Lex Gort. IV 18-23.
78. This may be the legal meaning of Lex Gort. II 20-4; but it is not the grammatical meaning (the grammar refers not to the woman's family, but to the scene of the crime), and other interpretations have been proposed.
79. ibid. VI 2-31.
80. The father is probably not mentioned there: see above, p.49.
81. Willetts, ad loc., misinterprets the clause τὰ μὲν κρέματα ἐπὶ τᾶι ματρὶ ἔμεν κ' ἐπὶ τᾶι γυναικί ('the property is to belong to the mother and to the wife') when he writes, 'The father or son is deprived of all rights over the property of other members of the family as a first penalty'. The entire point of the law is that no such rights exist – not that they belong to the husband, but are transferred to the wife if he should exercise them!
82. Isae. 6.38.
83. Men. *Dysc.* 731-40.
84. IG VII 3309, 3312.
85. γέροντας...ἀφειμένους: Arist. *Pol.* 1275 a 14-19. See further Lacey, 130-1.
86. That a woman might be able to handle property before marriage is indicated by the provision empowering the *patroiokos* to sell or mortgage property ἐ αὐ[τὰν ἐ διὰ τὸν]ς πάτροαν[ς καὶ τὸ]νς μάτροανς ('either in person or through her paternal or maternal relatives') in order to free her estate of debt (Lex Gort. IX 1-7). Whether the girl was to sell the property herself or through her relatives probably depended on her age; but her relatives are prohibited in any event from selling or mortgaging her property beyond the value of the debt (this is presumably what is forbidden by ibid. 7-24). This restriction is another innovation (ibid. 15-17), quite in line with the others we have discussed.
87. ibid. IV 23-7.
88. cf. Cicero, *Pro Flacco* 30.74; Gaius, *Inst.* I 193. The 'Greek law' of the Ptolemaic and Roman empires included the *kyrios* in a somewhat changed and limited role: see M. R. Taubenschlag, 'La compétence du κύριος dans le droit gréco-égyptien', *Archives d'histoire du droit oriental* 2 (1938) 293-314.

CHAPTER 5 : EXCHANGE AND DISPOSITION

1. Scholia on Ar. *Plut.* 426, 1120 restrict the term *kapelis* to a wine-seller, but Aristophanes himself (*Plut.* 1121-2) contradicts them. Cf. the *pandokeutriai* of id. *Ran.* 549-78, and the inventory a demigod could consume: sixteen loaves of bread, twenty pieces of boiled meat at half an obol apiece, all that garlic – not to mention all that smoked fish, and the poor green cheese!
2. Herfst, 40-8. The seller of reeds is Artemis from Piraeus, IG II² 1672, line 64, of whom more later; the caps (πῖλοι) were sold by Thettale, ibid. lines 70-1. A few more trades of the same sort can be added from later sources: see Herfst, loc. cit.
3. SIG³ 1177 (=IG III¹ App. 69).
4. IG II² 1561, lines 22-30.
5. Dem. 57.31: 'We admit . . . that we sell ribbons'.
6. Pherecrates, fr. 64 Kock; but see below. The fragment adds that 'no one has ever seen a butcheress or a fishmongress'.
7. See the list of trades in Herfst, 48-52. The terms ἀρτόπωλις, λαχανόπωλις

and λεκιθόπωλις should be included on the feminine side on page 49, cf. pp.42-3. Perhaps *σκοροδόπωλις ('garlic seller'), too, should be inferred from Aristophanes' invention σκοροδοπανδοκευτριαρτοπώλιδες (*Lys.* 458); Herfst counts, for example, the ἰσχαδόπωλις of ibid. 564, who is really no less imaginary. Not every masculine noun implies a masculine tradesman (Ar. fr. 256 Kock, for example, μήτ' ἄρα μ' εὖαι ἐγκριδοπώλην, attests a male character in a comedy, not a male cake-seller in the market), and not every entry in a mediaeval lexicon informs us of the sex of the people referred to; but even restricting ourselves to tradesmen identified by sex in ancient sources, we find a predominance of men.

The belief of Becker (*Charikles*, neu bearbeitet von Hermann Göll (Berlin 1877-88) II, 199-202) that there was a special section of the market, the *gynaikeia agora*, set aside for women merchants is not likely: see Herfst, 38-40.

8. Ath. XIII 612 a-e (=Lys. fr. 1 Thalheim), XV 687 a.
9. IG II^2 1672, lines 282-3. This is a price set by the *demos* for the sale of grain by the treasurers of the Eleusinian goddesses, and it may be artificially low. At an earlier period the price seems to have been even lower. Blepyrus could have bought a sixth of a medimnus of wheat with his three obols from the ecclesia (Ar. *Eccl.* 547-8) at the beginning of the century, which would give three drachmas for a medimnus and less, presumably, for a medimnus of barley. The price of a medimnus – we are not told of what – in Solon's day was one drachma (Plut. *Solon* 23).
10. A third of 18 ((Dem.) 42.20, 31); we should not press the exactitude of this figure.
11. ibid.
12. Ar. *Ran.* 553-4. This was not quite all he ate, but I suspect it would have been quite enough for mortal customers – perhaps even for an immortal of moderate appetite.
13. id. *Vesp.* 1391. Kuenen-Janssens, 'Some Notes upon the Competence of the Athenian Woman to Conduct a Transaction', *Mnemosyne*, Third Series, 9 (1941) 213, suggests that this was her whole inventory, but he has no grounds for this, as he admits. We do not know how large the inventory of a booth in the *agora* might have been, nor would this passage help, even were it dealing with a real personnage.
14. IG II^2 1672, lines 70-1.
15. Such was the trade in animals, metal goods, clothing, and building materials.
16. Ar. *Ran.* 857-8.
17. Id. *Plut.* 426-8. Herfst, 105 cites in a similar vein id. *Vesp.* 36, *Lys.* 456-60.
18. Herfst, loc.cit., cites *Thesm.* 347-8, *Plut.* 435-6, and Pl. *Leg.* XI 918 d; but he fails to notice the class prejudice of the remarks. This was surely not how the tradesmen saw themselves, and they were not a negligible portion of the *demos*.
19. Dem. 57.31.
20. δουλικὰ καὶ ταπεινὰ πράγματα, ibid. 45, cf. Xen. *Mem.* 2.7.6.
21. Dem., loc. cit. 30. That such a law had to be passed at all is an indication that tradeswomen were still susceptible to abuse. 'Respectability' is always relative.

22. ibid. 31, 34. If the law adduced in 31 has been correctly quoted, it would appear from 34 to have been superseded.
23. IG XII 1 1210-1441, 2 577-638. The one that seems to be a woman is 1 1402, 2 617 Τιμοῦς (=gen. of Τιμώ). Most of these amphorae originate from Rhodes.
24. ibid. IV² 1 102-20, SEG XI 417a, XV 207, 208, XXIV 227, XXV 383-406. One woman receives six drachmas for bleaching linen (SEG XV 208 A, line 70), the other five drachmas, 2½ obols for, probably, the same task (ibid. line 71).
25. See the inscriptions collected by M. Crosby, 'The Leases of the Laureion Mines', *Hesperia* 19 (1950) 189-312, and the index provided on pages 298-306.
26. IG XI 2 161 A, line 93; 203 A, line 65. The meaning of ταινία in the Delos inscriptions is not certain (see LSJ s.v.).
27. Ins. Dél. 440 A, line 35; cf. 447, line 13.
28. ibid. 442 A, lines 206-7. The woman of Ar. *Ran.* 1346-51, on the other hand, appears to have sold her work herself.
29. *Fouilles de Delphes* III, fasc. 5, nos.19-77.
30. IG I² 373-4.
31. IG II² 1672, lines 64, 71. There are no women in ibid. 1673.
32. IG II² 11254. For the relative value of a *himation* and a medimnus of barley, cf. ibid. 1672, lines 282-3 (where a medimnus of barley sells for three drachmas) and 1673, lines 45-6 (where *exomides*, skimpy outer garments, sell for seven drachmas and change). A *himation* (probably a good one, and perhaps comically inflated) costs twenty drachmas in Ar. *Plut.* 982-3.
33. Neither name is attested for an Attic citizen woman; and the normal style for a demeswoman of Piraeus would have been ἡ δεῖνα τοῦ δεῖνος Πειραιῶς (as in IG II² 7162, 7171/2, 7177, 7200), not (as here) ἡ δεῖνα ἐκ Πειραιῶς.
34. IG VII 3172.
35. This is not stated in the *hyperameriai*, the overdue promissory notes, in lines 162-76; but these are presented in very abbreviated form. The *kyrios* is mentioned in other documents of the series, lines 2-4, 49-51.
36. This explanation, which is that of Dittenberger in IG, presumes that there was not another loan whose terms were omitted after the word σουνάλλαγμα in line 176. If there was (see RIJG I, 280n.1, and 294-5), Nicareta may have made no profit at all on the loan.
37. Note the plural τᾶν οὐπεραμεριάων τᾶν ἐπὶ Ξενοκρίτω, 'the overdue notes from the year of Xenocritus' archonship' (lines 58-60, cf. 73-5, 98, 123-4, 157-8), though only one of the notes is so dated; but this probably refers to all the debts ('the notes since Xenocritus was archon'), since it is used interchangeably with τὰς οὐπεραμερίας ἃς ἔχι κατ τὰς πόλιος, 'the overdue notes which she holds against the city' (lines 73-4, cf. 80-1, 115, 133-4, 146-7), and the others would not have been inscribed if they were not part of the agreement.
38. Two years is a minimum, from Alalcomenius of the archonship of Xenocritus at Thespiae (line 162) to Alalcomenius of the year of Epiteles (line 94), with the year of Luciscus (lines 166, 169, 176) intervening; the time elapsed may have been longer. The sum of 1247 dr. 4 ob. is, on the other hand, a maximum; see above, n.36.

39. The Boeotian calendar was presumably the same for all parts of Boeotia, and I do not know the procedure for intercalation; but it is possible that the town of Orchomenus may have requested the extra month from the responsible body.
40. The inscription dates from between 222 and 200 (Dittenberger ad loc.).
41. SEG XXII 432.
42. IG VII 3054.
43. ibid. 2383.
44. SEG III 356, 359.
45. IG VII 3171, 3173.
46. SEG III 342.
47. SIG³ 544.
48. Ar. *Thesm.* 839-45.
49. Dem. 41.7-9, 21.
50. Segre, *Annuario della Regio scuola archeologica italiana di Atene* 15-16 (1932-3) page 298, no.6 (=Finley, no.10), from Lemnos. τὴν θεμένην is to be supplied as the subject of ἔχεω καὶ κρατεῖν, as in IG II² 2758 and 2759, the only other *horoi* in which a similar provision appears. It is not entirely certain that a woman is the creditor; cf. Segre, loc. cit., 299.
51. See Finley, pp.12-13.
52. IG XII 7 412, from Amorgos. Two other *horoi* of Amorgos in which women seem to take part in the loan are not actually dealing with their property: see below, p.85.
53. The sources mention the payment of a fine (Antiph. *Tetr.* A β 9), redemption from captivity ((Dem.) 52.8, 11), the buying of a slave's freedom (id. 59.31) and the dowering of a daughter (Nep. *Epam.* 3.5); there must have been other cases as well.
54. Fine, chapter 1, no.28; cf. the comments of Finley, 188. The *eranos* mentioned in IG XII 7 58, line 8 is usually taken to be a fraternal association which is acting as a creditor. Finley, 101-2, attempts to explain it as an *eranos*-loan, but his explanation leaves many questions unanswered. Most importantly for us, he provides no plausible explanation for the presence of the wife of the 'president' (the *archeranos*) if we are in fact dealing with a loan made by an ad hoc group, rather than a club in which women had a regular place. The presence of the borrower's wife, on the other hand, is normal, particularly if the loan was secured by land mortgaged for her dowry.
55. (Dem.) 59.31.
56. IG XI 2 135-289; Ins. Dél. 290-498.
57. Included in this category are one man who borrows with the agreement of another man (IG XI 2 287 A, line 127), one whose *kyrios* is his father (apparently a minor, Ins. Dél. 372 A, line 132), one whose partner is unidentifiable (ibid. 396 A, line 38), a borrower whose sex is unknown, whose loan is agreed to by a man and wife (ibid. 407, line 31), and a borrower of uncertain sex who borrows with a *kyrios* (ibid. 442 A, line 217). Other borrowers of uncertain sex are not tabulated.
58. IG XI 2 158 A, line 26; cf. ibid. 161 A, line 30.
59. ibid. 158 A, line 27, and 161 A, lines 31-2.
60. ibid. 199 A, line 11.
61. ibid. C, line 97.

62. ibid. 287 A, line 186.
63. ibid., lines 14-15.
64. Ins. Dél. 354, line 41.
65. ibid., line 52.
66. ibid. 362 B, line 11.
67. At least, all those we can trace; the *kyrios* of Astyphose (ibid. 407, line 39) has not been preserved.
68. ibid. 406 B, lines 25, 49; 442 A, line 213 (cf. ibid. p.347, note ad loc.).
69. The evidence for the period of Athenian domination (IG I^2 377, II^2 1633-53) does not show any women debtors, but it is too fragmentary to be of use.
70. Lex Gort. XI 18-19.
71. Isae. 7.25. Wyse doubts even as much as is asserted by Isaeus ('That an adoption affected in no respect a man's legal relations with his mother, must not be accepted as an axiom of Athenian law merely because it is asserted by Isaeus', 563). There is, however, no reason to deny it, and Wyse himself is willing to use it against Isaeus (669, ad Isae. 10.25). Note that the speaker of (Dem.) 43 – himself, of course, no impartial witness – appears to claim the same when he styles his own son the son of Eubulides and of Phylomache (ibid. 49).
72. Isae. 10.10.
73. We must remember on the one hand that the archon apparently disagreed with him about the validity of the adoption (Wyse, 651), and on the other, that his opponents were not claiming to inherit through a will made by a minor, so he had no reason to misrepresent the law.
74. Thus, rightly, de Ste. Croix, 'Some Observations on the Property Rights of Athenian Women', CR 20 (N.S.) (1970) 274.
75. Lys. 31.21.
76. For the men's rights (at least), see Arist. *Pol.* 1270 a 21.
77. IG IV^1 840. The inscription never mentions the fact that it is a will, but its editors have rightly presumed it to be one; biennial sacrifices in one's own name were not, as far as I know, established for the living. Cf. ibid. 841, where a man and wife jointly make a similar dedication.
78. IG XII 3 330. Ibid. 329 probably also refers to a will.
79. ibid. 7 57.
80. Thus Dareste et al., II, 114.
81. Schulin, *Das griechische Testament verglichen mit dem römischen* (Basel 1882) 43.
82. Lex Gort. IV 43-6.
83. ibid. VI 31-46.
84. See above, pp.58-60.
85. It is usually presumed that she returned to her brothers' house, making them her *kyrioi*; but this opinion, derived from Dem. 41.9, is not justified by that passage (see above, pp.55-6). There was no reason for Polyeuctus' wife to leave her children's house – she did not remarry – and I doubt whether she did.
86. Dem. 36.32.
87. ibid. 14-15.
88. Davies, 434, reckons that since the items mentioned at the beginning of the

will (all that was technically included in the dowry, according to Wolff's
punctuation (Wolff, RE, 138), which Davies does not mention) are worth
3 tal. 4000 dr., and since Apollodorus' quarter-share was 5000 dr., 'the
whole cannot have much exceeded the value of the major items'; but in fact
on this calculation the whole would have to be less than the sum of the
'major items', and the speaker of Dem. 36 has no reason to minimize the
sums Apollodorus has already received. In fact, the 5000 dr. consisted, as
the speaker says (Dem. 36.14), of two claims, one for 2000 dr. and one for
3000 dr. The first was a claim for his quarter-share of the 'maids and the
jewelry', which were indeed worth 8000 dr. (cf. προῖκα πέντε τάλανϑ',
(Dem.) 45.74; this calculation is suggested by Davies, loc. cit., but he rejects
it because he presumes that the dowry is in question) and of which Phormio's sons had already received their portion; the 3000 dr. was a separate
claim, perhaps based on the last clause of the will ('whatever else she has in
my house').

89. (Dem.) 46.19.
90. ibid. 50.60.
91. Ar. *Plut.* 975-92.
92. Dem. 25.56.
93. SGDI 5366.
94. ibid. 1260, 1261. Later, these gifts became more common: examples are
    given by Thompson, 169n.3.
95. Polyb. 38.15.6 (ed. Buettner-Wobst).
96. The donors, of course, dedicated the whole statue, but in most cases only
    the inscribed base is identifiable.
97. There are exceptions: a few victresses (see above, p.13), or a woman dedi-
    cating a relative's trophy, as in IG IV^1 801.
98. e.g., ibid. IV^2 1 208. The number of dedication-inscriptions is far too vast
    to permit a complete survey within the confines of this study; I shall restrict
    myself, in the footnotes, to giving an illustration of each point mentioned.
99. IG VII 55.
100. IG V 2 551.
101. IG VII 43.
102. IG V 2 461.
103. IG IV^1 840.
104. ibid. 241; IG VII 55, 249.
105. IG V 2 74.
106. ibid. 68.
107. IG VII 303, line 57.
108. IG II^2 1338 A, lines 37-9.
109. Roehl, *Inscriptiones Graecae Antiquissimae* (Berlin 1882) nos.45, 407.
110. IG II^2 1338 A, lines 24-6. 1300 drachmas = about six kilograms, figuring
     the drachma = 4.57 grams (Metrologicorum Scriptorum Reliquiae, ed.
     F. Hultsch (Leipzig 1864), *non vidi*; cited in M. Lang and M. Crosby, *The
     Athenian Agora vol. X: Weights, Measures and Tokens* (Princeton 1964)
     44n.10).
111. IG II^2 776. Her husband was crowned, too, though no special benefactions
     of his are mentioned.

112. IG XII 5 186.
113. IG VII 303.
114. ibid. 3498.
115. By Foucart, 'Mémoire sur l'affranchissement des esclaves, par forme de vente à une divinité, d'après les inscriptions de Delphes', *Archive des missions scientifiques et littéraires*, 2ᵉ série, 3 (1866) 379-80, and by T. W. Beasley, loc. cit. (above, p.130n.4) 251.
116. IG XII 1 764, lines 98-9, 118-19; see further the references above, p.132n.29.
117. IG XII 7 57. The words καὶ κυρίου Ναυκράτους were omitted in the original publication, causing later scholars (as Beasley, loc. cit.) to draw precisely the wrong conclusions.
118. IG XII 3 330, lines 3-4. The *kyrios* is repeated in the following decree (lines 110-12); no *kyrios* is mentioned in ibid. 329, a similar decree without the text of the will.
119. IG VII 43.
120. IG IV¹ 840. Beasley adds an example from Mantinea of Roman date.
121. Men. *Dysc*. 262-3.
122. A similar argument forbids us to draw conclusions from tombstones set up by women (as, e.g., IG IV¹ 801 or SEG XI 1139).

CHAPTER 6 : THE DOWRY

1. Men. *Peric*. 1013-14; cf. id. *Dysc*. 842-3, *Mis*. 444-5, *Sam*. 727.
2. (Dem.) 46.18, cf. Dem. 36.32.
3. Family relationship, And. 1.119; because of her family's character or pedigree, Lys. 19.14, 16, Pl. *Politicus* 310 b-c; for her money, Men. fr. 593 Koerte (=654 Kock); for her good nature, Men. fr. 581 Koerte (= 532 Kock); and, of course, for love, throughout New Comedy. Plato, loc. cit., recommends choosing a wife whose virtues are opposite to your own; like most eugenic schemes, this does not seem to have been followed by many.
4. Family relationship, Isae. 7.11-12, (Dem.) 44.10; family friendship, Isoc. 19. 46; his money, Didot Papyrus I 20-21 (= (Eur.) fr. 953 Nauck); his character, Lys. 19.15. Compare the criterion of the Grouch: (GORGIAS.) He says he will give her away in marriage when he gets a groom whose manners are like his. (SOSTRATUS.) You mean never. (Men. *Dysc*. 336-8).
5. This is the order in which they are cited in the law of betrothal in (Dem.) 46.18. It is not specified that the later-mentioned function only in absence of the former, and it is possible that no other law said so either; but that appears to have been the normal case. The plot of Plautus' *Trinummus* implies that the father could delegate his power for the period of his absence, as Charmides does to Callicles.
6. The entire subject of the dowry has been very ably treated by Wolff, RE, to which the interested reader is referred. The present discussion will concern itself with the dowry only in its effects upon the woman 'along with' whom it was given.
7. For the range of attested dowries, see Appendix I.
8. Lysias 19.14, 16.
9. Isae. 7.11.
10. (Dem.) 59.8; cf. ibid. 112-13, id. 40.4, Dem. 28.21.

11. Herodotus 6.122.2. This paragraph, which does not appear in the best manuscripts, has been bracketed by editors, but whether or not it is by Herodotus, it is certainly of ancient and not mediaeval origin. The author of the paragraph is attempting to demonstrate the wealth and magnificence of Callias; this is why he mentions his Olympic and Pythian victories, and why he calls his gift to his daughters μεγαλοπρεπεστάτην.

12. Isoc. 16.31.

13. Isae. 3.25, 29; 11.40; cf. Wolff, RE, 141. Menander mentions the importance of a dowry in choosing a wife; Stobaeus, typically, has preserved fragments of his both opposing (fr. 581 Koerte (=532 Kock)) and supporting it (fr. 593 Koerte (=654 Kock)).

14. Dem. 27.15.

15. For the clearest explanation of the suit for maintenance (δίκη σίτου) see Wolff, RE, 154-6.

16. Wolff, *Traditio*, 63; id., RE, 147-50; cf. Lipsius, 484.

17. Men. *Epit.* 1063-7.

18. (Dem.) 47.56-8, for all the woman's objections, gives no sign of any legal claim she could advance against the creditors; and the entire case of Demosthenes against Onetor (Dem. 30-1) rests upon his right to attach Aphobus' wife's dowry – a right that was not questioned by the opposition.

19. For the last, see Lys. 19.32.

20. (Dem.) 47.57.

21. id. 40.25.

22. Dem. 30.12. The contradiction between these passages and the well-attested rights of the husband led to a good deal of debate between those (e.g. Caillemer, Dar.-Sag. II a s.v. Dos, p.392 (1892)) who saw the husband as possessing rights in a dowry that was technically the wife's property, and those (most recently Wolff, *Traditio*, 53-60) for whom the dowry, though inseparable from certain obligations of the husband's, was nevertheless his property. Recent English-speaking scholars have resorted to vagueness: 'In a sense, the wife "owned" the dowry' says Finley, 50, and he is echoed by Harrison I, 113: 'her dowry was in some sense *hers*'. Wolff is, I believe, correct in asserting that the Athenians had no concept of *ius in re aliena*; in fact, they dealt little with conceptualized law. The question to ask in Athens is not 'who owns this?' but 'who can do what with this?' – a question that includes Wolff's ('who is *kyrios*?'), but by not limiting itself to formal legal power permits us to see why, and in what sense, an Athenian woman might consider her dowry to be 'hers'.

23. A slave, of course, was likely to be more attached to the mistress in whose house he grew up than to the master; such is Clytemnestra's slave, whom she calls 'mine', in Eur. *Iph. Aul.* 870.

24. Men. fr. 579 Koerte (=583 Kock); cf. id. fr. 577 Koerte (=582 Kock).

25. Plut. *Mor.* 13 f.

26. Eur. fr. 775 Nauck (=lines 158-9 in Eur., *Phaethon*, ed. James Diggle (Cambridge 1970); cf. Diggle's comments ad loc. His interpretation of the line is not, of course, certain as long as its context is missing. The word used here is φερνή, instead of the usual προίξ. On the difference see Appendix II.

27. cf. also Anaxandrides fr. 52 Kock, lines 4-6; Antiphanes fr. 329 Kock; Plaut.

As. 87, *Aul.* 167-9, 583, *Men.* 766-7; and Plato's claim that in his state, where dowries would be abolished, 'there would be less abuse of wives and less base and servile money-induced slavery for the husbands' (*Leg.* VI 775 c).

28. What he had to return was not the particular items given to him, but their monetary value, which was estimated at the time the dowry was given (τιμήσας, Isae. 3.35); see Wolff, RE 137.

29. Xen. *Oec.* 7.13.

30. Men. *Dysc.* 827-34.

31. Theoph. *Char.* 28.4; cf. ibid. 22.10. There is some uncertainty as to which day, exactly, is meant by the Greek expression I have rendered as 'New Year's Day', but all the candidates are in the winter.

32. Men. *Epit.* 134-7.

33. For his power to do so, for which the chief evidence is this play, see R. Taubenschlag in *Zeitschrift der Savigny-Stiftung für Rechtsgeschichte, Romanistische Abteilung* 46 (1926) 75, and Harrison I, 30-1; Wolff, *Traditio*, 47 n.23 hesitates to rely on the available evidence, none of which is clearly dealing with legal rights.

34. Men. *Epit.* 714-15.

35. Ten talents, plus another ten talents at the birth of a son. To get an idea of the size of this dowry, see Appendix I. The largest sum otherwise attested for the classical period, excluding testamentary dowries, is 100 minae, or 1.67 talents (Dem. 45.66; Boeotus may have claimed a slightly larger dowry, (Dem.) 40.20, but cf. ibid. 7, 14). Note here, too, the implication that the behaviour was the more heinous in one who had received such a dowry.

36. (And.) 4.14.

37. Plut. *Alc.* 8.6.

38. See Appendix I. These may not always represent the whole dowry.

39. Lys. 19.14, cf. Isae. 3.38. Isae. 2.5 and (Dem.) 40.20-7 have litigants denying the claim that their mother had no dowry. The dowry was apparently common enough in the class from which the orators (and the dicasts, if they were writing for their audience) came; but while they treat its absence as a sign that no marriage took place in the case at hand, none of them makes the claim (which would be much simpler, could it have been put over) that there were no marriages without dowries. Poor women in the comedies may lack dowries: see Men. *Dysc.* 842-7, Ter. *Adel.* 729.

40. Finley, 80.

41. Isae. 8.35. This figure is stated after payment of the dowry, and it excludes debts owed to Ciron at his death; his total fortune at the time of the marriage (assuming that no great changes had taken place since then) would have been somewhat more than two talents. For much of the following discussion I am indebted to Thompson, 106-13.

42. ibid. 8.

43. Isae. 3.49, 51. The emphasis is on εἰσποίητος, 'adopted': since the estate would have gone to her children had he not been adopted, he would not be so inconsiderate as to give her a niggardly dowry from it. The speaker is assuming in 49 what he correctly denies in 50, that an adopted brother could give away a legitimate sister. He is not contradicting himself, but merely arguing, 'Even could Endius have given her away, he would hardly

have dared do it like this. But in fact he could not give her away at all and still keep the estate.'

44. Dem. 30.10, 31.1.
45. id. 27.5, 11-13.
46. Lys. 32.6, cf. ibid. 15.
47. (Dem.) 45.74; cf. above, p.140n.88.
48. Dem. 36.5.
49. This is probably not the upper limit. There obviously must have been some such limit; noteworthy in this connection is Apollodorus' attack on Stephanus, that 'having a fortune great enough to give 100 minae's dowry with his daughter, he has not been seen to perform any liturgy whatsoever for (the city)' (Dem. 45.66). Since an estate would have to amount to less than three talents to be exempt from liturgies (Isae. 3.80), Apollodorus clearly does not think that so small an estate was 'great enough to give 100 minae's dowry', more than half the total. This, then, will give us an idea of how large a proportion of the estate might be, at least in this class, considered out of the question at Athens (Thompson, 107). Of course, it is possible that even a much smaller proportion would have provoked similar comment.
50. See Appendix I.
51. Stratocles, who left five talents and thirty minae (Isaeus 11.42), left his son a fortune which Theopompus claimed was as large as his own (ibid. 39) — that is, about 3 talents and 40 minae (ibid. 44), which means that the dowries of his four daughters (ibid. 37) came to about 110 minae or less — less than 30 minae apiece (thus Thompson, 110-11). Had he had only one daughter, her dowry would probably have been more than thirty minae, but surely less than 110.
52. See pp.142n.11, 77 and 143n.34. Cf. Davies, pp.254-70.
53. SIG^3 1215, where a number of fathers do not have the money in hand at all.
54. Men. *Dysc*. 842-7. Gorgias is offering a poor man's dowry; in the real world it would be a princely sum, but in the inflated world of Menander, no smaller sum is attested.
55. Plut. *Solon* 20.6.
56. See Appendix III.
57. SIG^3 1215, lines 7-8, 17, 23-4.
58. Lys.19.59.
59. Wyse, 651.
60. ὤν...χρηστός, Men. *Aspis* 130.
61. Pl. *Epist*. 13 361 d-e. The authenticity of the letter is disputed; if it is a forgery, it cannot tell us any more than that such consideration was conceivable, which, of course, we already knew.
62. Dem. 19.192-6.
63. ibid. 195.
64. Dem. 45.54, 75; Isae. 11.37.
65. Aeschin. 3.258, Plut. *Arist*. 27.1-2, cf. ibid. 6; Thompson, 111-12. The story is suspect (cf. Davies, 51-2), but it became firmly established in Athenian myth. In an inscription of the year 228, we read that 'the laws command (for) all those whom the Athenian people . . . have honored with maintenance in the *prytaneion*, that the senate and the people should take care of them and their descendants, and that the people should give as large a dowry

as they wish for the marriage of their daughters and for setting right their personal affairs as befits each of their benefactions' (IG II^2 832).

66. (Dem.) 59.71.

67. Lacey, 115-16, sees a case of concubinage 'with the maximum endowment permitted by law for one who was not a legitimate wife'. By 'maximum endowment' he appears to be referring to the limit on *notheia*, but *notheia* – bequests to a bastard child, not gifts to a concubine – have no relevance here. We know of no legal limit on the dowering of daughters at Athens, whether legitimate, illegitimate, or someone else's, except for the Solonian law mentioned above, which was surely a dead letter by the time of the orators. Epaenetus was very much able, legally, to pay more: that was precisely what he was trying to avoid in his dispute with Stephanus. Furthermore, Phano did not become a concubine at all ((Dem.) 59.122 surely implies a more regular relationship than what is envisioned here); she was simply available to Epaenetus when he was in town.

68. Although the law seems to have provided for that possibility in numbering the suit for return of the dowry among the *emmenoi*, suits that could be initiated each month, and were processed speedily (see E. E. Cohen, *Ancient Athenian Maritime Courts* (Princeton University Press 1973) 9-42). It is possible that an elderly widow, returning to a household from which she had long been separated, might manage her own finances; for women like this, and for women whose *kyrioi* were too poor to support them, the return of the dowry will have been a matter of more direct concern.

69. (Dem.) 42.27, 46.20. She did not always do so; Cleomedon's wife, for example, returned to her brothers' house, taking her dowry with her ((Dem.) 40.6).

70. Dem. 27.17. It is less likely that she was maintained by her brother-in-law Demochares; he did, indeed, according to Demosthenes (ibid. 15), complain to Aphobus, but he presumably did this on behalf either of the children whose estate was being spent, or of the mother who was being stingily supported.

71. Arist. *Ath. Pol.* 56.7, (Dem.) 43.75.

72. Dem. 28.11.

73. ibid. 27.65. Demosthenes was not, of course, going to impress upon the court a wish that the blackguard Aphobus had married his mother; but he might have urged Aphobus' responsibility either to marry her or to give her away. By the time of the speech, she was no longer marriageable, and Demosthenes thought only of his sister (ibid. 29.21).

74. e.g., Dem. 30.33, 41.4, (Dem.) 40.6, Isae. 2.9, 7.7, 8.8, 9.27.

75. Dem. 27.5, 36.8. Wolff, *Traditio*, 61-2, believes that the husband had to give a dowry at least as high as the first, since if he had made no provision, the entire dowry would have passed to the wife's *kyrios*.

76. Isae. 8.8.

77. (Dem.) 40.25. The only case we know of in which the second husband received less than the first, other than these two, is that of Polyeuctus' younger daughter, whose first husband Leocrates was adopted by Polyeuctus, thereby becoming heir to his entire estate, while her second husband, Spudias, received only thirty minae and ten minae of trousseau. Since there were no

sons, the daughters were *epikleroi*, and so Spudias also became custodian of half the estate when they were not claimed at Polyeuctus' death. The speaker of Dem. 41 is, however, sufficiently embarassed by the smallness of Spudias' dowry (ibid. 27-9) that he calls no attention to the comparison with Leocrates.

78. (Dem.) 42.27.
79. The fact that, according to the speaker, he claimed to owe the money 'to her' (ταύτῃ) is not decisive, since the Athenians were loose in this terminology. A third possibility – that Phaenippus was contemplating his mother's changing her mind and going back to her father's house – has at least as little to recommend it as the two offered in the text.
80. SEG XII 100.
81. (Dem.) 59.52.
82. ibid.
83. For a curious misapprehension of the situation, see Beauchet I, 319: 'Il résulte du plaidoyer de Démosthène contre Nééra que le mari n'est point ... autorisé à retenir la dot. Lorsqu'en effet Phrastor, reconnaissant son erreur, répudie Nééra [sic] qu'il croyait citoyenne, il veut garder la dot. Mais Stéphanos lui intente aussitôt une action, à l'occasion de laquelle l'orateur nous dit, "qu'aux termes de la loi, celui qui renvoie sa femme doit rendre la dot". C'est donc que la restitution est obligatoire dans tous les cas. Aussi la suite du plaidoyer nous apprend-elle que si Stéphanos a renoncé à la dot, c'est par une transaction et pour que Phrastor se désistât de son côté d'une accusation qui pouvait exposer Stéphanos à des peines très sévères.' Stephanus, of course, maintained that Phano (not Neaera) was a citizen and his daughter, and it was presumably on this basis that he instituted his suit, as it was on this basis that he defended himself against the speech we have. It is hardly likely that he planned to go to court and admit that he was liable to *atimia* in order to recover his money.
84. SIG^3 364, line 57; Achilles Tatius 8.8. For the claim of Wolff, RE, 168, that this is a law of the φερνή, not the προίξ, see Appendix II.
85. Wolff, *Traditio*, 61n.95.
86. Beauchet I, 318-19.
87. Lacey, 115, has indeed drawn this conclusion, but seems to see nothing odd about it. It may be noted, in passing, that the law in (Dem.) 59.86-7 does not say that the husband must divorce the woman, but that he may not remain married to her (μὴ ἐξέστω...συνοικεῖν). It could perhaps be argued by a legal mind that the marriage was dissolved automatically, and the rules applying to divorce – ἀπόπεμψις and ἀπόλειψις – would not apply in this case, so that, specifically, the dowry would not be returnable. For the reasons explained in the text, I have little confidence in the value of such an explanation for Attic law.
88. There were those who claimed that Solon had intentionally made the laws ambiguous so as to maximize the freedom of the jurors: Arist, *Ath. Pol.*, 9.2.
89. On the Athenian courts see further R. J. Bonner, *Lawyers and Litigants in Ancient Athens* (Chicago 1927, reissued Barnes & Noble, New York 1969).
90. Aeschin. 1.28.

91. Arist. *Ath. Pol.* 56.6; cf. Harpocration s.v. κακώσεως. Cf. Lipsius, 344n.17 for further references.
92. Arist. *Ath. Pol.*, loc. cit. and 58.3; cf. (Dem.) 35.48.
93. Aeschin. 1.28. The penalty, in fact, included a lot more: cf. U. Paoli, *Studi di diritto attico* (R. Bemporad, Florence 1930) 316 ff., and Harrison I, 78.
94. Aeschin. 1.99.
95. Ar. *Vesp.* 1354-9. In SGDI 1708, an inscription of Delphi, a girl is manumitted on condition that she care for her parents if they should need it; the parents are permitted to punish her if she fails to do so. These provisions are presumably to protect the parents, who remained slaves, from being left without recourse if abandoned by their free daughter.
96. For the last, see Dem. 24.107, Xen. *Mem.* 2.2.13.
97. Their responsibility applied only to direct ascendants, as mentioned in Isae. 8.32.
98. IG XI 2 287 A, line 127 (from 250 B.C.E.).
99. Ins. Dél. 298 A, lines 186-7 (from 240); 365, line 21 (from 208).
100. ibid. 290, line 131 (from 246).
101. ibid. 396 A, lines 44, 51, 55, 59 (from 194); 406 B, line 35 (from *c.* 190); 407, lines 23, 25, 28, 32, 34 (from *c.* 190); 442 A, line 213 (from 179); 449, line 36 (from 175).
102. ibid. 396 A, line 49 (from 194).
103. ibid. 407, line 31 (from *c.* 190).
104. IG XII 7 58.
105. ibid. 55.
106. ibid. 57. Wolff's explanation of the stone − 'the disposition was contained in a will and was not to become valid before the death of Nicesarete, that is to say, before Naucrates had to give up his right to the προίξ at any rate' (Wolff, *Traditio*, 60) − does not succeed in bringing the stone into line with Attic practice. In Athens, the husband would remain in control of the dowry if the woman died with children (cf. Appendix IV), and if she had no children, would have to return the money to her former *kyrios*, who might not be put off by the statement that husband and wife had dedicated the land to a goddess. To end the husband's responsibility, we should have required the agreement of the former *kyrios*, as on the other stones; but even then we should be surprised that it is the wife who dedicates and the husband who consents, for land title was usually clearly defined, even between man and wife, and this land was − by Athenian law − the husband's.
107. Wolff, RE, 166-7.
108. Lex Gort. II 46-54.
109. ibid. IV 43-6.
110. ibid. IV 48-V 1. The present participle ὀπυιομέναι may also mean 'the married daughter' (cf. ibid. IV 19). Some editors believe that the words 'of the paternal property' have been erased.
111. ibid. V 51 - VI 2.
112. See Harrison I, 50.
113. Whether or not this is explicitly stated in the law depends upon the interpretation of IV 52 - V 1 (quoted above in the text). The common, and rather more probable, view is that πρόϑϑ' (here translated 'already') means,

as it does in its other appearances in the code (V 8, VI 24, XI 21), 'before the enactment of this law'; but it is also possible that it meant 'before the father's death'. Even if the accepted interpretation is correct, it is clear that the purpose of the legislation is to prevent the daughter from getting a larger share than half that of a son, a purpose which would be defeated if the daughter could afterward receive her full share of the inheritance.

114. This had not always been the case: ibid. V 1-9 speaks of women who have no money 'given or pledged by a father or brother, or inherited as of when (or 'since'; see edd. ad loc.) the *startos* of Aithalos with Kyllos were *kosmoi*', which indicates that dowering by brothers had taken place before the enactment of the law. In the code itself, however, we find reference only to dowering by the father, or the dowering of a widow by her dying husband or her son (ibid. X 14-17, XII 1-5; cf. below). The mention of inheritances before the present law does not necessarily mean that daughters inherited in the presence of sons at that time; there will still have been (besides *patroiokoi*) sisters who inherited in the absence of brothers, etc.

115. Ephorus ap. Strab. 10.4.20 (=FGrH 70 fr. 149).

116. Lex Gort. IV 31-43. On the question of what, exactly, is excepted by this provision, see edd. ad loc.

117. ibid. III 17-30. The law presumes, in the case where there are children, that she will leave only to get married; it makes no statement as to where she will go when she has no children, since it is dealing only with her separation from her husband's household. Note also that where there are children they remain in control of the household, and she takes with her only τὰ Ϝὰ αὐτᾶς, 'her own property', i.e., her dowry (or inheritance) and what her husband has added, not the share of the produce to which she was entitled in case of childless death or divorce.

118. ibid. III 18-22, cf. 29-30.

119. ibid. II 45 - III 12.

120. See Appendix I.

121. This is Demosthenes' mother, who came to his father with fifty minae (Dem. 27.4) and was given away by him to Aphobus with eighty (ibid. 5).

122. Lex Gort. X 14-20.

123. On the difference between these two terms, see Appendix II.

124. Lex Gort. VI 9-12.

125. No recent scholar, at any rate, has suspected such a law for Athens: see Beauchet I, 262-6; Lipsius, 489; Erdmann, 307; Wolff, *Traditio*, 62n.100. That the father was free to determine the size of the dowry is stated by Demosthenes 41.26, and is further evidenced by passages such as Isae. 3.49, (Dem.) 40.25, etc., none of which could have been written if the size of the dowry were fixed by law.

126. Lex Gort. IV 51-2, X 14-20.

127. Arist. *Pol.* 1270 a 11-31. The testimony of Aelian (*Var. Hist.* 6.6) and Hermippus (ap. Athen. XIII 555 c) that Spartan women had no dowries is not to be relied on. Hermippus was apparently discussing the 'Lycurgan constitution', not the situation in his day, as the quote is from his *Nomothetae*; and Aelian is much too late.

128. Xen. *Ages.* 9.6.
129. Plut. *Agis* 4; 7.4; and cf. 9.3.
130. According to Spartan tradition, in fact, the laws of Sparta had been model-
     led on those of Crete (Herodotus 1.65.4, Arist. *Pol.* 1271 b 22-30; cf. Eph-
     orus ap. Strab. 10.4.17-19, Polyb. 6.45-6); the similarity of institutions may
     be connected with their common Dorian heritage, though the ancients do
     not seem to have thought so.

CHAPTER 7 : PATTERNS IN WOMEN'S ECONOMICS

1. Most directly, Arist. *Pol.* 1254 b 13-16.
2. (Eur.) fr. 953 Nauck (also available in D. L. Page, *Greek Literary Papyri*
   (Loeb Classical Library; Harvard University Press, Cambridge, Mass. 1942)
   184-9) I, 9-12.
3. By A. W. Gomme, 'The Position of Women in Athens in the Fifth and Fourth
   Centuries B.C.', CP 20 (1925) 1-25, reprinted in his *Essays in Greek History
   and Literature* (Blackwell, Oxford 1937) 89-115.
4. My thanks are due to Ms. Ellen Bravo, then of St Mary's University of Mary-
   land for pointing out to me that the women of tragedy, on whom Gomme
   bases much of his argument, fulfil in effect particularly feminine roles of
   virtue and conflict with behaviour that would be out of place in a man. A
   man would have to give more consideration to reasons of state than Antigone does; but Antigone is hardly contemptible.
5. Erdmann, 50.
6. (Dem.) 59.9, Isoc. 18.52, Lycurg. *In Leoc.* 65 (in the name of the ἀρχαῖοι
   νομοθέται); cf. MacDowell, *Athenian Homicide Law* (Manchester University
   Press 1963) 69.
7. Dem. 21.47.
8. Arist. *Ath. Pol.* 56.6-7.
9. Herodotus 6.122. Cf. Eupolis, fr. 100 Kock, where a young girl's falling in
   love has apparently ended in marriage. Therapontigonus, in Plautus' *Cur-
   culio*, asks his sister's agreement before betrothing her (line 673), but he has
   known her only a short time, and is in no position to be high-handed.
10. (Eur.) fr. 953 Nauck, I 20-2.
11. Dem. 21.158.
12. Dem. 36.45. The implications of freeing or dowering a *hetaera* (about whom,
    popular myth to the contrary, there was nothing respectable) are much the
    same as those that would attach today to the giving of large gifts to a wom-
    an of bad reputation.
13. Plut. *Alc.* 8.3.
14. Dem. 25.55.
15. See C. Préaux, 'Le statut de la femme à l'époque hellénistique, principale-
    ment en Egypte', *Recueils de la société Jean Bodin* 11, part 1 (Brussels 1959)
    139-47, 164-9.
16. Nothing reveals the decline of the Gortynian family as clearly as the provi-
    sion permitting the heirs to refuse to accept a debt-laden inheritance (Lex
    Gort. XI 31-45). No Athenian could have escaped his father's debts so
    easily.

APPENDIX I : SIZE OF DOWRIES

1. Sums on the border have been reckoned in the lower class; thus a dowry of 500 dr. would be listed on the top line.
2. The sources for each column are: Attic *horoi*: IG II² 2659-83; Fine, chapter 1, no. 7, chapter 2, nos. 8-10; SEG XXI 653-4, XXIV 206-7, *Hesperia* 41 (1972) 275-6. Other *horoi*: IG XII 7 56, ibid. Supp. 195. Tenos: IG XII 5 873. Myconos: SIG³ 1215. Orators: Dem. and (Dem.) 27.4, 30.7 (where I have treated the dowry as between one and two talents), 40.6-7, 20 (cf. 14; again I have treated it as being between one and two talents), 41.3-4, 45.66, 59.50; Isae. 2.3, 5, 3.49, 5.26-7, 8.8, 11.40; Lys. 16.10, 19.15, 32.6, Hypereides (ed. Jensen) 2.13. Literary sources: Plato *Epist*. 13; Plut. *Mor*. 179 f, *Arist*. 27.1; I have also included here Alcibiades' dowry of ten talents, mentioned both in (And.) 4.14 and in Plut. *Alc*. 8.6. Wills: Dem. 29.43, 45.28; Lys. 32.5-6. Menander: *Aspis* 135-6; *Dysc*. 844-5; *Epit*. 134; *Con*. 3 (the sum is conjectural, but is two talents or more; I have placed it between two and three, though it may be five); *Mis*. 446; *Peric*. 1015. Not included: Men. *Sam*. 727-8 (entire estate, after death); SIG³ 1215, lines 26-8 (house, after death); such items from the Hellenistic courts as Plut. *Pyrrh*. 9 (Corcyra) and Polyb. 28.20.9 (ed. Buettner-Wobst) (Coele Syria); and women with no dowries.
3. i.e., literary sources other than the orators and Menander.
4. i.e., dowries stipulated by a husband on his deathbed. These are all from the orators.

APPENDIX II : ΠΡΟΙΞ AND ΦΕΡΝΗ

1. Eur. *Med*. 955-7, of the poisoned robe sent to Glauce; *Ion* 298, φερνὰς πολέμου of the wife herself.
2. E. Gans, *Das Erbrecht in weltgeschichtlicher Entwickelung*, vol. I (1824) 302; Beauchet I, 255-6; Lipsius, 488n.61; Schulthess, φερνή, RE 19 B (1938) 2040-1; Wolff, RE, 167-9.
3. Aeschin. 2.31. There are well over a hundred occurrences of προίξ.
4. Hippothoon fr.6 Nauck (p.828); cf. Nauck's note ad loc.
5. Herodotus 1.93.4; Ephorus ap. Strab. 10.4.20 (= FGrH 70, fr.149).
6. See Schulthess, φερνή, RE 19 B (1938) 2041-2.
7. *Od*. 13.15, 17.413.
8. Eustath. 743.3.
9. cf. C. Vatin, *Recherches sur le mariage et la condition de la femme mariée à l'époque hellénistique* (Paris 1970) 199-200.

APPENDIX III : DOWRY AND TROUSSEAU

1. Isae. 2.9, 8.8; Dem. 41.27; Men. *Con*. 2-5; cf. ἐσθής in Plato *Leg*. 774 d, SIG³ 1215, Strabo 4.1.5, and ἱμάτια...καὶ σκεύη in Plut. *Solon* 20.6.
2. See Wyse, 245-6; Lipsius, 491; Erdmann, 317-8. Beauchet I, 289-90, appears to imply the same.
3. Isae. 3.35. For the actual working of this provision, see above, pp.10-12.
4. Wolff, *Traditio*, 54-8; repeated in RE, 137-9.

5. Most clearly Isae. 2.9 (Gerner, *Beiträge zum Recht der Parapherna* (vol. 37 of *Münchener Beiträge zur Papyrusforschung und antiken Rechtsgeschichte*; Munich 1954) 41-2, would like to discount this passage, but his suggestion that the ἱμάτια...καὶ...χρυσίδια refer to some *other* clothing and jewelry hardly seems likely); also apparently Dem. 45.28, Lys. 32.5-6 (cf. Wolff, RE, 138), and Men. *Con.* 2-5.

6. SIG³ 1215.

7. i.e., the *eranos* (mutual loan) made up of contributions of five hundred drachmas apiece.

8. viz., that these were 'ein dem Manne in natura geleisteter Beitrag zum Unterhalt der Frau' (RE, 139). How such a 'payment in kind' differs from a trousseau I cannot see – except, of course, that one is included in the dowry and the other (according to Wolff) is not.

9. Wolff, RE, 138 ('20 Minen' in col. 140 is an error).

10. This was first noticed by Tycho Mommsen, *Beiträge zu der Lehre von den griechischen Präpositionen* (1895) 368 ff., and has since found a place in all the major Greek grammars, as E. Schwyzer, *Griechische Grammatik* (C. H. Beck, Munich 1939-50), II, 488, or H. W. Smythe (rev. G. M. Messing), *Greek Grammar* (Harvard University Press, Cambridge, Mass. 1956) 386.

11. The same phrase occurs in the law of intestate succession, (Dem.) 43.51.

12. 'But you have no less (than I), as I will show. First of all, take the testimony as to the conditions on which she was given in marriage to this man. (The testimony is read.) (27) Now someone may say: how can (I say that) he has no less, if in his dowry the clothing and jewelry worth a thousand drachmas were reckoned in with the forty minae, while in mine the ten minae were added in addition? That is precisely what I am about to say. For Spudias, gentlemen of the jury, took his wife from Leocrates along with her clothing and jewelry, for which Polycrates paid to Leocrates the additional sum of more than a thousand; but as for me – if one were to compare what was sent to me beside the dowry (speaking only of what I have), to what was given to this man, he will find that they are approximately equal, except for what was mortgaged for the thousand. (28) So that probably there was reckoned in the forty minae that sum which had been paid to Leocrates and was more than what was given to me. Now first of all, take this deposition and tell them precisely what each of us has, and after that the testimony of the arbitrators, so that they may see that he has quite a bit more money than I, and Leocrates sued him over it, and the arbitrators gave this judgment. Read it.'

13. Wolff, *Traditio*, 55.

14. ibid. 56.

15. Dem. 27.13.

APPENDIX IV : INHERITANCE OF THE DOWRY

1. Isae. 8.34.

2. This is shown by (Dem.) 40.14, where the two sons of Mantias do not present claims to their mothers' dowries until his death, although Mantitheus' mother had died many years earlier (ibid. 50). It is also implied by the fact that a

woman's children by her first husband did not inherit her dowry if she had remarried.

3. For neither mother nor children, apparently, was maintenance guaranteed by law as long as they were in the husband's *oikos*. We know of no child-neglect laws at Athens, and there is no evidence that the wife's dowry compelled the husband to maintain her children; they – as, indeed, their mother – would have difficulty bringing a suit against their *kyrios* in any case, and whether their maternal grandfather or uncles could have interfered success-fully is doubtful. But I know of no example at Athens of a father failing to feed his children once he had decided to raise them, so the question may be moot. That the mother's dowry might be considered in connection with her children's maintenance is shown by (Dem.) 40.50: 'now, my mother died when I was a child, so that it sufficed for me to be fed and educated from the interest of her dowry'. This passage does not, of course, prove or even imply any *legal* obligations to the speaker arising from his mother's dowry.

4. We have no evidence as to whether an only daughter of her mother who was also an *epikleros* might have inherited her mother's dowry; but it seems reasonable – at least on my understanding of the epiclerate – to presume so; cf. Wolff, RE, 152-3.

5. Thus the dowry of Mantitheus' mother in (Dem.) 40 was claimed entirely by him; her son by a previous marriage, Cleon, had no more right to it.

Glossary

• •
•

agora – the market-place, which was also the centre of social activity.

anchisteus (pl. *anchisteis*) – the next-of-kin, who was entitled by law to claim the hand of the *epikleros* in marriage. At Gortyn he was called the *epiballon*, pl. *epiballontes*.

archon – technically, any member of the board of archons that nominally shared the power of the ancient Athenian kings; in general usage, and in this book, the term refers to the eponymous archon, the member of the board after whom the year was named ('in the year when so-and-so was archon'). At one time the chief officer of the state, he had become, by the time of the orators and Aristotle, a magistrate whose chief function was the supervision of family matters.

atimia – deprivation of civil rights, generally as punishment for a crime.

demos – either 'the common people' (as opposed to the aristocracy), or 'the people' (conceived as a single body), or 'the assembly of the people' (convened as a law-making body).

epiballon – see *anchisteus*.

epidikasia – the adjudication of an *epikleros* or of an inheritance to the nearest relative of the deceased.

epikleros (pl. *epikleroi*) – a woman who, having no brothers, is married upon her father's death to his nearest male relative, with the father's estate eventually passing to their children. The corresponding Gortynian term is *patroiokos*, pl. *patroiokoi.*

epiklerou kakosis – abuse of an *epikleros*, a crime at Athens.

heliastic court – a subdivision of the *heliaea*, the 'popular court' at Athens which had 6000 'judges', but generally met in smaller courts of some 200, 300, or 500 judges.

herms – images consisting of an oblong block with (generally) a head and a phallus.

hetaera (pl. *hetaerae*) – a prostitute. The term is actually of wide variation, ranging from virtual streetwalkers to what we should perhaps call *demi-mondaines*; but in none of its applications does it denote a respectable woman, even in the eyes of the Greeks.

hieropoios (pl. *hieropoioi*) – the overseer of a temple.

hieros, hiera (pl. *hieroi* (m.), *hierai* (f.)) – a member of a religious guild.

kyrios (pl. *kyrioi*; fem. *kyria*) – the head of a family, who also enjoyed certain legal rights over the family property(see chapter 4); his authority is known as *kyrieia.*

liturgy – the performance by a rich citizen of one of a certain number of civic burdens (equipping a ship, producing games or a tragedy, and others), which were imposed as a form of taxation upon the richest citizens. This word when used in this book always has the above meaning, and never its modern ecclesiastical one.

medimnus – a dry measure equivalent to about 52½ litres (M. Lang and M. Crosby, *The Athenian Agora, vol. X: Weights, Measures and Tokens* (Princeton 1964) 44-5).

oikos (pl. *oikoi*) – household. The Greek household was conceived as passing from father to son, with marriage involving the transfer of the bride from her father's *oikos* to her husband's.

patroiokos – see *epikleros*.

polemarch – an official of various Greek cities. Originally the term referred to an official who served as general in time of war, but by the classical period this function had been lost in many places, and replaced by various others.

polis (pl. *poleis*) – a Greek city-state.

prasis epi lysei – a form of primitive mortgage disguised as a sale: the borrower 'sells' his land to the lender, with the option of buying it back by a given date – until which the land remains in his hand. In effect, this is no different from a loan with real collateral.

proxenos – a 'public friend' of the state; particularly, one who represents the interests of a foreign state in his own community is a *proxenos* of the foreign state.

prytaneion – the hall where the *prytaneis*, the representatives who presided in rotation over the Athenian senate, met and ate. Various public benefactors were honoured from time to time by being granted the perpetual right to free meals in the *prytaneion*.

thirty tyrants – the group of oligarchs who seized control of the Athenian state for a short period after the end of the Peloponnesian War.

xenos – either a 'foreigner', or a 'non-citizen' (even though he may have lived all his life in the city), or a friend (that is, a foreigner with whom ties of hospitality have been established).

Index of Sources

• •

References in italic are to pages in this book. Items in footnotes are indexed under the page to which the footnote refers

General Index

• •